Praise for *Black Market Billions*

"Most people wouldn't think that buying an off-the-truck designer bag could fund terrorism. In my three decades of experience as a former Detective Investigator with the NYPD and now running a private investigation firm, I can say that Hitha understands and explains why this is a dangerous mentality to have. In *Black Market Billions*, she spells out why the mindset that a stolen designer handbag is a bargain disappears once you consider that your purchase may be funding a deadly organized crime group."

> —**Thomas Ruskin**, Former NYPD Detective Investigator and President of CMP Protective and Investigative Group, Inc.

"Written like a financial thriller, *Black Market Billions* shines a bright light on the dark side of capitalism. The book opened my eyes to what really goes on behind the scenes in high-end retail, and the best part is you can feel her courage and passion on every page."

> —**Lawrence G. McDonald**, *The New York Times* Bestselling Author, *A Colossal Failure of Common Sense*

"*Black Market Billions* is a must-read for all government policymakers, business leaders, opinion makers, and consumers. With global markets in chaos, states in recession, and extremists waging war against civilization, few topics are as vital to our security as the nexus between organized retail crime and terrorism. This book will change the debate as we come to understand just how much terrorism depends on funds raised by crime. This is an immensely important book for understanding why terrorism remains part of modern politics and why societies must find ways to cut off the financial tentacles of support."

> —**William C. Martel**, Associate Professor of International Security Studies, The Fletcher School of Law and Diplomacy, Tufts University

Black Market Billions

How Organized Retail Crime
Funds Global Terrorists

Hitha Prabhakar

Vice President, Publisher: Tim Moore
Associate Publisher and Director of Marketing: Amy Neidlinger
Executive Editor: Jeanne Glasser
Editorial Assistant: Pamela Boland
Development Editor: Russ Hall
Operations Specialist: Jodi Kemper
Senior Marketing Manager: Julie Phifer
Assistant Marketing Manager: Megan Graue
Cover Designer: Alan Clements
Managing Editor: Kristy Hart
Project Editors: Jess DeGabriele and Jovana San Nicolas-Shirley
Copy Editor: Gayle Johnson
Proofreader: Seth Kerney
Indexer: Erika Millen
Compositor: Nonie Ratcliff
Manufacturing Buyer: Dan Uhrig

© 2012 by Hitha Prabhakar

Publishing as FT Press
Upper Saddle River, New Jersey 07458

FT Press offers excellent discounts on this book when ordered in quantity for bulk purchases or special sales. For more information, please contact U.S. Corporate and Government Sales, 1-800-382-3419, corpsales@pearsontechgroup.com. For sales outside the U.S., please contact International Sales at international@pearson.com.

Printed in the United States of America

First Printing November 2011

ISBN-10: 0-13-218024-3
ISBN-13: 978-0-13-218024-5

Pearson Education LTD.
Pearson Education Australia PTY, Limited.
Pearson Education Singapore, Pte. Ltd.
Pearson Education Asia, Ltd.
Pearson Education Canada, Ltd.
Pearson Educación de Mexico, S.A. de C.V.
Pearson Education—Japan
Pearson Education Malaysia, Pte. Ltd.

Library of Congress Cataloging-in-Publication Data:
Prabhakar, Hitha, 1975-
  Black market billions : how organized retail crime funds global terrorists / Hitha Prabhakar.
    p. cm.
  Includes bibliographical references and index.
  ISBN 978-0-13-218024-5 (hbk. : alk. paper)
  1. Black market. 2. Shoplifting. 3. Smuggling. 4. Organized crime. 5. Terrorism--Finance.
I. Title.
  HF5482.6.P73 2012
  363.325--dc23
                        2011023166

*This book is dedicated to the memory of
my grandmother Susila
—the ultimate truth teller.*

Contents

Introduction 1

Part I   **The Piracy Economy**

Chapter 1   **Organized Retail Crime Goes Global** 9

   Why Is ORC Such a Threat? 11

   The Promised Land: Money Talks 13

   Made in America: Homegrown Terrorism. 17

   Recruiting from the Inside. 19

   From Prison to Gangs to the World's Most Notorious
   Terrorist Group. 21

   Access to Funding Gets Creative. 25

   Burrowing In: The Hezbollah Finds a Home in the
   U.S. and South America 27

   From America to South America: Ties Get Stronger
   in the Tri-Border Region 28

Chapter 2   **When a Deal Isn't a Deal**. 31

   Getting a Slice of Luxury the Cheapest Way Possible 34

   The "Real Deal" 36

   Dying for a Deal: The Recession Doesn't Make
   Aspirations Go Away. 38

   Big Takedowns Take Precedence Over
   Smaller Offenders. 39

   Counterfeiters and ORC Move Their Operations Online. . . 40

   eBay's Swift Response. 42

   Too Little, Too Late 44

   Lurking in the Shadows: Stolen Gift Cards
   Bought Online. 45

   Easy to Obtain, Easy to Sell 46

   Fake-out: Retailers Fronting as Legitimate Stores 48

   Protecting Yourself: Know the Signs of E-fencing/ORC . . . 51

Chapter 3   **The Cost to the Stores** 53

   The Blame Game 54

   Insider Information: Employee Theft and ORC. 54

Human Resources Fail: Hiring the Wrong People 56
Wholesale Scam: Terrorist-Affiliated Warehouses Sell
to the Little Guy 61
Taking a Bite Out of the Balance Sheet:
Economic Downturn Fosters Cargo Theft 64
Coordinating Information in Real Time: LAPD
and APD Case Studies 67

Part II   Follow the Money

Chapter 4   The Money Trail and the Business of
Cross-Border Trade 77
The Warehouse: Ground Zero for
Cross-Border Trade 80
Profile of a Purchaser 81
Keeping Shelves Stocked Through
Cargo Theft 83
Coveted Items: Over-the-Counter Drugs 84
Profile of a Cargo Thief 86
"Shell Stores": A Conduit for Organized Retail Crime 87
Shell Stores Move Online 89
A Hotbed of Stolen Merchandise: Flea Markets 91
Nabbing the Bad Guys: Classifying Organized Retail
Crime as a Felony 91
Insurance Companies: The Missing Link 93
The Gray Market: Another Retail Facilitator of ORC 94
Laws Have Been Passed, But Are They Helping? 95

Chapter 5   Profile of a Booster and a Fence 97
Moving the Merchandise: The Role of a Fence 100
Being Convicted as a Level 1 Fence: More Like
a Slap on the Wrist Than a Slap in the Face 101
The Level 2 Booster: Inside the Mind of
a Potentially Dangerous Criminal 104
Other Forms of Theft from a Level 2 Booster 106
Level 3 Boosters and Fences: A High-Level
Organization Equals High Profits 108
Level 3 Boosters: Frequently Lifted Merchandise 112
Curbing Boosters and Fences: What Does
and Doesn't Work 115

Chapter 6   Family Ties. 119
              When Family Funds Support Terrorism 121
              Assad Muhammad Barakat and
              His "Family" 123
              Illegal Entry into the U.S. Is Not Difficult—
              if You Have Money 127
              The Great Entrepreneurs: Terrorists. 132
              The Trust Factor: The Basis of Any Organized
              Retail Crime Ring. 136

Chapter 7   Money Laundering 2.0 139
              The Three Stages of Money Laundering. 141
              Organized Retail Crime and Latin America 151
              Funneling Money Through the Black Market
              Peso Exchange 152
              The South American, Mexican, and African Connection . . 155

Chapter 8   The Political Agenda 159
              Homegrown Terrorism: How Retail Theft
              and Piracy Has Funded Terrorist Operations 160
              Rebel Kids: Extremist Ideas Financed Through
              International ORC 163
              When Things Went Awry 164
              ORC Funding by Way of Somalia: A Tale of
              Two Misguided Kids. 165
              As Local as Down the Street 168
              Funding Evil Under the Guise of Charitable
              Contributions: The Mosques 168
              Muslim Charities: Capitalizing on Natural Disaster
              and Religious Empathy 169
              Terrorist Fund-Raising Via Charities Finds Roots
              in the U.S. 172
              Charitable Donation Loopholes: How the IRS and
              Banking Systems Failed to Prevent Fraudulent
              ORC Funds from Financing Terrorist Groups 173
              Charities Turn to a Cyber Audience 175
              Why the Government Can't Regulate Charities 175

Chapter 9   Strange Bedfellows 179
              How Banned TVs Funded Bombings 180
              The Business of Cigarette Smuggling 183

The EC Versus R.J. Reynolds Tobacco 185

The Role of Money Brokers and Money Launderers 186

The History of Cigarette Smuggling 188

Cigarette Smuggling Funds Local Terrorism
Around the World. 189

Chiquita International Brands: "Either You Pay Me,
or I Am Going to Kill You." 192

Dole Foods' Involvement with the Colombian
Paramilitary. 195

Part III   Putting a Band-Aid on a Broken Leg

Chapter 10   The Failure of Preventative Measures 201

Acting Locally, Thinking Globally 202

Types of ORC Theft Prevention That Are
Supposed to Work But Don't. 204

A Bottom-Line Breakdown of Costs 207

Legal Issues: Defining ORC Versus Shoplifting
and Shrinkage 215

Regulating the Resale Market 216

Chapter 11   Letting the Bad Guy Get Away 219

Regulation Epic Fail: How Banking BSAs and
AML Programs Let Terrorist Funding Slip
Through the Cracks 222

Continued Failure to Regulate IFTs: The Costs to
Local and Federal Governments as Well as Retailers. 223

Failure to Regulate Hawalas 224

IFTs Get Sophisticated: Stored Value Cards. 227

Bulk Cash Smuggling Comes in a Smaller Package 228

Retailers Feel the Pain of SVC Fraud 230

Credit Card Fraud Is Even Worse. 231

RICO Defined 234

Why ORC Rings Still Exist: Money Laundering
and the RICO Statute. 235

More Problems with RICO: It's in the Definition 236

Laws That Once Protected Potential Terrorists
Have Changed. 239

Defining "Material Support" and "Coordination" 239

Epilogue 243

Glossary 247

Endnotes 271

Index 299

Acknowledgments

Like many large projects, writing a book takes the support of many great people. *Black Market Billions* could not have been written without the indefatigable help and support of many people in the public sector, including the Los Angeles Police Department, Albuquerque Police Department, Immigration and Customs Enforcement, the Federal Bureau of Investigation, the National Retail Federation, the Secret Service, and the Retail Industry Leaders Association. Captain Bill Williams and Detective Kent Oda of the Commercial Crimes Division put their trust in me based on a quick in-person conversation and a lengthy e-mail. They gave me unprecedented access to people, places, and divisions for days on end. Thanks to Kevin Tyrrell at Immigration and Customs Enforcement and to Cori Bassett, who took the time and had the patience to set up meetings, explain every little detail about money laundering instruments, and advise me on overseas travel to undisclosed locations. Karen Fischer and Commander Harold Prudencio also allowed me to come behind the doors of the APD, letting me ask questions about cases, incidents, and people who had never been discussed with outside sources.

This book started out as an idea based on an instant-message conversation I had with a former colleague. But the foundation of the research came from Joe LaRocca and Kathy Grannis at the National Retail Federation, as well as Elizabeth Jennings at the Retail Industry Leaders Association. These retail industry stars helped me sort through piles of documents, countless reports, and congressional testimony to get to the right sources. From the private sector, I cannot thank Jerry Biggs and Gary Weisbecker from the loss prevention team at Walgreens enough. The number of hours spent on the phone discussing, strategizing, and helping me understand how an organized retail crime group works, from the psychology of a Level 1 booster and fence to a Level 3 shell warehouse owner, was instrumental in creating the foundation for this book. Likewise, I owe a large amount of gratitude to the public relations and loss prevention teams at LVMH, Deckers, eBay, Target, and Limited Brands for fielding questions and requests for interviews and making sure every fact was correct.

I interviewed hundreds of sources, many on background, who helped me "follow the money," so to speak. Although the majority of them requested anonymity, I would like to thank Professor Willam Martel at the Fletcher School of Law and Diplomacy for reviewing chapters, adding input, and convincing me "not to bury the lede." Likewise, Kris Buckner's input and wealth of information on the counterfeiting industry was insurmountable. And to my anonymous sources, thank you for your help.

Behind every good author is a great editor, and Jeanne Glasser is the best. The book would not have happened if it weren't for her editorial advice, foresight, and direction. Through Jeanne I not only gained inspiration, but I made a friend for life. Thank you to the editorial and production team at Pearson North America: Tim Moore, Russ Hall, Jess DeGabriele, and Jovana Shirley. Their hard work in the last stages of the book got us to the finish line. I was lucky enough to have Molly Novero agree to be my research assistant even though she was a full-time law student. Words cannot express how grateful I am for her dedication and hours spent going through thousands of court documents, tracking down the names of attorneys, and interpreting Supreme Court decisions for me. Thank you to Adam Kirschner, Nik Deogun, and Nick Dunn for having the faith in me that I could be on television, run a research company, and write a book at the same time. And, I wanted to give an extra special thank you to my colleagues at Bloomberg Television, especially to Mark White, Dan Colarusso, Andrew Morse, and Andy Lack for their support.

Last, but not least, I want to thank my friends and family for their love and support. To my parents, Sonia, Giri and Betsy, Michele P. and Nathan B., Andrew T., Sarah Mary, Stacey S., RKB, Lori, Meena,

Shane, Megan A., Alexis R., Ernest, and Fero, thank you for being there at all hours of the night and day to listen to my ideas, offer advice, make me laugh, and, when needed, offer a shoulder to cry on. To my teachers Jon B., Liz M., and Kim N. for imparting your writing wisdom on me throughout the years. And to Seth. This book happened because you are my rock, love, and light. Thank you.

About the Author

Hitha Prabhakar is a New York-based reporter for Bloomberg Television, covering business news and financial markets with a particular focus on retail. Before joining Bloomberg Television in 2011, Prabhakar was founder and principal of The Stylefile Group, a retail consulting firm based in New York City, where she served as an advisor to hedge funds and other clients with long-term holdings in retail companies. Prior to that, Prabhakar served as a retail reporter for Forbes Media, covering the luxury industry as well as men's fashion. She has written for *Time*, *People*, MSNBC.com, *ELLE India*, and Metro newspapers, among other publications. Prabhakar was formerly a contributor on CNBC and has had numerous television appearances as a retail analyst on networks including CBS, CNN, Fox News, Sky News, and Bravo. She holds degrees in philosophy and economics from Smith College and a master's degree from Columbia University Graduate School of Journalism. She also studied at the London School of Economics.

Introduction

Was he kidding?

Sitting at my computer on December 26, 2007, I couldn't believe what I was reading in my instant message window. I was checking my e-mail when a bizarre series of messages[1] from a former colleague and friend appeared like a flashing For Sale sign in the middle of my screen. (I've changed my contact's name and IM address to protect his identity, as well as that of the retailer in question.)

HermCGC: Did i ever tell you i have hook ups sometimes with bags?

I had no idea what that meant. Did Herman have a direct connection to Marc Jacobs? Did he lose his job in the IT department of my former company and get a job at Neiman Marcus? Did he have some inside track to a sample sale unknown to fashion insiders? I had to find out.

HithaPrabhakar:	you do???
HithaPrabhakar:	where??
HermCGC:	right now i have 2 bags for sale
HithaPrabhakar:	is it black market
HermCGC:	yes
HithaPrabhakar:	wait. what??
HithaPrabhakar:	how did you get them?
HermCGC:	a hook up

HithaPrabhakar: what does that mean?

HermCGC: How about a Givenchy Grained Leather Bettina and that one in black just like its shown

HithaPrabhakar: i love the givenchy bag!! where did you get these??

HermCGC: They fell off the truck

HithaPrabhakar: HERMAN!!

HermCGC: he wants $300 for the Givenchy and $400 for the Lanvin

HithaPrabhakar: really?

HermCGC: i just sell them! i dont have nothing else to do with it

HermCGC: when i need a hookup its there for me

Having covered the retail and fashion industry the majority of my career, I had heard of fashionistas acquiring merchandise through less-than-legitimate sources. There was always a friend of a friend who worked at a luxury designer who had a glut of last year's "it" handbag that didn't sell well and who was trying to get rid of them so that she didn't have 20 of the same handbag in her closet. I'd also heard of "handbag parties," usually hosted by a middle-aged mom in a fancy apartment or home. She would somehow get ahold of 40 or 50 real Fendi, Coach, or Louis Vuitton handbags, or in some cases fakes, and sell them to her friends while they ate paté topped Wasa crackers and drank Dom Perignon. I never inquired where these bags came from because, quite frankly, I wasn't interested in buying them. But, for some reason, I had to know what Herman meant when he said, "when i need a hookup its there for me."

HithaPrabhakar: totally off the record

HithaPrabhakar: did he steal them?

HermCGC: yes

HithaPrabhakar: NO seriously??

HermCGC:	dont get my hookup in trouble
HithaPrabhakar:	i would never. what is he doing stealing bags? i could definitely NOT buy the bag
HermCGC:	actually from what they tell me... their entire staff does it.
HermCGC:	alot get caught and alot dont
HithaPrabhakar:	wow
HermCGC:	they also told me most of their bags they get for 2/3rds cheaper than what they sell them for

When Herman confirmed that stealing from a luxury retailer was not uncommon and that the entire staff was stealing from the store, I knew there was more to the story. This wasn't a minor case of petty employee theft. Clearly a theft ring was at work. I had to find out who was behind it, why it was so easy to steal the merchandise, and, more importantly, what they were doing with the proceeds once the merchandise was sold. I couldn't understand how a retailer that had such high-end clientele was skimping on the most basic fixed cost a retailer could have: good security.

"Stores literally go out of business because of theft," says Alan Herbach, president at American Theft Prevention Products, in an interview with me. "And the more technology you add [to the item], the more expensive it is. Someone is not going to put a $10 security tag on a $50 coat and pass the price hike on to the customer. They would rather have the merchandise sit out unprotected than put on an additional cost."

I found out two facts as I did more research. First, it wasn't just the store where Herman's hookup worked that was having a security problem. It was retailers from Walgreens to Bloomingdale's. Second, this kind of theft had a name: organized retail crime (ORC).

Organized crime has been a part of the American and global landscape for centuries. Back in the 1800s, Italian crime families started to surface and weave their way into the global economic fabric.

Although extortion, bootlegging alcohol, and having shell businesses fronting for illegal activity are often affiliated with crime rings, ORC has started gaining traction. On the surface, ORC looks like your average petty theft, often equated with shoplifting. However, this brand of crime costs retailers nearly $30 billion a year. And states lose billions more in sales taxes. (Ohio, for example, recently reported $61 billion in lost sales taxes due to retail theft.[2]) This is a lot more damaging than just a couple items being lifted from a store.

Since 9/11, ORC has grown exponentially, with the global recession as a catalyst. Crime ring members realized (like Herman and his criminal cohorts) that unsuspecting women like me hadn't lost the desire to carry around an expensive handbag just because the economy was tanking. On a different level, these crime rings also realized that parents who were losing their jobs and being forced to cut back on staples such as baby formula were seeking deals on over-the-counter drugs and beauty items as mundane as Crest White Strips and Prilosec OTC.

"Why would anyone care if people are buying stolen merchandise at cheaper prices?" asked a friend over lunch one day.

She admitted purchasing makeup at a local makeup wholesaler in midtown Manhattan, and she didn't see anything wrong with doing so. It was true: the American consumer's purchasing psyche had changed as stock prices dropped and unemployment rates hit their highest levels since the Great Depression. During the recession, it was every person for himself. Uncertainty dominated how people spent. Most importantly, it was all about saving as much as you could. So why would anyone care when the objective was conserving dollars? But while the consumer was busy pinching pennies, something more sinister was going on that would have a significant impact on the economy at a global, national, and individual level.

Retailers and consumers were being duped by sophisticated schemes created by ORC rings. These rings were communicating via the Internet, disposable cell phones, and social media to move stolen merchandise from the store to a warehouse and back to another seemingly legitimate retailer within hours. These schemes had opened the floodgates for international criminals based in the U.S. to steal upwards of $2 million in merchandise in one hit alone. The worst part was that these crime rings were funding terrorist cells such as Hezbollah, the IRA, Hamas, Harkat-ul-Mujahideen, and al Qaeda. That's right—the discounted designer handbags, soap, and baby formula that people were buying to save a buck were funding terrorism. To prove it, I decided to follow the money trail.

Part I
The Piracy Economy

Organized Retail Crime Goes Global   9

When a Deal Isn't a Deal   31

The Cost to the Stores   53

1

Organized Retail Crime Goes Global

A hush falls over the room as a man in a designer suit jacket walks to the podium. The man is tall and well spoken and is comfortable addressing an audience of 30,000. Methodically pointing to charts projected onto a screen using high-tech equipment, he reviews how much this organization spent within the last year, its new financial targets, how it can make more money in the upcoming year, and, most importantly, how the American army fighting across the border in Afghanistan is no match for his organization. In the wings, spokespeople for the organization take notes furiously, ready to communicate the main points of the meeting to the rest of the world.[1]

This man isn't the chief executive of a Fortune 500 company. He is Baitullah Mehsud, head of Pakistan's Tehreek-e-Taliban terrorist group.[2] (Mehsud was subsequently killed in August of 2009 along the Afghan border in U.S. air strikes.)

As it turns out, consumers and businesses weren't the only ones suffering from the repercussions of the global recession. Terrorist organizations such as al Qaeda that once brought in close to $30 million a year before the 9/11 attacks felt the financial pinch just like legitimate businesses around the world. Abd al Hamid Al Mujil, known as al Qaeda's "million dollar man,"[3] at one point turned to charitable donations to raise money for the terrorist group. When the U.S. government realized in 2006 that he was using his position as the executive director of the eastern province branch of the International Islamic Relief Organization (IIRO) to funnel money back to al Qaeda, he was removed from his post, costing the IIRO millions of dollars

9

in potential donations. With its once large bank account dwindling, al Qaeda decided to decentralize. Instead of having one major unit functioning in the Afghanistan and Pakistan regions, al Qaeda suddenly had affiliates all over the world that shared the same ideals but planned and executed their own terrorist attacks.

Professor Bill Martel of Tufts University's The Fletcher School of Law and Diplomacy told me, "Pre-9/11, the conventional wisdom was that groups like al Qaeda were tightly organized with clear lines of control from its leadership. What's happening now is that al Qaeda has lost central control [of] its power as well as its financing. Once the U.S. began to attack al Qaeda, it became a very dynamic organization with a constantly evolving set of networks all connected to the core group. These subgroups are all highly adaptable as well and take it upon themselves to recruit from within—convincing their own people that supporting their group is one step closer to God while using the Internet for self recruitment, planning and financing."[4]

Martell notes that al Qaeda wasn't the only organization facing a funds shortage once these groups started to come under greater scrutiny and attack. After all, they declared war on the U.S. and attacked it, and in response the U.S. attacked al Qaeda and its financial means of support. Hezbollah and the Taliban also became decentralized, creating an opportunity for subgroups to crop up in unsuspecting areas such as Latin America, Africa, South and Southeast Asia, and even the U.S. These affiliated groups supported the main organization and indoctrinated extremist ideals shared by their members worldwide. However, they were on their own when it came to getting money to fund attacks. They raised funds by increasing the cocaine trade, carrying out kidnappings, and running scams that bilked donors out of money meant for charitable organizations. Transferring funds via *hawalas*[5] was commonplace and in fact was a standard way of accumulating money.

What wasn't typical was that the Lashkar-e-Taiba (LeT), al Shabaab, and South American cells of Hezbollah[6] were increasingly relying on gangs, cartels, and international sympathizers to build their bank accounts. One of the main sources of money was organized retail crime (ORC).

Why Is ORC Such a Threat?

Once known to the retail community as the minor crime of shoplifting, in the past decade ORC has grown into an estimated $38 billion a year black market operation.[7] U.S. government agencies such as Immigration and Customs Enforcement (ICE), the Federal Bureau of Investigation (FBI), and the Department of Homeland Security (DHS) have all tracked ORC synchronized teams that steal from our economy and use the money to attack us and support international terrorist groups. These groups include Partiya Karkeren Kurdistan (PKK) in Iraq (led by Saddam Hussein's son, Uday, until his death), the FARC (Revolutionary Armed Forces of Colombia), the IRA in Ireland, as well as Hezbollah, Hamas, and Lashkar-e-Taiba (Pakistan/ India).[8]

These terrorist organizations are hell-bent on destroying not only the lives of the people within their own countries who don't stand with them (or their mission) but also the American economy, its people, and its way of life. While it is difficult for government organizations to track exactly how much money is actually being made, the National Retail Federation (NRF), ICE and FBI estimates the proceeds from stolen goods equal $600 million dollars annually and have been funding everything from weapons, to fake visas and passports, to paramilitary equipment.[9] ORC is one of the easiest and least detectable ways for criminals to make money quickly and send it to terrorist groups overseas. What's even more disturbing is that these terrorist organizations are using grassroots tactics to recruit people into ORC rings. According to Joe LaRocca, spokesperson for the NRF's ORC initiative, the rise in ORC, especially within the past two years, has had to do with the economy. Consumers were quite literally "dying for a deal" by purchasing items that were stolen by crime rings with links to terrorist organizations overseas—they just didn't realize it.

"The economy played a big role in the organized retail crime and the resale market," says LaRocca. "Consumers who were cashed-strapped and lost their jobs looked for alternative places to purchase everyday items at an affordable cost. When places like Walmart, Target, and Walgreens became too expensive for them, the only option was to tap into resale markets, flea markets, pawn shops, and online web sites. These consumers forfeited their comfort and trust with retailers they knew, and chose those [retailers] who had what they were looking for at lower prices in order to save some money. And when the economy is tight like that, consumers made those tough choices. Suddenly, shopping at a desolate warehouse or purchasing a clearly fake or stolen purse at a handbag party thrown by a friend seemed like a good idea, regardless of who or what the ripple effect may be [impacting]."[10]

LaRocca sat down with me one humid afternoon at the Atlanta National Retail Foundation conference on loss prevention. He explained how domestic ORC groups were fully aware of American consumers' spending vulnerabilities and took advantage of them. "People were forced to do more with less, and these guys were smart enough to make money off of it," he said. LaRocca also pointed out that with the economic downsizing that was taking place, retailers had to cut back, creating an endless cycle of understaffed stores that aided criminal acts.

Another reason why these crimes are so attractive to ORC rings is that they are not looked upon as federal crimes. Retail theft falls into the category of "property theft" and takes on a lesser charge than an offense that would fall within the jurisdiction of the major crimes division. Despite ORC rings stealing upwards of $1 million in a couple of months, they are still viewed as petty thefts in some instances.

One ORC ring, which was busted in Polk County, Florida in 2008, involved an orchestrated group who stole $100 million in over-the-counter (OTC) drugs, beauty products, and baby formula, reported Casey Chroust, executive vice president of retail operations at the Retail Industry Leaders Association (RILA).[11] This group was a well-organized crime ring, masterminded by someone who knew how the system worked. They worked as a team, blocking cameras and using boosters (someone who steals items from a store) to steal the merchandise, making handsome profits.

Up the coast in New York City, another ORC leader established and oversaw a ring of about 75 to 100 people. Jerry Biggs, director of the organized retail crime division at Walgreens, called this man "Samuel Elias." Elias' ring stole upwards of $2.5 million in merchandise from Walgreens per hit and used it to fund everything from his gambling addiction to overseas accounts based in Jordan.

Both of these rings are similar in how they organized and executed and profited from ORC. However, neither was prosecuted under federal statutes despite engaging in anti-American acts for years, including sending money overseas to support terrorist organizations.

These are just small examples of a larger issue that spans three continents and involves people and cultures from around the world, including the U.S.

Although some involved in ORC are doing it for personal financial gain, most are motivated by the idea of *jihad* and having a hand (small or large) in plotting the demise of one of the world's greatest superpowers—the United States of America.

The Promised Land: Money Talks

Chris from the Congo[12] arrived in New York only to get caught up in the world of counterfeit handbag sales. He told me his story on a July day in 2010 as we sat on a stoop on Lespinard Street, just steps from Chinatown. Let me assure you that although Chris is involved in retail crime, he is not part of any terrorist cell.

Chris hails from the Congo by way of Paris. Although he is only 28, he already has a strong business sense. He looks like a normal, well-educated member of high society. When I met up with him, his shorts were tailored and pressed. His basic white T-shirt was crisp and fit perfectly and was tucked into his shorts. Chris even sported a pair of Prada driving moccasins, often seen on the feet of Upper East Side chief executives, not downtown on Chinatown street merchants. In his right ear was a lattice-patterned earring made of diamonds.

Chris comes from a professional family. His sister works in financial services at a bank in London. His brother is in medical school. Following in his sister's footsteps, Chris came to the U.S. to get a business degree from Pace University in New York City. His family believes this is all he is doing. But the truth is that upon arriving to the city, a contact told him to get in touch with a man from Somalia who ran a couple of businesses and could potentially give him a job. "I didn't come to New York *not* to make money," said Chris. "I had everything in Paris—free healthcare, free social security and benefits. The only reason you would leave that is if you wanted to make real money, and you can do that here."

When Chris arrived in New York, he hooked up with a warehouse owner, from whom he would purchase handbags for $20. He then sold each bag for $60, making $40 in profit per bag. When he first started out, he was moving 30 to 40 bags a day on average. Now, he sells approximately 100 to 150 bags a day at $60 per bag and keeps almost all of the profits. Let me reiterate at this point that Chris keeps the money he earns and is not involved with terrorist rings, but he is very familiar with those who do send their earnings to such groups.

Chris and I made our way to a nearby Starbucks, where he paid for the two drinks on his business debit card from JP Morgan Chase. He explained that he also runs another clothing business, where he sells pants, shoes, and shorts online. "If I am not making money on my web site, then I want to be making money doing this. If I am not working here, I am learning. I have to constantly be improving my situation."

Just as he said this, Chris got a phone call on his cell. It was a colleague of his who also sells handbags in the same Chinatown area, telling him the cops are near. "Come on; we have to go," he said as he gathered his bags, took a last gulp of coffee, and headed out the door. Chris and I ran to the street corner to gather the rest of his merchandise before it could be confiscated by the patrolling NYPD. Chris is constantly moving around; he doesn't have a stand (like some handbag sellers) for fear that he will get arrested. In fact, most of his colleagues operate their businesses like this.

He said some people bring in so much money that they feel they have no choice but to stay in this industry. Chris explained, "When I was put in touch with the warehouse owner, I didn't realize how much money people could make doing this. While I brought in about $10,000 a month, enough to pay for my living expenses and tuition, some people bring in close to fifty or sixty thousand dollars a week, specifically those who have sellers working under them. And you better believe they are the ones sending the money home through the mosques and family members via hawalas. Their American dollars are supporting their economies and political groups back home."

Most of Chris's colleagues who come from Somalia and send money back to their homeland spend their days voicing their disdain toward the U.S. Many of the gripes center around the U.S.'s perpetuation of capitalism and the "in your face" display of money by Americans, in addition to how they spend it. According to Chris, many of his colleagues have a love/hate relationship with that aspect of the U.S. Likewise, the racial undertones that make it more difficult for immigrants to establish themselves as business owners or to get jobs is a topic of heated conversation. "The United States isn't the easiest place for immigrants if they want to establish themselves," said

Chris. "I think all of the rules and regulations, mixed in with overt racism and a general disdain for Muslims, perpetuates a feeling that we not only need to make and take money from this country, but we need to use it to help our home countries. It's the right thing to do."

Given the political state of the Somali government, it's understandable how anti-American sentiment could rise quickly. In a Bertelsmann Transformation Index report conducted by Bertelsmann Stifung over two years ending in 2010, Somalia experienced escalating violence and a deteriorating level of security. This has led to massive population displacements and the worst humanitarian crisis in the country since 1991–1992. Not only did the Transitional Federal Government fail to establish national unity, but it also has been involved in a war against insurgent groups, including Islamists and clan-based militias, such as al Shabaab.[13]

Speaking to several of Chris's colleagues confirmed the anti-American sentiment. One man I spoke to (we'll call him "Edward") told me that after years of economic and social oppression by the government, America was seen as "The Promised Land" where upon arrival, success, security and most importantly monetary gain would happen almost instantly. And while Edward acknowledged his situation was much better once he arrived to New York, it's not up to the standards he had dreamed of. "I thought my big house came the minute I walked off the plane," said Edward laughing slightly. "It wasn't like that to say the least. I have problems here too. It's almost as if the American Dream is just that—a dream."

The country was also significantly affected by the global economic crisis. As many Arab nations felt the sting of sinking oil prices, local stock markets cut in half the value of investments in the global marketplace, with Somalia catching the brunt of it. While most of the population lived in poverty, the crisis catapulted them into extreme poverty, living lives of shocking insecurity.[14] Somalia's labor force of nearly 3.5 million contains few skilled laborers, and its GDP is $2.731 billion. Given these factors, the country has had to sustain itself on an informal economy that is based on livestock, remittance/money transfer companies, and telecommunications.[15]

Somalia isn't the only country brewing with instability and anti-American feeling. We saw this same sentiment expressed by Faisal Shahzad during his initial indictment hearing in June 2010. Shahzad, a Pakistani-born U.S. citizen, devised a plot to detonate a bomb in Times Square—a plan that took two years for him to come up with. It involved multiple trips back to Pakistan, covert ways of obtaining funding for the plot, and, most importantly, a deep disdain for the country of which he was a citizen.

"I want to plead guilty, and I'm going to plead guilty a hundred times forward, because until the U.S. pulls its forces from Iraq and Afghanistan and stops the drone strikes in Somalia and Yemen and in Pakistan and stops the occupation of Muslim lands and stops killing the Muslims and stops reporting the Muslims to its government, we will be attacking the U.S., and I plead guilty to that,"[16] said Shahzad as he pled guilty to ten counts of attempted bombing and engaging in terrorist training.

His statements weren't altogether surprising. Hating America had become the driving force and justification for extremist organizations to plan attacks. But what was shocking was that this hatred was brewing on American soil and sprouting seeds of domestic terrorism.

Made in America: Homegrown Terrorism

Suspected New Jersey terrorists Mohamed Mahmood Alessa and Carlos Eduardo Almonte also felt the need to wage a domestic attack on the U.S. They traveled to Somalia by way of Egypt to train with al Shabaab. According to a friend who belonged to the same mosque, as well as an informant who tipped off the FBI, these troubled young men were talking about "waging a violent jihad." They kept saying that all Americans are their enemies, that everyone other than their

Islamic followers are their enemies, and they all must be killed.[17] Both suspected terrorists were funded by money raised from the sale of merchandise stolen from retailers.[18]

Muslim extremists do not think of themselves as members of separate countries. Rather, they belong to a greater organization whose sole purpose is to create a world free of non-Islamists. This sentiment was expressed by a senior Taliban commander, Mullah Minbullah, in Nuristan in an interview with a pro-Islamist web site. "First of all, Muslims are one," says Minibullah. "Among us there are no foreign and inlanders. We are all Muslims, and I can gladly tell you that nobody can match Afghans in fighting. No Iranians, Arabs, or anyone can fight like we do. But the important fact is that we are, thanks to Allah, Muslims. And for us Muslims, it doesn't matter if you are Afghan, Arab, Pakistani, Tajik, or whatever... and in every household in every corner weapons are present. And the expenses of these weapons are not so expensive to prevent us from financing them ourselves. We get financial aid from people...Muslims from all around the world."[19]

To engage in a full-out jihad, you need weapons, and weapons cost money. As funds are raised by illicit means (such as by selling counterfeit handbags, contraband merchandise, or stolen product), the money made from these illegal sales is being sent back by sympathizers. Taliban groups, such as al Shabaab and Tehreek-e-Taliban, used the funds to train people such as Shahzad in explosives training while he was in Pakistan. The Federally Administered Tribal Areas (FATA) of Pakistan, widely known as a safe haven for al Qaeda fugitives and a staging area for Taliban forces, is largely financed by smuggling goods and persons across the border.[20]

Likewise, two compounds were located within the U.S.—one known as "Islamberg," in Hancock, New York, and the other, a commune called "Red House," in Virginia. Both have ties to the Jamaat al Fuqra, the terrorist group known for kidnapping and killing journalist Daniel Pearl, and both were known to have their own ORC rings involved in the sale of stolen and counterfeit products. According to sources, members of the Islamberg community supplied Shahzad with explosives for his failed attempt to detonate a bomb in Times Square.[21]

Members of the Red House compound (an alleged Muslim 50-acre compound in Charlotte County, Virginia) were recently involved in a $7 million fraud scheme. Under the name Talib's Sportswear, they sold counterfeit-label clothing to retail merchants throughout the country. The probe into the Talib firm led to the arrests of Ronald Gerald "Talib" Roundtree and his wives Berna Robbin, Terri Lynn Singleton, and Keisha Janelle Simms, who reside on "Fatima Lane" in Red House.[22]

"American-based operatives of terrorist groups have increasingly turned to criminal endeavors to finance their murderous actions,"[23] Stephen I. Landsman, director of National Security Law and Policy on the Investigative Project on Terrorism, told me. Whether through drug trafficking, ORC and black-market smuggling, the production and sale of counterfeit name-brand goods, or car theft rings, terrorists have demonstrated that they are willing and able to resort to the types of activities normally reserved for street gangs for financial support. U.S. law enforcement has stopped and should continue to stop these activities with the same proven techniques it has always relied on to combat illicit financial activity. Those efforts, however, must be accompanied by measures aimed at preventing the actual flow of money supporting terrorism—and thwarting the means used to recruit potential ORC ring members.[24]

Recruiting from the Inside

On a hot day in the Santa Ana California State prison, a group of men congregate in the prison's parole yard area. Although they look like typical prison inmates in orange jumpsuits, what they are talking about is anything but ordinary. They are part of a group called the Jam'iyyat Ul-Islam Is-Saheeh (JIS), which translates as "the Assembly for Authentic Islam."[25]

The group was started by Kevin Lamar James, a wiry African-American who sports cornrows, oval-shaped glasses, and an untrimmed goatee. James has what is known in Muslim circles as a "raisin" in the middle of his forehead—a symbol of a pious man who grinds his forehead to the ground during prayer.[26] A California native and 32 years old at the time, James was sentenced for plotting attacks on military recruitment centers, synagogues, the Israeli consulate, and Jewish facilities in 2005. While imprisoned in Folsom in 1997 for gang-related armed robbery, he recruited Levar Washington and Gregory Patterson, who were also sentenced to jail time for assisting James in these attacks. According to an FBI press release, James recruited Washington into the organization by making him swear an oath of loyalty to him and the JIS. A couple weeks after he took the oath, Washington was released from prison and subsequently recruited Patterson and a fourth accomplice, Hammad Samana (a Pakistani native), to form a cell. The three would rob gas stations (because of oil and its political symbolism). They took everything from money to personal care items and over-the-counter medicine for the purpose of reselling it and raising money for the organization. The men stole upwards of $50,000 within ten months. And that's just three people.

"Prisons literally provide a captive audience of disaffected young men easily influenced by charismatic extremist leaders," explained FBI Deputy Assistant Director Donald Van Duyn in a statement before the Senate Committee on Homeland Security and Governmental Affairs and Related Agencies. "These inmates, mostly minorities, feel that the United States has discriminated against them or against minorities and Muslims overseas. This perceived oppression, combined with a limited knowledge of Islam, makes this population vulnerable for extremists looking to radicalize and recruit."[27]

Anti-American sentiment has been historically prevalent in immigrant communities—especially Latin American communities—dating as far back as the early 19th century. A poll done by UNESCO and USIA provided statistical confirmation that U.S. values had great appeal for much of the world's population.[28] Data from the 1958 National Intelligence Estimate found that Latin American attitudes "expressed envy by disparaging U.S. materialism, yet wanted our consumer goods and capital; they espoused pan-Americanism, but engaged in petty nationalism; they chafed at our military power but wanted our protection."[29] Clearly anti-American sentiment has been long-standing and was deep-rooted. (9/11 only accelerated this sentiment worldwide. In a survey done by the Pew Trust in 2001, opinion leaders in many countries stated that U.S. policies were a principal cause of the 9/11 attacks. 58% of the Latin Americans who responded in the survey agreed.[30])

James wasn't the only inmate to recruit or be recruited out of a California prison. Jose Padilla, a native Puerto Rican who was also a U.S. citizen, converted to a radical form of Islam while in jail. He had been involved in many crimes connected to gang activities in Chicago. Padilla (aka Abdullah al Muhajir) admitted he had ties to the Maniac Latin Disciples, the largest Latin street gang in Chicago. He was arrested at Chicago O'Hare airport for plotting a terrorist attack with a dirty bomb.[31] According to Chicago authorities, Padilla was tagged as a potential al Qaeda terrorist and trained with the network.[32]

From Prison to Gangs to the World's Most Notorious Terrorist Group

The MS-13 (Mara Salvatrucha) gang's[33] connection to al Qaeda was facilitated after 9/11 when the terrorist group realized the gang could help smuggle operatives and weapons into the U.S. over the

Mexican border. According to Steven McCraw, the former assistant director of the FBI's Office of Intelligence and current director of the Texas Department of Public Safety, a *matricula* consular[34] provides an opportunity for terrorists to move freely within the U.S. without triggering name-based watch lists.[35]

The cross-border gangs, known as the Maras, came about in the early 1980s when conflict-ridden zones in Central America, such as El Salvador, Guatemala, and Nicaragua, caused hundreds of thousands of people to migrate north to the U.S.—especially into California, Arizona, and New Mexico—as illegal aliens. Once in America, these immigrants (mostly men) encountered difficult work and social situations in terms of integrating into other ethnic-based gangs such as the Crips, Bloods, and Mexican Mafia. Some joined the M-18 (also known as the 18th Street gang, named after a street in Los Angeles), and others created their own gang, the MS-13. The number 13 also refers to a street in Los Angeles. Trained and very familiar with military combat and guns due to the insurgency in their countries, the MS-13 would wage war in the streets of Los Angeles, involving themselves in violent crimes, theft, and drug dealing. When they were arrested and put in jail, MS-13 members would use their time to recruit more members, hone gang identities and criminal skills, and make their cells stronger.[36]

As soon as the peace process ended the strife in El Salvador in 1992, many of the Maras members (who were now M-18 and MS-13 members) were deported and sent back to their homeland. While in their war-torn cities of Guatemala City, San Pedro Sula, and San Salvador, they reestablished themselves and have been expanding their cells all over the world ever since.[37] Today the MS-13 has more than 11,000 active members (compared to the 8,000 members of M-18), with a regional total of 69,145 members in 920 groups.[38]

MS-13 quickly became globally ranked for criminal activity, along with drug trafficking organizations (DTOs) and Mexican Zetas, according to Samuel Logan, author of *This Is for the Mara Salvatrucha:*

Inside the MS-13, America's Most Violent Gang. Despite being from various parts of Central and South America, these gangs have one thing in common. Their strong paramilitary backgrounds allow them to structure themselves into "cliques", individual groups that can number in the hundreds, which operate together within a common network to wage violence with militaristic fervor. Their structures are elaborate, flexible, and sustainable, with solid leadership at the helm and another person to back it up. They function as networks with extensive transnational linkages. Their internal functions are broken into groups and include recruiting, logistics, battle, intelligence (gathering and propaganda), and juvenile delinquents. These are the ones engaging in ORC, in addition to extortion, selling drugs, and committing homicide for pay.[39]

Similar to how non-Afghan mujahideen soldiers eventually formed Al-Qaeda, the Zetas originated from ex-Mexican Special Forces operatives. Not only were these soldiers trained in the art of psychological warfare, but they also were trained to kill like combat forces. "These special forces soldiers just got too close to the money and defected," says Logan. "They are the most sophisticated and well run as far as organized crime rings go. Leaps and bounds over Pablo Escobar (a late Colombian drug lord once know as "the world's greatest outlaw" and certainly the richest). And because of their level of sophistication, they were able to take on the Mexican government head on." Members of these organizations are also known to be heavily armed, with weapons including M-16s, AK-47s, and grenades.[40]

But weapons cost money, and so does running a 69,000-member organization.

To have consistent cash flow to pay for hotel rooms, cars, transportation, and overhead costs, the MS-13 raised funds by escorting people across the U.S. border for thousands of dollars per person. If they are crossing through Mexico, they work with Mexican organized crime rings such as the Zetas or the Tijuana, Juarez, or Gulf drug cartels. The organizations and cartels monitor who the MS-13 traffics in because they take an increased percentage per head depending on whether those crossing are Chinese, Central Americans, or Mexicans. To bring an Arab into the U.S., the "tax" and percentage per person is much higher.[41]

"It is possible that the MS-13 is working with Hezbollah as well as the al Qaeda to smuggle [operatives] into this country. The question is to what extent they are involved and if Hezbollah or al Qaeda really requires their help," says Logan. "There are some Latinos who are becoming Islamic radicals and are engaged in activities that support the Hezbollah. Because of the MS-13's strong ties to Latin and Central America, and because their organization is so vast, adaptable, flexible, and connected, the U.S. government would have a hard enough time going up against them. Forget about the Mexican government. It makes sense that the [MS-13s] would be the main facilitators of illegal entry into the United States."[42] Logan points out that in illegal border crossings, rarely do people give their correct names, nor are they asked what their real names are. "Based on what is happening in Latin America, in countries where the Hezbollah have a strong presence as well as the MS-13, you can't assume they're not working together."[43]

In addition to making money from smuggling people into the U.S., some of whom could be sympathetic to terrorist organizations, many members of the MS-13 are members of or have created organized crime rings (OCRs). This helps them generate income for paying off drug cartel border taxes in their country of origin. They also use the money to help support their families back where they came from. Members who are based in port cities, such as Los Angeles, Miami, New York, Chicago, and Houston, operate rings that fence everything from baby formula to pirated DVDs and cigarettes.

"I wouldn't be surprised if it [organized retail crime] makes up 5% to 6% of what they earn," says Logan. "Half of their extortion, one quarter of the proceeds, comes from being hired hit men; the other 20% or so of the income pie is derived from between five or six things, like drug sales and shady business deals. But ORC is definitely a significant portion of their income because it's a lucrative business. They will steal several quarts of baby formula, cut it with generic powdered milk like they would a powdered drug, and repackage it so that they get more quantity. If you steal a kilo, you can make pretty good money with it."[44]

Members of the MS-13 are obliged to support other members' families, wives, girlfriends, and children if those fellow members are in prison. Logan estimates that almost 60% of the MS-13 funds made through ORC is sent back to El Salvador or other countries via underground banking systems. There is very little accountability, so it's hard to determine exactly how much is sent back per month. However, Logan estimates that thousands of dollars per week per clique could be sent back, with payouts to families in amounts that range from $500 to $800 a week, so that they are taken care of and don't get turned out on the street. In addition, funds are used to pay off corrupt judges within their countries of origin. Logan notes that 20 MS-13 members were essentially let out of jail because their sentences were paid off by other members of the organization. What's more, judgments are made based on what facts a judge writes in a statement. Bribes are often paid to change the facts or sway the judge in favor of the person on trial. Logan recalls one judge getting paid nearly $30,000 to let a single MS-13 member go free.

Access to Funding Gets Creative

Avoiding banking systems is the modus operandi of most homegrown terrorists. For example, Faisal Shahzad worked with four other men in Pakistan as well as the U.S. to move money to and from Pakistan to fund his failed Times Square terrorist plot in May 2010.

According to a report on terrorist financing by the U.S. General Accounting Office, the use of informal banking systems is one of the ways in which organizations earn, move, and store assets. Like other criminals, terrorists focus on crimes of opportunity in vulnerable locations and seek to operate in relative obscurity by taking advantage of close networks of people.[45] The Financial Action Task Force (FATF) requires all member countries to ensure that individuals and entities providing money transmission services must be licensed and registered and subjected to the international standards set out by the FATF.[46] But as seen in the case of Shahzad, countries, including the U.S., have a difficult time regulating money transfers.

Terrorist organizations have to stay two steps ahead of law enforcement even when it comes to the transferring of money. Federal law may cover bulk cash transfers over borders, "just like Tony Montana did in *Scarface*,"[47] says John Tobon, Unit Chief of Financial Programs of the Cornerstone Unit of Immigration and Customs Enforcement. These perpetrators are prosecuted in a federal court if they are caught. Laws do not take into account just how technologically advanced money transfers are becoming and that they are evolving rapidly. The use of stored value cards, PayPal, and wire transfers in conjunction with hawalas allows potential terrorists to move money quickly and remain undetected. When there is more than $10,000 on a stored value card in someone's wallet, customs enforcement doesn't know about it.

In an interview with me in July 2010, Tobon explained how his unit tracks 20 different initiatives by looking at the utilization of shell corporations. These corporations are fronts, acting as legitimate businesses so that terrorist cells can transfer laundered money more readily and easily. Tobon spends his time investigating wire transfers, Ponzi schemes, and ATM fraud—the real issue he says is the generation gap between law enforcement and the criminals.

"We are dealing with a group of people where the virtual world is the only world they know," says Tobon. "Law enforcement is full of 37-year-old guys, all of whom didn't grow up with the Internet and are at times slow adapters. This is where we see the generational gap widen. In a recent financial fraud case, a loose confederation of very bright and young men all under 25 got together every six to eight months to defraud customers via stealing their identities and credit card numbers online. The shocking part was that they were making $20 to $25 million a year just on their ability to manipulate web sites. We are going to see that more and more, especially within terrorist cells and networks. In order to arrest them, we have to know them, and the only way we are going to do that is to technologically evolve."

Burrowing In: The Hezbollah Finds a Home in the U.S. and South America

As terrorist organizations such as al Qaeda, Hezbollah, and Hamas began to disassemble, cells of the organizations started to crop up in unlikely areas of the world. The Tri-Border Area in South America (the border intersection of Argentina, Brazil, and Paraguay) piqued the interest of the FBI and ICE in 2002 when word got out that terrorist operatives were meeting in the area. Meetings took place in and around Cuidad del Este that were attended by representatives of the Hezbollah and other groups sympathetic to Osama bin Laden's terrorist network.[48] Capitalizing on the frustrations of about 25,000 Arab and Lebanese residents living in the area, the Hezbollah set up shop in the South American region. It used the millions of dollars it raised via counterfeit and stolen product smuggling schemes to fund terrorist training camps, propaganda operations, and bomb attacks in South America.[49]

With porous, ill-patrolled borders within the region, U.S. officials fear the rate of potential terrorists entering the U.S. via Brazil or Mexico is extremely high.

Cars, motorcycles, and people can slip between countries' borders without documents being checked. According to the CIA, the Hezbollah militiamen are less likely to raise suspicions because they have Latin American passports, speak Spanish, and look like Hispanic tourists.[50] In addition, many of the alien smuggling networks that move non-Mexican aliens over the borders have ties to Muslim communities in Mexico. According to a 2004 paper on terrorism threats from the CIA's Counterterrorism Center, "Non-Mexicans often are more difficult to intercept because they typically pay high-end smugglers a large sum of money to efficiently assist them across the border, rather than haphazardly traverse it on their own."[51]

Even more significant than members of terrorist organizations getting smuggled into the U.S. is how they are getting the money to pay for it.

Supporting the Enemy Through Charitable Donations

Muslims are required to give away 2.5% of their earnings as a form of *zakat*, or alms. Hezbollah, al Qaeda, and al Shabaab sympathizers concur wholeheartedly with this sentiment. Since zakat guidance is broad, alms can be given to whomever or whatever organization donors see as worthy. For example, when a *fatwa*[52] was issued by the late Ayatollah Khomeini, it legitimized the use of zakat funds to finance the resistance movement against Israel.[53]

This gesture is more for charitable giving and supporting those in need. However, the lines get blurred when it comes to Hezbollah, al Qaeda, and al Shabaab sympathizers who willingly give zakat to fund terrorist acts and shroud this as a religious duty. In testimony given by Dr. Matthew Levitt, senior fellow and director of terrorism studies at the Washington Institute for Near East Studies, Hezbollah receives significant financial support from Hezbollah sympathizers living abroad, especially from Lebanese nationals living in Africa, South America, and other places with large Lebanese Shia expatriate communities. Hezbollah's main income, according to Hezbollah Parliamentarian Mohammad Raad, comes from the group's own investment portfolios and wealthy Shias.[54]

From America to South America: Ties Get Stronger in the Tri-Border Region

South America's Tri-Border Area has been a lucrative region for Hezbollah. Because of its dense population, designated free-trade area, access to ports (Puerto Iguazu, Argentina), hidden air strips, and minimal law enforcement presence, smuggling merchandise is a significant way in which sympathizers raise funds. And it's taking place within U.S. borders.

The connection to the Tri-Border Area has deep roots in the U.S. Within a couple months of each other, two men were arrested in connection with providing material support to the Hezbollah in the Tri-Border Area in the form of smuggled and stolen merchandise. Moussa Ali Hamdan, a 38-year-old native of Lebanon, was a naturalized citizen of the U.S. By day he worked as a carpet installer from 2007 to 2008. He then operated a low-end car dealership. During that period he bought more than $154,000 worth of what he thought were stolen electronics and cars from undercover agents.[55] While he sold some of the stolen product for personal profit, he was allegedly smuggling merchandise to South America, with the proceeds benefitting the Hezbollah, according to court documents.

What Hamdan didn't know was that his smuggling was also playing a pivotal role in helping law enforcement investigate high-level Hezbollah operatives who were selling counterfeit cash to purchase assault weapons to be shipped overseas. Using the money made from the sale of stolen and smuggled merchandise, Hezbollah operatives worked "18 hours a day producing high-quality counterfeit currency for the Hezbollah."[56] In addition, Hamdan helped his co-conspirator and well-connected Hezbollah operative, Dib Hani Harb (who was also involved in producing the counterfeit currency), broker a meeting between the FBI informant and Hassan Hodroj, a member of Hezbollah's political bureau in Beirut. Hodroj requested 1,200 Colt M4 machine guns, a model used by U.S. special forces, for which Hodroj said he would pay $1,800 per gun.[57] "His arrest there underscores the global nature and reach of Hezbollah's financial and logistic support," said Levitt in an interview with me.

Prior to Hamdan's arrest, three men in Miami were also arrested for selling stolen Sony PlayStation 2 consoles, cameras, and other electronics to the Galeria Page mall in Cuidad del Este in Paraguay, which we will delve into later in the book. The men, Khaled T. Safadi, Ulises Talavera, and Emilio Gonzalez-Neira, created a sophisticated ring that involved buyers, sellers, and freight forwarders, as well as people who could create fake documents and invoices.

"While engaging in criminal activity often increases a group's vulnerability by further exposing them to scrutiny of law enforcement authorities, Hezbollah's reliance on fellow sympathizers and members of local expatriate communities minimizes that potential exposure," says Levitt. "Hezbollah is very criminally oriented for its fundraising in the U.S., including legitimate and illegitimate business activities."[58]

These cases are just the tip of the iceberg. With such a large portion of money from ORC theft up for grabs and because of the federal government's unwillingness to prosecute these criminals as felons, the problem continues to grow at an astronomical rate. Retailers and government officials have one option—step up their game, or keep putting their country at risk.

And as if the state of national security weren't enough, another group is also being severely affected by ORC—the consumer.

2

When a Deal Isn't a Deal

On one of the hottest days of the year in 2009, a line of women clad in Louboutin heels and thousand-dollar outfits wait patiently in the 100-degree heat. The doors to the much-anticipated Fendi warehouse sale in New York City are about to open. Women have come from as far away as Australia to stand in the sweltering sun to get first dibs on the best merchandise. The estimated wait time is well over four hours. The markdowns on the prior year's ready-to-wear shoes and accessories will be "well worth the wait" according to one well-heeled customer, who insists that this year will be way better than past years.[1]

"No one was shopping this year [2009], so unlike years past, there is going to be an abundance of merchandise," squeals one customer who has brought extra bags in anticipation of carrying out a larger-than-usual haul. "Most retailers were hesitant to mark anything down last season, and those that did still priced out pieces way too high. For all those girls who stifled their inner Carrie Bradshaw, this [sale] is our way of getting back at those retailers!"

In 2009, Fendi, whose parent company is LVMH, like most other brands had seen declining profits due to the global recession in markets that included the U.S. and Europe. In fact, it wasn't until February 2010 that Fendi chief executive Michael Burke announced in an interview that for the first time in a long time, the company had grown in all geographic zones around the world.[2] However, the plummet in demand the company experienced up until that point had to do with a general sentiment that consumption of luxury items was seen as uncouth in the wake of a sinking economy, Ponzi schemes, a crashing housing market, and employment uncertainty. This was according to Milton Pedraza,[3] principal at the Luxury Institute, a luxury consulting company in New York City. Fendi tried to regain a foothold in the retail space by launching new products such as the chic handbag the Fendi Peekaboo that enjoyed robust sales around the world during the spring of 2010. However, this means of generating profits also gave way to sinister practices—counterfeit merchandise and the resale of stolen handbags.

China's economic boom was fueled by overseas companies looking to take advantage of the low costs and high productivity of China's factories. Companies that outsourced were able to retain most of the retail value of their products, while Chinese manufacturing firms retained a smaller share, according to a report from the United Nations Office on Drugs and Crime (UNODC). However, manufacturers and designers living in two different countries had a hard time policing design fraud. That fact, combined with a high demand for luxury goods and the ability to produce large quantities at a cheaper price along with a cut in manufacturing costs, made the illicit production and sale of goods an attractive proposition. Sales of accessories such as shoes and ready-to-wear from legitimate luxury brands suffered tremendously in the U.S. because the market was saturated with fake and stolen merchandise. What's more, the rise in unlicensed street vendors, web sites, and illegitimate discount stores selling contraband merchandise made these products readily available with little consequence if they were purchased.

And terrorist cells such as al Shabaab and Hezbollah took note.

I learned from two sources who are close to LVMH, that during the global recession Fendi executives met with their design teams, management consultants, and manufacturers on a regular basis to figure out how to decrease their exposure to organized retail crime. All the while, Chong Lam and Siu Yung Chan, aka Joyce Chan, a middle-aged pair who looked more like my best friend's parents, were importing and selling more than $100 million of counterfeit goods by way of China to the U.S.

In fact, Lam and Chan controlled 13 different companies in the U.S. and China and operated "at least eight separate factories dedicated to producing handbags, including large quantities of counterfeit bags," according to an ICE investigator.[4] Investigators raided the offices of Coco USA (Chan and Lam's primary storage warehouse and shell company), located in Manhattan close to the wholesale district of Broadway and 28th. On a blustery January day in 2008, they executed search warrants and seized approximately 1,500 cartons of alleged counterfeit and other illegal items. The total value of the corresponding luxury goods (meaning items that are real and not fakes) manufactured by Burberry, Louis Vuitton, Gucci, Coach, Fendi, Chanel, and others was estimated to be more than $100 million.[5] In addition to housing counterfeit items, Lam and Chan's warehouse contained crates full of stolen merchandise, including iPhones, high-end clothing, and beauty products. It also contained handbags that would be purchased by smaller warehouses that were known Hezbollah and Hamas sympathizers, said an investigator close to the case.[6] (When I pressed the NYPD for details about with whom Lam and Chan were doing deals, they mentioned that many of their "buyers" were in the same neighborhood. What's more, a detective working on the case confirmed that a percentage of the money made was being sent to overseas accounts in the Middle East.)

But it wasn't just the smaller retailers and vendors who were in on the illegal activity.

Starting in 2005, Fendi tried to address the problem with a very public lawsuit against retailers such as Filene's Basement (which was once owned by Retail Ventures Inc. [RVI] and subsequently went bankrupt) and Burlington Coat Factory. The lawsuit alleged that the retailers were selling counterfeit and stolen Fendi items including handbags, shoes, and clothes. After close to five years,[7] Fendi received a $2.5 million settlement against Retail Ventures Inc. in June

2010, resolving allegations that the former Filene's chain bought and sold counterfeit Fendi goods with RVI involvement. The settlement also provided an injunction that permanently barred RVI from selling Fendi products without prior permission. The settlement came after a $4.7 million contempt judgment against Burlington Coat Factory that cited the company for willfully selling counterfeit and previously sold merchandise. In October 2010, Fendi settled with Burlington Coat Factory for an estimated $10 million after a judge ordered Burlington to pay Fendi $5.6 million in "treble damages, attorneys' fees, and costs for willful counterfeiting."[8] These settlements sent a strong message. As Michael Burke, Chairman and CEO of Fendi said at the time of the settlement, "It's particularly reassuring that the district court made clear in its rulings in this case that the retailer is responsible for making sure that the trademarked products sold to the public are authentic, and that the consequences when a retailer sells counterfeit goods are serious."[9] Despite the retail industry's success with the Burlington Coat Factory verdict, its efforts in trying to curtail the problem from the loss prevention side, not to mention the millions of dollars LVMH spent on legal fees, its actions were in vain. The problem went far beyond the walls of this high-end retailer.

Going after big-box retailers when it comes to selling fake and stolen merchandise was just the beginning.

Getting a Slice of Luxury the Cheapest Way Possible

The consumer, desperate to get luxury items at a discounted cost, saw no harm in using alternative channels to obtain merchandise. Loss prevention executives soon realized that big-box retailers selling counterfeit and stolen merchandise accounted for only a very small percentage of their profit loss. Smaller discount stores, storefronts, and street vendors (such as warehouses and stores that purchased from the Lam/Chan operation in New York, Los Angeles, or Boston) set up stands on large avenues with a glut of tourists. By selling counterfeit and stolen items, they (street vendors) made $500 million a month. What's more, government agencies estimated at least $25 million was going to fund terrorist cells overseas.

Back in New York, I'm standing out of breath with Chris from the Congo minutes after we've dodged NYPD cops. He begins to explain how much Chinatown alone is profiting from the sale of stolen and fake merchandise. "I need some water," I gasp, while noticing that the strap on my four-inch heel is broken. Convinced I will pass out from heatstroke, I look for an awning where I can fix my shoe, replenish electrolytes, and come to terms with the fact that we are two seconds away from getting arrested. The temperature is Hades hot; it is a sweltering 98 degrees. "A couple of blocks from here is Wall Street," says Chris, pointing in the direction of the Statue of Liberty. (Chris looks just as calm as he did when we were in Starbucks 10 minutes earlier, despite our 400-meter dash through Chinatown.) "Down there they made more than half a trillion dollars last year. The black market for counterfeit and stolen goods is making billions, and that's just in Chinatown alone! If we added up how much each city was generating in sales of black market items, it would be a lot more than half a trillion dollars [he estimates]."

It seems that Fendi and LVMH Group weren't the only ones to be affected by pirated and counterfeit merchandise (in addition to the global recession). The streets of Manhattan were filled with all manner of discounted high-end items. But the problem isn't isolated to the Big Apple.

In May 2010, Coach sued the city of Chicago for allowing fake handbags to be sold on Maxwell Street—a bustling tourist thoroughfare filled with vendors selling knockoff bags, leather goods, perfumes, and toiletries. The public company claimed that by allowing these handbags to be sold, the city of Chicago was costing Coach (whose annual global sales exceed $3 billion) millions. Coach also alleged that the city did nothing to prevent these bags from being sold, which was a trademark violation of nearly 50 logo copyrights, according to the lawsuit filed in federal court. The total cost of this breach was close to $98 million.[10]

But copyright infringement, corporate lawsuits, and city-wide crackdowns on fake handbags are the furthest thing from the minds of the sample salegoers in New York. And, as the women wait patiently in line to make their annual purchases of legitimate merchandise, Chris from the Congo sets up his selection of counterfeit and stolen Fendi and Coach handbags. He expects to rake in three times the profit that the Fendi sample sale will bring selling handbags alone. When pressed about the authenticity of his bags, he admits that most of what he sells is fake.

"The fake ones are the less expensive ones," he says, pointing to modified versions of logos for Coach, Fendi, and Louis Vuitton handbags. "If you want the 'real' ones, well, those are going to cost you some money."

Nearly $400, to be exact.

The "Real Deal"

Most vendors selling counterfeit goods have the "real deal" (another name for a counterfeit bag that's made more properly) in the back room. Chris from the Congo gives out his cell phone number, with a New York area code. "If you call me, I can make sure I have all the items with me and will meet you wherever you like," he says. This personal delivery of merchandise ensures that Chris and his cohorts remain virtually anonymous, says a detective with the NYPD when I asked why the vendors do business like that. Not only does this make him virtually indispensable to his customers, it also makes him hard to catch. "If a store is selling something fake or stolen out of a back room for an extended amount of time, they create a transactional trail that makes it easier for us to bust the store. When vendors move around, obtain merchandise from different wholesalers, or sell stolen items, it's virtually impossible to trace."[11]

A couple days later on a Sunday, I visit Chris again. This time, when we walk along Lispenard Street, vendors openly display designer (albeit fake or stolen) handbags, accessories, and electronics on the sidewalk. Swarms of women surround them, haggling over prices with two or three bags dangling from each arm.

"What is going on here?" I ask, befuddled. Surely a cop would come bounding out of nowhere, and I was ready to bolt—this time in the appropriate footwear.

"No cops on Sundays; therefore, the environment is more relaxed," says Chris. His speech has a slight, clipped British overtone I hadn't noticed before. Meanwhile, I spot the all-too-familiar NYPD uniform across the street. The officer is directing traffic.

"What about him?" I squawk. The thought of dashing through the streets again is less than appealing.

"Be cool," Chris says. "That's just a traffic cop. They don't care!"

According to Chris, in the five years he's been selling counterfeit goods, he's seen a rise in clients. Prior to the recession in 2007, demand for counterfeit and stolen "real deal" handbags was already high. However, as the job and real estate markets started to sink and uncertainty about everyone's collective financial future settled in, Chris saw demand for his handbags increase so much that he could barely keep them in stock. "My customers live on Park Avenue but shop down here. 99% of the time you can't tell the difference between a bag they bought through me and a bag their friends are carrying."

Dying for a Deal: The Recession Doesn't Make Aspirations Go Away

According to the Bureau of Economic Analysis, consumer spending dipped to its lowest level in December 2008, the worst year for consumer spending in 47 years. Expenditures on durable goods, such as motor vehicles and parts, furnishings and durable household equipment, and recreational goods and vehicles, hit their lowest points. In the nondurable market (also known as discretionary expenditures), clothing and footwear dipped to a measly negative 8.9%, as the consumer reallocated funds toward purchases such as gasoline and other energy goods.[12]

The definition of discretionary versus nondiscretionary items was rapidly morphing as the recession pressed on. Prior to the recession, clothing, footwear, and even certain beauty products such as makeup and shampoo were considered nondiscretionary. The "aspirational shopper," the woman who occasionally splurges on an expensive handbag, pair of shoes, or piece of clothing, no longer had discretionary income to allocate to those purchases. Instead, she turned to merchants like Chris from the Congo and stores like Collette in East Hampton, New York to fulfill her need for designer wear at a less expensive price.

"Luxury merchants can no longer count on the sheer increase in the number of affluent consumers to ensure the (at least near-term) viability of their brands and their companies," says Richard Baker, chief executive of Premium Knowledge Group, a luxury market research company. "[In 2008] neither could they count on the current number of affluent shoppers to spend the way they did. Current conditions, and the probability that these conditions will last for some time, make the task of the luxury marketer more difficult. No longer will 'a rising tide lift all yachts.'"[13]

The Organisation for Economic Co-operation and Development estimated the value of counterfeit and pirated goods that are traded internationally to be 2% of the world trade in goods, or $176 billion in 2007.[14] The U.S. estimated that 14,841 seizures valued at $261 million were made by authorities in fiscal year 2009 alone.[15] Although the most pirated and reproduced products are usually electronics, clothing and apparel are a close second. Piracy compromises the rigorous testing for lead, toxic materials, and workmanship, thus creating potential hazards for the consumer. What's more, counterfeiters often employ sweatshop labor and engage in environmentally unsound manufacturing processes.

Similar to selling pirated items, counterfeit and ORC rings further maximize profits by evading import duties through customs fraud and avoid paying sales taxes by selling items through informal means (vendors, unlicensed and unauthorized retailers, and the Internet). The counterfeit consumer route can be traced from East Asia to Europe and sees two billion pirated and counterfeit articles a year[16] being shipped via sea through transit hubs in Dubai. Groups involved with the trafficking of product originate in China, South Asia, and Eastern Europe. The United Nations sees this trend increasing in the next five to ten years.[17]

Big Takedowns Take Precedence Over Smaller Offenders

In 2005, the NYPD carried out one of the largest takedowns in the city's history when they raided and removed $40 million worth of merchandise from a warehouse identified as the Epoch USA Trading Company, located in the heart of the city's wholesale district. Police raided nine floors of the building and removed counterfeit goods that ranged from handbags and wallets to shirts and baseball caps with the Lacoste, Coach, and major league sports team logos emblazoned on them. The warehouse supplied these goods to many of the NYC street vendors. Although many rings exist in urban areas, law enforcement tends to go for the larger, more "newsworthy" takedowns. The larger the bust, it seemed, the more accolades the detectives, officers, and investigators received said a detective I spoke with.

"We aren't concerned so much with people like Chris from the Congo and the stuff they sell on the street. What we are concerned with is the warehouse that is importing and distributing and then supplying Chris with his merchandise," says John Tobon, ICE Unit Chief of Financial Programs at the Cornerstone Unit, a group created within the ICE to investigate financial crimes. "The NYPD has roughly 28,000 to 38,000 cops on the street. ICE has 7,000 worldwide. Unfortunately, we don't have the manpower to go and get every single vendor who is selling potentially illegal merchandise. But we can get to the heart of the problem, which are these illegal warehouses and distribution centers."

Counterfeiters and ORC Move Their Operations Online

Keeping a terrorist group going takes money. From 2007 to 2009, traffickers and ORC ringleaders cut costs by selling contraband merchandise on web sites while maintaining high margins. Online, merchandise can be sold seamlessly, anonymously, and with minimal investment on the seller's behalf. The market for goods also increases, because auction sites have an international reach. The UN estimates that the number of people using the Internet has gone from seven million users in 1992 to almost two billion across 233 countries in 2008.[18]

Online auction fraud was the most reported crime in 2009, comprising almost 52% of reported complaints, compared to 44.9% in pre-recession 2007.[19] The rapid growth of a service that is free and accessible virtually everywhere in the world gave rise to *cyber crime*. This term describes anything from offenses against computer data and systems (hacking and phishing) to content offenses and, in the case of selling pirated and counterfeit items, copyright offenses. Retail losses due to cybercrime were estimated to be as much as $1 trillion in 2008. 70% specifically focused on the sale of pirated items. What I didn't realize is that most of these pirated items were items that could be found in my medicine cabinet.

The cybercrime of e-fencing is one of the main ways terrorist cells such as al Shabaab in Somalia obtain funding. Likewise, Lashkar-e-Taiba (LeT) has been known to engage in Internet piracy to fund terrorist cells.[20] *E-fencing* is a term used to describe the activities of boosters who sell stolen items on Internet sites such as eBay, DHgate, and Alibaba. The process is fairly simple for boosters engaged in ORC. First, items that are stolen are organized and photographed, and then the photos are uploaded to the auction site. In most cases, the boosters have multiple code names to sell items ranging from over-the-counter and counterfeit medicine to razor blades and electronics. They create these code names to throw off regulators and to price the merchandise well below market value and lure the unsuspecting consumer.

In a recent search I did on eBay, more than 300 auctions were dedicated to the sale of over-the-counter drugs originating in India. Three auctions were at wholesale prices (ten boxes minimum, with 42 tablets in each), with a starting price of $1.99. Likewise, there were more than 40 auctions for coupons for Prilosec OTC for up to $3 off, with coupons selling for $0.99 to $7.49.

Shocked and perplexed, I did some research and found that India has become one of the main sources of drugs (both stolen and counterfeit) sold through illegally operating Internet pharmacies, according to a UN report.[21] Orders placed with such pharmacies are often dispatched to buyers in other countries using courier or postal services. Since 2002, Indian law enforcement agencies have detected and disbanded several groups that were operating illegal Internet pharmacies. However, many still operate, which can have devastating health effects on consumers.

"The problem arises when e-commerce sites don't police themselves," says Jack Gee, a detective and founder of the Coalition of Law Enforcement and Retail (CLEAR), a partnering organization between law enforcement and loss prevention professionals. "Figuring out who is selling this stolen and counterfeit merchandise is within their jurisdiction, despite the fact that their sellers are not centralized—they are from all across the country and the world. They [e-commerce sites] weren't catching it themselves—they were being reactive instead of being proactive. [We found] someone selling 40 or 50 gift cards, or most recently [we nabbed a] guy who in a year made $60,000 selling GPS devices online, or another guy who made $2.5 million over two years selling razor blades through eBay and another company that was posting on Amazon. When we followed the funds, we found that he was sending money back home through a charitable organization linked to the Harakat al Shabaab.[22] If nothing else, it should raise an eyebrow to these e-commerce sites that something more dire is going on here."[23]

eBay's Swift Response

"Whenever stolen property is put on eBay, it is to some extent [a national fence problem]," says Rob Chesnut, former eBay senior vice president of trust and safety. "And there is no question in my mind that eBay gets abused by people who've got stolen property."

Chesnut explains that eBay's business model is built on trust between buyers and sellers. "If crime happens on the site, and buyers don't trust the sellers, they will simply go elsewhere," he says.

Recently (after coming under intense scrutiny from the retail community), eBay created a group within the company to monitor, identify, and report potential criminals and ORC ring members posing as legitimate sellers. The group was formed in 2009 and is headed by the retail industry's loss prevention luminary Paul Jones. His long career in loss prevention spans working at Limited Brands to being an executive at the Retail Industry Leaders Association (RILA). Jones knew he had a lot to prove. In the second quarter of 2009, eBay's reported revenues were $2.10 billion with a profit of $377 million, historically a low point in the company's run during the "Great Recession."[24] Amazon was quickly encroaching on the company's market share with its $40 million acquisition of Zappos.com. All departments in eBay's marketplace division (which includes eBay.com, shopping. com, and ticket resale and exchange site StubHub), PayPal (its payment arm), and the loss prevention team at eBay knew they had to step up their game. "I was scared," Jones admits to me when I met with him in Atlanta at the 2010 NRF Loss Prevention Conference Expo. "In the past there was a shrouded approach to what eBay was doing in terms of curbing any criminal activity. People (here Paul was referring to those from the Loss Prevention and Retail industries) immediately thought eBay was the place for criminals and crooks to go when they wanted to unload their stuff, and PayPal was facilitating it. I had to let them know we were doing everything in our power to ensure we were monitoring the situation. When people ask to see what we are doing, I am happy to take them through the eBay system, show them exactly who is buying what, and how we flag potential criminals. In order to be effective, we needed to be transparent."[25]

To bolster his point, Jones, along with other members of his team, invites me to look at my PayPal account as well as others. He pulls up PayPal accounts of sellers who have been flagged as alleged criminals. Jones and his team look at four primary characteristics when flagging an account as suspicious: selling history, price anomalies, quantities, and information of losses due to theft from eBay's retail partners. Showing me an account that is selling razor blades, Jones points out, "Usually when a seller is trying to get rid of something they own, it's not sold in these quantities," he explains. Pointing to the eBay report that charts how many bulk items the seller has uploaded to be sold, the report also shows how many times the seller has done so during the year. He goes on to explain that "PayPal adheres to the same regulations a commercial bank must adhere to. We immediately flag accounts that are moving $10,000 or more from one account to another."

Jones also says that the data mined by eBay and PayPal is shared with the government on request, subpoena, pursuant to banking regulations, or when eBay determines there is a crime. This includes the seller's name, address, what items are being bought and sold and at what price, and how many transactions the seller participates in within the week, month, year, and five years. "If you think Amazon and Google aren't sharing the same information with the government, then you are mistaken," asserts Jones.

Too Little, Too Late

While some loss prevention experts like Jack Gee admit the addition of Jones and the creation of his team have benefited the retail community greatly, some in the industry feel that eBay is still not doing enough to curtail the sale of stolen or counterfeit items. Kris Buckner, private investigator and ORC and counterfeiting consultant to brands such as Deckers, says the problem with auction-based e-commerce sites like eBay is the lack of cooperation and information sharing. Investigators and law enforcement officials agree. "They only give us the information when we ask for it, which is usually after these criminals have not only swindled their buyers, but they've made their money and transferred it elsewhere. Their timing in identifying these criminals is ten steps behind everyone else. If they could self-police more, instead of contacting law enforcement to police after the fact, their system would be more effective," Buckner tells me.[26]

Lurking in the Shadows: Stolen Gift Cards Bought Online

Former Colorado State Representative Alice Borodkin, a Denver Democrat, introduced a bill that would make it illegal to sell manufacturer or store coupons and prescription drugs on auction sites. (This occurred after Colorado experienced a loss of approximately $533 million in retail sales in 2008.) This legislation has yet to pass.

Auction sites and fake online stores may help stolen products magically become untraceable cash. They also facilitate the transfer and sale of gift cards to fund terrorist activity. This system is also called "shadow banking," a term coined by FBI chief Robert Mueller. Instead of moving large amounts of cash (over the $10,000 limit) in duffle bags, which are heavy and can easily be identified, criminals use gift and cash cards to easily slip tens of thousands of dollars through customs. The cards, which look like credit cards, can sidestep banking regulations, which state that cash or "money instruments" such as shared certificates, travelers checks, and money orders must be declared if they are being moved across borders. Carrying $100,000 on a gift or cash card is perfectly legal, and they can be used without fear of documentation, identification, law enforcement suspicion, or seizure.[27]

By some estimates, the stored value card is a $300 billion-a-year industry and is growing exponentially. At a congressional hearing in March 2010, Mueller said, "Recent money laundering investigations have revealed a trend by criminals to use stored devices, such as prepaid gift cards and reloadable debit cards in order to move criminal proceeds."[28] With money laundering accounting for 2%–5% of the world's GDP, according to the International Monetary Fund (IMF),[29] stored value cards are becoming a larger part of the global money laundering problem. Obtaining them is just a matter of a few mouse clicks.

Auction sites tend to be the first place ORC thieves unload their stolen merchandise, but these sites also sell stored value cards, gift cards, gift receipts, and store credit. Unlike traditional auctions, for the most part they are unregulated.

Easy to Obtain, Easy to Sell

At the National Retail Federation's annual Loss Prevention conference in Atlanta in June 2010, a group of 60 loss prevention retail executives packed into a frigid conference room to discuss the rising impact that stolen store gift cards and cash cards are having on their businesses. The leader of the discussion was Paul Cogswell, CPP, CFE, and vice president at Stored Value Solutions. He coaxed the executives to talk about their experiences—something they were hesitant to do. When no one spoke, he said, "I know some of you definitely have something to say about this topic. Some of you in this room have approached me outside of these doors. Come on; let's hear it. We are in a safe space."[30]

A tall, tan, youngish-looking man sheepishly raised his hand. All eyes were on him as he began telling his story. "This happens all the time, and I'm always so surprised when I see it," said the young executive. "People come in wanting to pay for items using their gift cards, and there is nothing on them. Instead of our clerks asking questions or running the number on the back of the card through the system, they just assume it was a mistake on behalf of the cardholder. If a couple checks were put in place, we as retailers would be able to regulate theft more."[31]

As with most ORC-related theft, retailers have problems communicating what is taking place in their stores. Their reasons range from embarrassment to store employees not realizing how grave the situation is. When it comes to stored value cards, loss prevention executives, as well as employees, often push aside the issue. The executive added, "Most of our people manning the cash registers are 18 years old and don't know any better. And with turnover being so high, it's hard for us to invest in proper training."

Purchasing items that aid in criminal activities isn't a new practice, as in the case of terrorism suspect Faisal Shahzad. He admitted to receiving $4,500 transferred to him from Pakistan through a *hawaladar* (someone who arranges a money transfer). Shahzad's co-conspirators, Pir and Aftab Khan, according to their attorneys, transferred money back to their home country of Pakistan using stored value cards in amounts of $20,000, $100,000, and $300,000. In addition, Mahmoud Reza Banki, a resident of New York City and a former management consultant with degrees from UC Berkeley and Princeton, was accused of receiving more than $3.4 million from the accounts of companies and individuals in Latvia, Slovenia, Russia, Sweden, Saudi Arabia, Kuwait, the Philippines, and the U.S. With the help of a business partner based in Tehran, he would transfer funds to recipients in Iran by using stored value cards, circumventing government regulations and processing fees.[32]

In 2009, retailers reported an increase in organized groups returning stolen merchandise and getting store credit in the form of a receipt or gift card and then putting the gift cards on online auction sites to sell. ICE estimates that $30 billion in remittance payments for open system cards goes to Latin America from the U.S. each year. The purchaser can put a certain amount of money on this kind of card, which often is branded with American Express, MasterCard, or Visa and operates like traditional credit or debit cards. Each year, $10 billion goes to Mexico alone to fund narcoterrorism groups.[33]

Joe LaRocca, senior loss prevention advisor at the National Retail Federation (NRF), notes that auction sites have made strides to try to close the gap in communication between law enforcement and retailers to police web sites. "What we need to do is keep an ear out for the blatant gift card and money card fraud that is going on, because those are open loopholes," says LaRocca. "Monitoring the amount of applied value that is going on the cards, as well as monitoring cards that don't work when they are presented at stores, is one thing. Monitoring these cards being sold on the Internet is another. Disclosure of amounts from the buying and selling on auction sites as well as at the redemption end is crucial."[34]

Fake-out: Retailers Fronting as Legitimate Stores

Urban jungles like New York, Chicago, and Los Angeles draw wanderlust tourists from the U.S. and around the globe. They also provide a market for counterfeit and stolen items to be sold through flea markets and pawn shops. In 2009, the city of New York saw demand for street vendor licenses increase by 60% from 2007 to 2009 when the economy started to plummet.[35] In New York, nearly 12,000 vendors applied for the coveted 853 merchandising vendor licenses the city provides to nonveterans. In addition, the wait list to get a license exceeded 7,000 in 2009.[36] Instead of waiting around to get their legitimate license, vendors took to the streets to sell their merchandise illegally. The makeup of their merchandise landscape varies from pirated DVDs and media to counterfeit high-end perfume and luxury items. Some set up shop at a table or stall on a street, but most carry their merchandise in bags that are easily transportable in case law enforcement comes through.

"Street vendors who sell counterfeit merchandise do it because it's the easiest way to turn a profit," says Ali Issa, a former staff organizer of The Street Vendor Project, which is part of the Urban Justice Center. "Consumers know when they are a buying a pirated item, and that's why they go to these street and flea market vendors. They want to get a deal without paying for the real thing."

U.S. Customs and Border Protection estimates that in 2008 the value of counterfeit items seized was worth $275 million in the U.S.

alone. This included footwear, consumer electronics, handbags, leather goods, and apparel. Ninety percent of those goods were sold through illegal street vendors.[37] The number dipped slightly (to $260 million) in 2009,[38] as imports into the U.S. decreased due to a global recession and limited supply. But the agency expects the numbers to rise again when the economy rebounds. Stolen merchandise is no different. In July 2010, a family-run ORC ring was busted in Kansas City, Missouri. They were hoarding almost $180,000 worth of health and beauty merchandise in a home and selling it at the local flea market, "Super Flea."[39]

Contrary to what most industry analysts might think, most consumers are unaware of where their purchases come from. They leave it up to the retailers to regulate sites and off-price venues to ensure the integrity of what they are purchasing, even though this assumption may seem naive. Although Chris from the Congo can tell me everything about handbags—down to the type of rivets Louis Vuitton uses on its signature monogram bag—he can't tell me where the knockoff manufacturer got such rivets, and he doesn't care. In fact, he explained to me that if I had $2,500 to spend, I too could create my own small business of selling these handbags with a markup of at least 150%. "As you can see, people make a lot of money," says Chris. I could see the appeal, especially if I were unemployed without any job prospects.

At the same time, flea market stall owners, pawn shop owners, as well as "mom and pop" stores all take advantage and sell items that are potentially funding terror cells. According to Dr. Read Hayes, director Loss Prevention Research Council and co-director Loss Prevention Research Team at the University of Florida, the most common hot beds of retailers selling counterfeit and stolen beauty, health, apparel, media and electronic items are souvenir shops in beach towns and tourist hot spots, such as Atlantic City, New Jersey; Orlando and Fort Lauderdale, Florida; and Ocean City, Maryland.[40] Owners take orders from boosters for items to stock their store shelves or to resell the items, and then the boosters go out and obtain the goods. The stores purchase the goods for a discounted price. Most of the time, stores purchasing the items have close ties to either the boosters stealing the items or the warehouses storing them. What's more, Hayes has proof that these merchants sent money that was used to fund bombings in India as well as Indonesia.

Thinking back to his bigger ORC cases, Jack Gee recalls a time prior to 9/11 when he was doing a sting operation in the Fort Lauderdale area. He received information that several small shops were purchasing stolen property; all of the operators happened to be from various countries in the Middle East. The operation involved many months of surveillance where, for instance, one law enforcement official listened in on a conversation spoken in Sudanese. "The men were discussing time zones in the U.S. and purchasing stolen property," recalls Gee. "But what struck me was, when we did the actual bust, not only did we find that these store owners were engaging in buying stolen merchandise, they were also purchasing ID sets in order to make fake identification cards. Further digging and calls to the FBI indicated that these guys were in fact on a terrorist watch list."[41]

Khaled T. Safadi, Ulises Talavera, and Emilio Gonzalez-Neira, three businessmen from the Miami area, were sure their funding of the Hezbollah via stolen Sony PlayStation 2 systems would go unnoticed by the U.S. government. The scheme entailed obtaining Sony PlayStation consoles and digital cameras and exporting them to the tune of $720,000. After three years, the men were finally arrested in February 2010 on charges of illegally exporting electronics to the Galeria Page mall in Ciudad del Este, Paraguay, which funnel profits to the Hezbollah. The Galeria Page mall has been flagged by the U.S. government and listed as a terrorist organization blamed for attacks on Israel, making it illegal to export items to the mall.

"We all have a terrorist task force any time I am doing a sting operation," says Gee. "Just about half are being watched by the task force for money laundering, ORC, false ID, or a combination of all three. It's safe to say there is a huge correlation between ORC and terrorism."

Protecting Yourself: Know the Signs of E-fencing/ORC

"You know the old adage 'If it's too good to be true, it probably is?' In this case, that should be a mantra the consumer should live by," says Jack Gee.

"I've been in swap shops where merchandise is priced way below market value, and you can pretty much guarantee it's stolen. The problem is that the everyday consumer looks at this like it's a good deal, but they are helping to commit a crime. Protect yourself. If a person is not letting you see the product in person, or through pictures, that person is probably not telling you the entire truth about the product." Gee gives an example of how a victim of e-fencing decided to purchase a dirt bike on eBay. The owner of the bike told the victim that the bike was in a storage facility in New York, and that if he put the money in escrow, he could check it out for himself. The victim put the money in the account but never saw the bike or his money again. Likewise, Gee says to look out for patterns of multiple or bulk items being sold at the same time by one person or a company, because most of the time those items have been stolen. "If a person is trying to sell you 30 packs of razor blades, or 20 packages of nicotine patches, then that should be a red flag, and take extra precaution when dealing with them," he says. Gee's last words of advice: Extremely high seller ratings don't help. "Take extra precaution when dealing with Internet sellers. You never know if it's their friends that are giving them such high ratings. You can't always trust that."[42]

It's hard for me not to wonder what the impact on the stores would be. Consumers thought they benefitted from purchasing lower priced items, but the benefit came to a screeching halt when retailers realized how much revenue they were losing from ORC. Someone had to make up the cost and it wasn't coming from the bottom lines of the retailer's balance sheets.

3

The Cost to the Stores

It happened again.

During a routine investigation in 2008 of a reported shoplifting incident at the Arden Fair Mall in Sacramento, California, Captain Daniel Hahn noticed there was more to the reported rip-off. The theft was part of a series of thefts carried out over a nine-month period by a group, not an individual. As Hahn delved deeper into the situation, he realized that what was deemed by store security as "a minor shop-lifting infraction" executed by one person was actually part of a larger ring of people. They could steal an estimated $46,000 worth of mer-chandise in three months, making the grand total $138,000.[1]

"This wasn't the first time I've seen something like this happen with retailers," Hahn told me,[2] shaking his head in disbelief. "Store security, loss prevention executives, even store management think one-off 'shoplifting' situations aren't part of a larger organizational scheme and end up getting swindled for millions of dollars."

When Hahn totaled all the estimated losses from theft at the store in a year, he realized the store had lost nearly $3 million to ORC from this ring alone.

"In this recession, that kind of loss can be the difference between a store staying open and closing down," he explains.

The lack of communication between government agencies, law enforcement, and retailers is one of the main reasons profit loss occurs. This scenario benefits, in part, an underground network of terrorist financing. The problem starts at the foundation. Internal, external, and operational theft combine with a failure to exchange information between employees and managers. As well, retail loss prevention managers don't share information with law enforcement.

The Blame Game

According to an NRF (National Retail Federation) survey from 2010, retailers lost $33.5 billion to "shrinkage"[3] —a term that refers to losses from internal theft, shoplifting, and other external criminal activity. What's more, only 49% of senior management in retailers have a firm grasp of how much is being stolen—the who, what, where, and when, as well as the seriousness of this issue—despite the billions in losses due to theft. The blame game goes on, with agencies such as the FBI, for example, blaming cargo fleets (such as semi-trucks and other shippers) for "not cleaning up their own businesses" when it comes to who is responsible for internal and external theft in addition to cargo theft.[4] Private fleet companies in turn blame law enforcement for not taking a more active role in identifying and prosecuting criminals. The circle of blame not only leads to losses, it also allows dangerous loopholes to exist where terrorist financing becomes easier to accomplish and nearly impossible to trace.

In many instances, a lapse in due diligence by retail companies leads to the establishment of crime rings and funding of potential terrorist organizations. According to the Department of Commerce, 75% of employee theft goes unnoticed.[5]

And I couldn't believe how widespread the problem has become.

Insider Information: Employee Theft and ORC

Let's go back to the instant message I got late in the afternoon of December 26, 2007 from a former colleague. When he asked if I wanted to purchase designer handbags for $300 and $400 that his friend had stolen from Barneys, I started to think about how these rings are run. His admitting to me that his friend was part of a larger ring at a high-end department store like Barneys was a story—and one that I planned on delving into. What struck me most about the conversation was that he said, "It happens all the time." If it was such a common occurrence, how much were stores losing in terms of revenue unbeknownst to them? "Rings are created within stores among friends," my former colleague explained. His friend happened to be the leader of the ring and had three or four people, all employees of Barneys, working with him. Like most ORC rings, this one was based on trust. The head of the ring recruited people with whom he had worked for at least a year. All members worked in different departments and hardly spoke to each other while they were working to give the illusion that they didn't really know each other. Outside the store, however, it was a different story. The group spoke daily through instant messaging (IM) chats or conference calls to talk about how many bags they'd sold that week and, most importantly, when the new shipments were coming in. Between the five of them, they were making $20,000 a week.

The Barneys New York ring was stealing primarily from the warehouses. In most cases, ORC is more prevalent in some stores than in others because of physical factors, such as type of merchandise, location of the store, and how the store is laid out. Items that can be easily lifted, concealed, sold, and repackaged are more likely to be stolen. Bigger items, such as furniture and large electronics, have low shoplifting rates. However, they tend to get lifted in cargo theft. Larger items that get lifted tend to follow the same pattern of demand as smaller items. "Hot products," a term coined by Ronald V. Clarke, professor of criminal justice at Rutgers University, are products that spark mini-crime waves due to their popularity. In the case of the Barneys crime ring in 2007, the Lanvin Olga Sac and the Givenchy Grained Leather Bettina handbags were the "it" bags of the year. The following year, the Chanel 2.55 and Balenciaga motorcycle bag were the hot items.

Timothy Elliot, a former spokesperson from Barneys, said in an official statement, "Barneys does not comment on matters having to do with LP,"[6] but longtime employees confirmed ORC has been going on for years. "The store [Barneys] is one of the easiest places to steal from because they don't have proper checks in the warehouses as well as on the floor," says my source. "Tags can easily be removed and discarded in a matter of seconds, and merchandise can be put in bags or even carried out of the store without anyone in security or management noticing."

Apart from Barneys, everyday retailers also stock items that have good resale value. For example, designer clothing, Benadryl, Crest White Strips, Prilosec, gift cards, electronics, DVDs, CDs, razor blades, over-the-counter medicines, beauty care items, and Similac baby formula[7] are often stolen by theft rings.

If a retailer is near a major highway or port, this allows ORC criminals easy access to get into the store, steal the merchandise, and make a quick escape within minutes. The store's layout also is a factor. If a store has multiple exits, without an employee or security guard nearby, or has many items on shelves in blind spots that help conceal boosters, theft increases. Without even realizing it, stores end up losing millions of dollars in merchandise a month.

Human Resources Fail: Hiring the Wrong People

Stores rarely hire the right talent to prevent loss , especially during a down economy. Store management, from human resources to the managerial level, does not do adequate research when it comes to the hiring process. Despite having established human resources departments, extensive interviewing processes, and background checks, retailers with the highest levels of internal theft still can miss crucial signals that they are hiring criminals. Most of the time, members of internal ORC rings have seemingly spotless resumes. But in reality, these retailers often hire illegal immigrants, employees with criminal records, or people who have been fired from other companies for theft. Longer and varying store hours, business fluctuations, and wage and benefit costs lead retailers to employ more part-time than full-time associates, resulting in more theft. That, combined with liberal return policies, allows ORC members to steal merchandise, return it without a receipt, and receive store credit, merchandise gift cards, or cash refunds.[8]

"You want to believe that when someone says they are who they are on a resume or in an interview, that is who you are going to get when they come to work for your company," says a human resources representative at Bloomingdale's in New York City who asked to remain anonymous. "But that's not always the case, and that's unfortunate. Likewise, with pressure to do more with little or no resources to hire the best talent, sometimes you end up meeting with and hiring people that, in a different situation, you may have outright rejected."[9]

A 23-year-old Saks Fifth Avenue sales clerk was caught ringing up $130,000 in false merchandise returns and siphoning the money onto a gift card. A 20-year-old cashier at Best Buy on Staten Island was arrested in December of 2009 for fraudulently ringing up gift cards totaling $600. In early 2009, a 20-year-old worker at Sears in Milford, Conn., was charged with manipulating the store's computers to divert more than $35,000 onto gift cards that were fraudulently activated.[10] But gift card fraud isn't specific to 20-something, associate-level employees. Tom Coughlin was a former Wal-Mart Stores vice chairman who rose through the ranks of the retail juggernaut by starting his career in the security division and becoming vice president of loss prevention. He pled guilty in a U.S. District Court in Arkansas in 2006 to fraud and tax charges while admitting that he stole money, gift cards, and merchandise from the company. The estimated loss was $500,000.[11]

Overall theft, estimated to be $36 billion a year in the industry, constitutes 1.5% of overall retail sales according to a 2008 National Retail Security survey conducted by the NRF. The national study, based on information obtained from 106 retail chains that responded to a questionnaire, said employees were responsible for 43% of stores' unexplained losses versus 36% for shoplifting. Employee theft constituted $15.5 billion in losses for the industry.[12]

According to Dr. Richard Hollinger, professor of Criminology, Law and Society at the University of Florida, retailers that experience high employee turnover run the greatest risk of internal employee theft. Retailers that employ a large number of part-time workers—who have less access to pensions, 401(k)s, promotional opportunities, and health insurance—tend to see less allegiance to the company.[13]

While hiring the wrong employees can lead to the possibility of staffing criminals in a retailer, inadequate employee training can have an equally devastating effect. The inability to identify ORC boosters, along with fraud concerning gift cards, returns, coupons, and receipts, results in another way retailers lose profits that fund terrorist rings. For example, most employees are unable to spot gift and cash card fraud and do not ask the proper questions, says Paul Cogswell, Vice President of Risk Management at Stored Value Systems. Employees aren't trained to ask the right questions from the beginning of the transaction, so suspicious activity goes undetected.[14]

"Retailers who buy and sell used items are what I like to call 'the blessedly ignorant,'" Jack Gee, founder of the Coalition of Law Enforcement and Retail (CLEAR), told me. "The blessedly ignorant includes secondhand dealers and pawn shops or, for example, retailers like GameStop and Cash for Gold that notoriously take in stolen property. Some of the employees and salespeople will actually take the merchandise and ask a couple extra questions to vet a potential thief, but most are happily ignorant—blessedly ignorant. If some of these salespeople were trained to ask the proper questions, I doubt we would see so much merchandise being stolen."[15]

In 2009, GameStop had an estimated 18,000 full-time employees and hired 15,000 to 21,000 temporary/seasonal employees nationwide, which was slightly down from 2008. The company invested $20–30 million in training its employees, an amount that was down by about 5%, according to a GameStop spokesperson. During its busiest few days Black Friday weekend, GameStop increased staff by only 30% compared to years past and, as a consequence, experienced its highest incidence of shrinkage. Revenues are made by selling new games, but GameStop also has a program in which it buys back used games, gaming consoles, and parts. Because GameStop sales staff don't undergo formal training on how to check whether these items came from a legitimate source or whether they were stolen, new employees made buybacks with no questions asked. In 2008, eight GameStop employees pled guilty to "theft of property" charges when an investigation uncovered they were purchasing stolen games. Sites such as online retailer Cash 4 Gold have encountered similar problems with identifying stolen merchandise.

Luxury stores such as Chanel, Tod's, and Coach saw staff cuts directly correlate to shrinkage in 2009 alone. Saks Fifth Avenue reported an estimated $20 million in employee theft. This happened at a time when bottom-line growth was being monitored carefully by Wall Street and investors.[16]

Not all ORC rings start inside stores. External rings account for the majority of shrinkage costs to retailers and are why 60% of terrorist funding comes from retail crime, according to Immigrations and Customs Enforcement (ICE).[17]

Post-9/11, several ORC rings were busted by the FBI's Joint Terrorism Task Force. One of the most well-known cases was Operation Blackbird, in which the FBI uncovered an ORC that specialized in reselling infant formula to warehouses. The proceeds were wired back to countries in the Middle East where the Hezbollah and Hamas were active. The FBI seized almost $3 million in stolen assets.[18] Then Operation Greenquest was set up to target financiers of al Qaeda and other international terrorist groups.[19] In May of 2003, federal authorities arrested nine individuals suspected of stealing baby formula and sending the proceeds to Jordan, Egypt, and Palestinian areas close to Israel.

Apart from Operation Greenquest, the FBI identified and interviewed 18 people led by families of Middle Eastern origin who bought and sold (in addition to infant formula) razor blades, nicotine patches, and Viagra stolen from supermarkets in north Texas between October and May. In addition to sending laundered funds via hawalas, these members moved money using diapers worn by infants on international flights, violating the Bank Secrecy Act of 1970.[20] Money was also laundered through import and export businesses dealing with automobile parts. According to FBI informants, Middle Easterners in the north Texas area who owned and operated convenience stores would purchase items from "a loosely knit group of repetitive thieves and drug addicts," repackage the merchandise, and sell it in their stores.

In the case of Maria, a former MS-13 gang member now jailed in Houston, her weekly haul along with her two other accomplices in Madison, Wisconsin, was nearly $200,000 retail, costing Walgreens close to $1.5 million a month. Although her route was through the Midwest, hitting mostly Walgreens stores from Houston all the way up to Madison, Maria would send the merchandise back to a warehouse in Louisville to be resold. Not only did the Louisville warehouse send the profits of the merchandise sold overseas to terrorist organizations, such as the Holy Land Foundation, the ORC ring also was funneling money back to the MS-13 group in Houston. This particular cell of the MS-13, according to the Houston Police Department and FBI, was known to take funds made from the sale of stolen over-the-counter drugs to fund other MS-13 units linked to the FARC (Revolutionary Armed Forces of Colombia), as well as Mexican terrorist organizations. From one ring, three different terrorist organizations were being funded over two continents.[21]

"This is a high-profit, low-risk crime, and it's safe to draw the conclusion that rings of people engaged in it are also engaged in something a lot more criminal with a larger-scale impact," explains Jerry Biggs from Walgreens. "You have boosters who either feed the warehouses and illicit wholesalers who purchase the merchandise or sell the merchandise on their own. In Maria's case, she and her ORC ring were not only sending merchandise to Alpha Trading out of Louisville, for which she was paid a flat rate of $300 to $500, she was also selling merchandise on the side, all of which funded numerous terrorist fronts. Did she have an idea that's what her efforts were being used for? Probably not, but on the higher levels people like her know exactly what they are doing."[22]

Walgreens engaged in a big case (an investigative case which then became a legal case) in North Carolina with Middle Eastern fences who had stolen nearly $1.5 million in a year, according to Gary Weisbecker, an executive in the organized retail crime division at Walgreens.[23] Most of the merchandise was stolen by a booster who passed it on to a Level 1 fence, who then moved the merchandise to a higher-level fence. These boosters and Level 1 fences, says Weisbecker, were part of a group of illegal immigrants from Mexico and Latin America. The higher fences were from the Middle East. Weisbecker also was told that the money the higher fences made from selling the stolen merchandise was being sent overseas to unmarked bank accounts.

Wholesale Scam: Terrorist-Affiliated Warehouses Sell to the Little Guy

Walking along Broadway near 28th Street in New York City, you see numerous small deli-like stores. You can buy pretty much anything you need at these stores, from laundry detergent to soap to perfume to medicine, all at severely discounted prices. But if you inspect the merchandise, something is a little off. What looks like Oil of Olay face wash has a slightly different font on the packaging, and its smell is altered. The price is $2.50, as opposed to the $8 I usually spend when I purchase Oil of Olay at the drugstore down the street from my apartment. Could this merchandise have been altered in one of Chong Lam and Siu Yung Chan's illegal warehouses?

"It's likely, especially in that area," says Weisbecker. He explained to me through a detailed drawing how a Level 1 fence who might own a small deli or bodega has a large enterprise in stolen beauty products and drugstore items. He sells them to a middle man Level 2 fence or goes directly to a larger Level 3 wholesaler such as Coco USA. The Level 3 wholesaler ends up selling back to the larger retailer in some cases. Weisbecker detailed the Queen of Sheba case in Queens, New York, run by a Bangladeshi by the name of Abdul Malik. Although the Queen of Sheba store looked like an unassuming local deli, Malik stored boxes of Prilosec OTC in his basement and back rooms, ready for resale that was originally Walgreens stock. He also had close to $14.5 million in the bank. "He definitely wasn't making that kind of money off of selling cans of 40s," Weisbecker says.

Dishonest wholesalers who deal with legitimate retailers, both small and big-box, have been known to sell stolen merchandise back to the same source. The 2009 Retail Industry Leaders Association (RILA) ORC Annual Report outlines how dishonest wholesalers use a number of methods to trick legitimate stores into purchasing their stolen goods. For example, some warehouses have been known to use lighter fluid and windshield fluid to remove price stickers and labels. They have access to packaging counterfeiters, who repackage the goods to make them look identical to their original packaging. Some fences go so far as to collude with chemists and engineers to get the colors and packaging correct. They repackage the items so there is no way law enforcement can tell whether an item was stolen from a specific store. Legitimate stores such as gas stations, convenience stores, beauty shops, bars, gyms, and music stores are all places that potentially purchase stolen goods and sell them to unassuming customers. The proceeds build up the bank accounts of dangerous groups.[24]

In 2007, retail department store Mervyns was hit by an ORC group in 2007 that lifted close to 63,000 pairs of Levi's, jeans to sell in the garment district of New York City. The crime rings would sweep the pants off store shelves and then run them out to a waiting car. The jeans were warehoused in the homes of the thieves, along with other stolen merchandise. The total cost to Mervyns was nearly $1 million.

Khaled T. Safadi, Ulises Talavera, and Emilio Gonzalez-Neira, whom we met in Chapter 1, "Organized Retail Crime Goes Global," were no strangers to repackaging and reselling stolen items. The three business partners from Miami had a warehouse dedicated to printing packaging for Sony PlayStation 2s and then putting the stolen sets in it. The men then used their contacts in the Tri-Border Area of Paraguay, a central location where counterfeiters as well as ORC criminals sell stolen merchandise. The group had contacts within the Galeria Page mall, owned by a Hezbollah sympathizer who employed other Hezbollah sympathizers to manage the mall, staff stores, and send money back to Iran to aid the terrorist group. Sony's estimated loss totaled several millions of dollars.[25]

States' budgets also are affected by ORC. Pennsylvania estimates that ORC costs the state $81 million a year in lost sales tax revenue. This was one of the arguments supporting the state's passing a law making ORC a felony. "We're talking about gangs targeting stores, moving quickly, and walking out with thousands of dollars worth of merchandise to resell. Before this week, if those criminals were caught, they faced a mere fine. Pennsylvania's become a target," says Pennsylvania Rep. Tom Caltagirone (D-Berks County), chairman of the House Judiciary Committee. "They can and will be put away for a number of years." Likewise, California has lost $228.5 million, Texas $153 million, and Florida $132 million. Of the 46 states that have a state sales tax, roughly $1.6 billion in sales tax revenue is lost each year.[26]

Taking a Bite Out of the Balance Sheet: Economic Downturn Fosters Cargo Theft

A December 2008 survey by RILA found that 80% of the retailers surveyed reported experiencing an increase in ORC since the start of the current economic downturn. In a 2008 survey of loss prevention executives performed by the NRF, 85% of the 114 retailers surveyed indicated that their company had been a victim of ORC in the past 12 months.[27] The majority of the losses came from cargo theft from semi-trucks, trains, shipments, baggage, and so on.[28]

In an unmarked LAPD car, Detective Kent Oda took me to meet Senior Detective Marc Zavala with BAD-CATS, the LAPD cargo theft squad, to see what they had obtained in a recent cargo theft bust. Zavala monitors an official warehouse the LAPD uses to store evidence obtained in raids and from busts of cargo theft rings. Its location is so secretive that Oda drove around the downtown area for an hour to sufficiently disorient me before we arrived at the site. And it worked.

The warehouse is an unassuming building in the heart of downtown Los Angeles. Gang graffiti decorates its concrete walls, and methadone addicts visit nearby dilapidated Victorian houses. Zavala, a fast-talking Lou Diamond Phillips look-alike, took me on a tour of the warehouse, where boxes were stacked seven feet high and as wide across, all filled with clothing, shoes, car parts, and electronics intercepted through raids. Many of the items were still in their original packaging. "Los Angeles is a prime target for cargo thieves because it's a port town," says Zavala. "Whether it's shipments by boat or if it is semi-trucks that are transporting the merchandise, some rings can get away with stealing hundreds of thousands of dollars in merchandise. Then they drive it across the border into Mexico, all within the same night. Recovery of any product is virtually impossible."

Many of the items are stolen by boosters, usually former drivers from countries such as Cuba, Colombia, Ecuador, and Mexico.

These boosters are hired by shell warehouses and are paid $500 to lift the merchandise, dispose of its packaging, and ship it to another address, where the warehouse then resells it. The warehouse claims that the merchandise was stolen and collects on the insurance, creating another opportunity for a fraudulent revenue stream.

"Proceeds from illicit activities like cargo theft have been traced back to people and organizations suspected of having terrorist ties overseas." Jared Palmer, AFN, LLC (formerly known as Advantage Freight Network) in-house counsel and cargo theft prevention expert, tells me. "There have been cases and ongoing investigations involving warehouses in Illinois that are used as the base of operations for cargo theft and retail theft fencing operations. These same fences who own the shell warehouses and sell millions of dollars of stolen goods, have been suspected of using the proceeds from these illegal operations to help fund terrorist organizations overseas. By the time law enforcement realizes that there is a complex criminal enterprise at work, the stolen goods have been sold, the fences have laundered their money, and the cargo thieves have already moved on to their next victim."[29]

Post-9/11, cargo theft has been estimated to be between $30 and $50 billion annually, and ORC accounts for almost half of these losses. Law enforcement agencies believe the majority of cargo theft involves current or former employees.[30] Again, the lack of communication between agencies facilitates theft between employees. To curtail the miscommunication, the trucking industry was regulated by the Federal Motor Carrier Safety Administration (FMCSA). However, after the establishment of the Transportation Security Administration (TSA), which was mostly formed to facilitate air travel safety, the government started focusing on the trucking industry as a potential breach in national security. George Rodriguez was appointed director of land and cargo security. Although the FMCSA set guidelines and security proposals for the trucking industry, the TSA did not do the same, which caused confusion. This led to a lack of initiatives between shippers, carriers, and customers that would have resulted in a virtual "checks and balances" system. This included complete background checks for new hires with references, photo IDs, secured terminals with adequate fences, driver awareness of suspicious activities, monitoring and remote locking systems, and security training for all personnel. But this system poked multiple holes in the process of safe and secure cargo delivery.

In 2010, retailers lost $30 billion to cargo theft; big-box retailers alone have lost nearly $10 billion.[31] In southern California, five men were charged with stealing nearly $200,000 worth of 3D televisions from a freight train. According to Detective Zavala, that type of crime is fairly common. He explains, "Flat-screen TVs and electronics are particularly popular items to steal, because of their resale value, but also because the penalty for getting caught is far less severe than if they got caught stealing and selling drugs. Picking someone up for stealing $400,000 worth of electronics from a freight train may put them away for ten years, versus picking someone up for stealing and selling 400 pounds of cocaine, where the resale street value is $9 million. These guys want to do the least amount of time possible."[32]

But prosecuting cargo thieves poses its own challenges.

The Patriot Act was established to help curtail terrorism by creating a federal law to prosecute criminals who finance terror. However, this law did not apply to cargo theft or the boosters and fencers involved. In July of 2005, legislation introduced by Florida Rep. Cliff Stearns (R-Ocala) allowed cargo theft to be included as part of the Patriot Act, and it was officially enacted. The idea behind the act was to enhance domestic security by cracking down on a growing criminal problem that was especially prevalent in ports in Jacksonville, Tampa, and Miami.

The provisions were supposed to increase criminal penalties for cargo theft and create an all-inclusive database on cargo theft, allowing state and local law enforcement to coordinate reports of cargo theft.[33] In addition (and arguably the most exciting aspect of the provision), cargo theft will be reflected as a separate category in the Uniform Crime Reporting System used by the FBI, enabling the tracking and monitoring of trends in the crime. However, the government has yet to establish how these criminals will be prosecuted. Likewise, Jared Palmer lobbied to enforce the law that required there to be a separate category to report cargo theft under the Patriot Act. According to Palmer, the law was already on the books but not enforced until January of 2010 after he and other members of the National Cargo Theft Task Force made several trips to Washington, D.C.

"Each state has their own crime reporting system that is used to report crime information using unique codes," Palmer says. In addition to the systems being siloed on a state-by-state basis, they have not been reprogrammed to accept the new cargo theft code. This is mostly because the states lack the proper funding. The irony is that in order to get more funding to combat cargo theft, the states need to report the problem to the feds. This vicious cycle continues to play into the hands of the cargo thieves, who continue to steal billions of dollars each year. To get an accurate idea of how big these numbers are, [years ago President Richard] Nixon commissioned a report that showed cargo theft was a $1 billion—$16 billion in today's money—annual problem. Almost 40 years later, and estimates show that the problem is around $15 billion a year, so not much has changed."[34]

To stay steps ahead of the thieves, the FBI and ICE have rolled out a database called Cargonet in conjunction with RILA and local police departments. From a financial standpoint, establishing a database will not only help connect law enforcement and businesses, but also will help reduce costs when it comes to insurance premiums on cargo trucks.

Coordinating Information in Real Time: LAPD and APD Case Studies

Miscommunication is an endemic problem—not only when it comes to cargo theft, but also for tracking ORC rings in general. Local law enforcement agencies have issues for several reasons. The first is timing. When a booster is caught, it takes a while for store management to recognize what is going on, figure out whether it is petty theft or something larger, and then charge the person. More than 85% of all reported criminal offenses are property crimes. These can lead to larger crimes, such as murder, drug trafficking, or, in some instances, terrorist financing.[35] Because the ways to track such thefts (such as by using software) are limited, law enforcement has a more difficult time finding patterns in theft that could potentially be the work of ORC rings. But agencies such as the Los Angeles Police Department and the Albuquerque Police Department are changing this situation by fostering communication in an online real-time environment.

Case Study: Los Angeles Police Department

In 1999, pinpointing, tracking, and fighting ORC was an uphill battle for the LAPD. Like social cliques in a high school, the government agencies and other participants in the fight against crime kept to themselves. The police department functioned autonomously, doing everything from going after criminal activity on their own to eating their meals and socializing as a group. Likewise, when the LA Sherriff's Department caught wind of a potential ORC theft, they would identify the case, track the crime, and keep it to themselves. Private security companies and investigators at retail stores weren't any better. According to James Hooper, a private investigator and consultant, if they got a tip regarding criminal activity, they would try to solve it on their own. "I think there were a lot of egos involved back then," says Hooper. "Everyone wanted to be the hero and take the glory for it. There wasn't a team mentality. The mission wasn't 'How can we collectively solve this crime together and make a massive impact?,' it was more about 'How can our group get the most kudos for the biggest case busted?'"[36]

Recognizing that change needed to be implemented, and quickly, the LAPD created the Law Enforcement and Private Security

(LEAPS) conference. It promotes discussions and information sharing between government agencies and private security entities within retailers. What they didn't realize was that communicating between themselves was also a preventive measure to stop terrorism.

During a walk-through of the city of Los Angeles' top-secret and ultra-high-tech management facility, James Featherstone, general manager of the city of Los Angeles Emergency Management Department, referred to the work of Rick Rescorla. (Rescorla is an Army veteran and former World Trade Center security chief for the financial services firm Morgan Stanley Dean Whitter who predicted the 9/11 attacks and published a report on evacuation procedures.) Featherstone explained how Rescorla's report wasn't just his call to action over something he believed was about to happen, but a painstaking plan he created focused on communication. This was something many of the local agencies and the private sector did not have at the time.[37] The report now serves as a foundation for the way the city of Los Angeles handles crisis management. "Rescorla had enough gumption not only to say something but to present a viable plan in the event something happened which posed a serious threat," says Featherstone. "He was a 'force multiplier.' He changed things not only to secure the safety of his firm, but to change the way New York and the rest of the country look at crisis and emergency management. It's not about fixing the situation after it happens; it's about taking preventative steps before something of that magnitude happens again. That concept resonated for me and the city of Los Angeles emergency preparedness department. We make sure all lines of communication are open between all agencies. That's the only effective way to manage crisis."[38]

As the LEAPS meetings started to gain momentum throughout the years, and especially after 9/11, agencies started to discover that by having conversations as short as two minutes and no longer than a couple of hours, they could connect the dots more effectively. FBI agents began collaborating with private investigators on cases. ICE agents frequently spoke to retail security. And the most significant change was that they were invited to join the fire department for a weekly dinner at the firehouse. "I told my guys that this was imperative if they wanted to work in our group," says Featherstone at a speech given at the LEAPS conference in Los Angeles.[39] The result was an efficient system with more terrorism-related ORC busts than any other police department in the country.[40]

"We realized just because a situation hadn't presented itself didn't mean it wasn't about to happen," said Assistant Chief Michael Moore, director of the office of special ops in the LAPD. "Conceptually, everyone understood what 'When you see something, say something' meant, but to put it into practice was a different story and took diligence and coordination on the parts of every government agency."[41]

Captain Bill Williams, a 30-year veteran of the LAPD, knew that even a good interagency communication system could become even more efficient. Commercial crimes as well as property crime tend to take a backseat to the larger, more "If it bleeds, it leads" crimes, such as murder, drug busts, and terrorism. What people didn't understand is that many large-scale crimes start with commercial crimes.[42] And Williams and his team were adamant about making sure different divisions could connect the dots if needed.

In January of 2009, Captain Williams and Detective Oda established the Los Angeles Area Organized Retail Crimes Association (LAAORCA). It has a database that tracks the frequency of certain ORC, where it happens, and possible perpetrators. LAAORCA communicates the information in real time to its agency and private-sector partners. The reasoning was to provide a proactive partnership between police and community. In addition, it exposes the root causes of crimes and disorder and creates efficiencies between prosecutors, legal entities and corrections.

The LAPD also established a private-sector partnership between law enforcement and the retail community so that each could learn from the other. This partnership had been in the works since 2008, according to Williams. Back then, it was just local communities gathering information and learning from each other in ways similar to LEAPS. In 2009 and 2010, LAAORCA began digitizing information and placing it in an easily accessible database. Retail, government, and state agencies could access the system and look up information about the perpetrator such as his age, hair color, description of the crime, how many stores he has hit, how many items he has lifted, and if he is working in a group or by himself. The database contains other information that the LAPD asked me not to disclose for the sake of protecting the system and their agents. In 2010, LAAORCA had more than 200 people from the business and the law enforcement communities attend meetings and log onto the database—not only to update it but to see whether there were any connections to the cases on which they were working. In 2011, the number went up to more than 800. Cornerstone (a financial division of ICE that deals with money laundering and fraud), the Department of Homeland Security, the Secret Service and the Federal Bureau of Investigation are two of the organizations on the international side working with LAAORCA. Both recently became involved because of the growth of ORC in which the profits were being moved overseas to countries such as Jordan, Lebanon, and Afghanistan, especially from major cities such as Los Angeles. "ICE has been involved in five of our most recent cases in Los Angeles, because the stolen property we've discovered inevitably goes overseas. In order to bust them, we not only seize their buildings, but we can also seize their property," says Williams.

The greatest success, says Captain Williams, was that after the establishment and help of LAAORCA, the LAPD saw declining crime rates. Property crime in Los Angeles dropped by 5%. The major-crimes unit also completed a bust called the Hernandez Operation. They nabbed a notorious Los Angeles-based ORC ring that was stealing $6 million worth of merchandise per year, including formula, diapers, health and beauty products, hair-care products, and over-the-counter medications. Four banking institutions also worked with the LAPD after the Los Angeles Superior Court issued search warrants to seize multiple accounts showing transactions equaling hundreds of thousands of dollars. San Francisco has rolled out its own system, called BAORCA, modeled after LAAORCA, and Chicago is putting together its own database as well, and another is about to roll out in Las Vegas and southern Nevada. Retailers who are members of LAAORCA saved an estimated $60 million in revenue lost to ORC in one year.[43]

Case Study: Albuquerque Police Department

Before LAAORCA existed, there was Karen Fischer.

Fischer, a high-energy mom of two, is considered a civilian but has worked with the Albuquerque Police Department for close to 25 years with the commercial crimes division. She bounces around her office at the Albuquerque Police Department, answering emails and checking her schedule to make sure she is not late to her daughter's soccer game. She is also checking on the latest ORC to hit retail stores. She pulls up a Google map, which looks like a digitized version of a wall map with pinpoints. On the right side of the screen is a picture of a perpetrator. In the middle are all the places they have hit. With a couple of mouse clicks, Fischer can find out how many crimes the person is being charged with, what was lifted from the stores, any bank accounts, and, most importantly, if the person was working with a group or was solo. "This is my baby," Fischer beams as she takes me on a virtual tour of the Albuquerque Retail Assets Protection Association (ARAPA). Fischer (who has a knack for thinking up acronyms while driving) is the brains behind ARAPA, a web site and partnership to further build the "local trust" for law enforcement and local Albuquerque Police personnel to feel comfortable in exchanging information on incidents. ARAPA is what LAAORCA is based on. She thought of the idea when she realized community watch programs such as Neighborhood Watch weren't as effective as they could be. "There is something to be said about community policing," she says. "The proactiveness and the willingness of everyone, including police departments, community organizers, and civilians to work together to fight crime. I wanted to create something where both law enforcement and retail partners could do that in real time."

Fischer describes the case of Marin Moreno. This Mexican native would steal Tide laundry detergent, razors, energy drinks, and toys from retailers such as Target and Walmart and send the money he made selling his haul in flea markets and online back to Mexico. When the APD finally arrested him, they found $30,000 worth of merchandise and $30,000 in cash.

Similar to Moreno, Nick Jojola, an unassuming skateboarder and subsequent meth addict, ran an ORC ring of adults who helped him steal nearly $1 million in DVDs, electronics, clothing, and Christian-themed merchandise. Nick was only 16 when ARAPA's information exchange began logging his license plate number every time he engaged in a "smash and grab" hit at retailers such as Kmart, Hastings, and Best Buy. What's more, the exchange was able to track the adults working with Jojola, thus creating a substantial case against that ring.

The system was so effective that the LAPD flew in Fischer and Kenneth Cox, director of loss prevention at Target in Albuquerque and the co-creator of ARAPA, so that they could give a three-day tutorial about how the LAPD could create their own system based on what Fischer created. As ORC prevention and communication between agencies and retailers becomes more technically savvy, police departments around the country and the world have Fischer and Cox to thank for their database.

"It's important to note that ARAPA is not intelligence," says Fischer. "There are other systems the APD uses that do that. ARAPA is a tool used by retailers and law enforcement that is ever evolving."

The ARAPA web site is one of a number of web areas the APD has inside of CONNECT (Community Oriented Notification Network Enforcement Communication Technology), which operates as a 24-hour crime watch for different business sectors. It also allows both law enforcement and retailers to track whether their "one-off" incident is actually part of a larger ring hitting the same or different stores in the area. Another example of a case busted by using the ARAPA system happened in 2009. A traveling booster and e-fencing operation had been hitting Marmaxx, JCPenny, and Toys "R" Us stores, shipping nearly $85,000 a month to fences in Texas for a total loss value of $2 million.

What the APD realized is that ORC rings travel, to nab criminals, law enforcement efforts must expand and build local trust. To complicate crime-fighting matters, criminals were communicating with each other in jail, in some instances coordinating hits as well as shipments from behind bars. To bring to light what the ORC rings were doing in Albuquerque, the APD put up wanted posters in malls and on billboards to let the community know who they were looking for. Kenneth Cox credits the use of ARAPA for saving his division an estimated $15 million in stolen merchandise related to ORC in 2010.

"Getting involved was crucial," says Albuquerque Police Chief Ray Schultz. "When Karen [Fischer] first proposed the idea of ARAPA, I knew as a police department, we had to be involved and get behind it. There is always turnover in police departments, and with that changing of the guard, there are new ways of going about dealing with ORC. While I was in charge, I wanted to implement a system that I knew would last and stay committed to our retail partners. As a public-sector organization, knowing how to work with your private-sector partners is very important."

The LAPD and APD might be great examples of how government agencies can effectively communicate with each other; however, the system is still new and has yet to be completely adopted and used on a national level. With that said, record numbers turned out for the annual LAAORCA conference in 2011, and Detective Oda expects the numbers to increase.

Part II
Follow the Money

The Money Trail and the Business of Cross-Border Trade   77

Profile of a Booster and a Fence   97

Family Ties   119

Money Laundering 2.0   139

The Political Agenda   159

Strange Bedfellows   179

4

The Money Trail and the Business of Cross-Border Trade

It's 5 a.m. on a Monday at a highway Super 8 motel near Madison, Wisconsin. Traffic is surprisingly heavy for such a sultry summer morning. Maria (an alias), a member of the Houston, Texas arm of the MS-13, works swiftly to load a U-Haul van, filling it with cardboard boxes full of OTC drugs such as Prilosec, Sudafed, and Zantac. She collected them while hitting the first of 12 Walgreens stores along her 1,200-mile route back to Houston. This early-morning ritual at a motel isn't anything new for Maria, who does this at least four times a week. What is new are the cameras on the outside of the building—something she hadn't noticed in the past. The slow, omniscient sway of the camera's lens will put a crimp in her stealth mission to load up and leave the motel undetected. Staying at the Super 8 allows her to pull up behind the motel late at night instead of having to walk through the lobby with all her goods. Likewise, renting a U-Haul under an alias helps keep Maria's mission under wraps. Why the secrecy? All the merchandise in Maria's U-Haul is stolen. The total value of her pull from one night is about $50,000 to $60,000 retail.

Maria moves fast. On average, it takes her three and a half to four minutes to steal $2,000 worth of merchandise from a store. After working as a booster for the MS-13 for almost nine years, Maria has her technique down to a science. First, she never hits the same store twice in one month or takes the same route. However, the stores she hits can be in the same area. Second, if a store manager or sales associate asks her if she needs help, she leaves. (Personal interaction equals attention, and Maria needs to remain as under the radar as possible.) Third, if she is required to work in a group, the maximum number of people is four. Any more people might raise a red flag and puts the hit at risk. It also prevents them from getting out of the store in less than five minutes. By the end of her four-day trip, Maria's rented van will be filled with an estimated $100,000 worth of merchandise. In a month, Maria makes this journey three times and on average picks up nearly $500,000 worth of merchandise at retail value.

But unlike the typical shoplifter, who, according to Jerry Biggs, director of the organized retail crime division at Walgreens, steals for his or her own benefit, Maria lifts merchandise to sell it and send funds to the MS-13 back in El Salvador. They have sent word they need $10,000 to pay off the El Salvadorian government and get a comrade out of jail. To make money quickly, Maria and several other women affiliated with the MS-13 are sent out to boost from retail stores such as Walgreens, Walmart, and Target, hitting ten to twelve stores in one day. After a day of lifting, these women go back to their hotel rooms (usually Super 8s or Motel 6s). They drive their U-Hauls[1] up to the door of their rooms, sort their merchandise with the efficiency of a skilled pilot, and box it up and ship it to a warehouse in the U.S.

Maria stays up all night with the help of a street-grade speed pill, writing down every piece of merchandise she lifted in a detailed log, which will be sent with the merchandise to the warehouse. The nearly 10,000 boxes of Prilosec and Tylenol, sorted by type and brand, form a wall around her, fencing her in as though she is in her own personal jail. The logs make it easy for the warehouse fences to analyze exactly what is coming in, how much is available, and if it's an item they need or can do without. In Maria's stash are more heartburn and stomach ailment medicines than in years past.

"These rings are run like small businesses," says Biggs. "On most days, warehouses get shipments of at least 200 to 300 boxes worth between $14,000 and $20,000, from boosters all over the country. By looking at their detailed log, they can tell what's in high demand and what they can move out of the warehouse quickly and get the most money from, selling it at 75 cents on the dollar. The profit margin ranges from 20% to 30% because they are paying very little for the merchandise."[2]

Like any well-run corporation, the structure and management are just as important to an ORC ring as the people who are running it. Biggs explains that the larger ring, the one Maria was affiliated with in Houston, was composed of three booster groups and four fencing operations. Forty to fifty women, also known as "runners," (which is essentially the same thing as a booster) would steal from retailers between Houston, Los Angeles, and Las Vegas and send the merchandise back to the "den"—a code word for the home base warehouse. Women are often chosen as boosters as well as runners because they are less suspicious than men and are more likely to get away with the crime.

Most women affiliated with the MS-13, like Maria, are considered property of the gang and are used only to boost merchandise. On this particular trip, Maria is getting ready to ship her merchandise to a warehouse called Alpha Trading, located in Louisville, Kentucky. It is owned by Abe Zakaria (who, according to Biggs, is from Jordan and is now a Level 3 fence of stolen goods). Zakaria will purchase the merchandise and then sell it to a retailer. Maria makes only a small percentage from this transaction. For every shipment delivered, she earns only $700, even though she boosts along the route from Wisconsin to Houston, hitting 20 to 30 more stores before the end of her trip. As she moves further from the scene of the crime, the merchandise becomes harder to trace back to its point of origin.

Maria isn't the only woman who takes on the role of booster as part of a larger organization. June (an alias), originally from Iran, belongs to a ring of 70 people. Her group is led by George (another alias), who has close ties to the Mujahadeen-e-Khalq (MEK) in Iran, according to Biggs. June was recruited to boost through George's connections to her family in Iran. As part of the MEK, she hits the Eastern Seaboard, going from Atlanta all the way to New Jersey. Her method is basically the same as Maria's. In a five-day span, June hits 12 to 15 Walmart stores, stealing $4,000 to $5,000 worth of merchandise per store; items include things such as Enfamil, diabetic test strips, and diapers. Her warehouse, in North Carolina, houses upwards of $150,000 worth of merchandise on pickup days. Although June gets paid only pennies on the dollar for her work, her Level 3 fence, to whom she sells, makes close to 80 cents on the dollar for every item sold. She does not share in the profit.

The Warehouse: Ground Zero for Cross-Border Trade

In most cases, warehouses can move stolen items across the border more quickly than boosters because they maintain a front to look like legitimate wholesale businesses that sell to retailers both offline and online. Smaller retailers looking for a price break, or ones that want to get around the minimum order requirement needed to buy directly from manufacturers, enlist the help of wholesalers, which have less stringent requirements than the manufacturer. For legitimate wholesalers, the more buyers they have for a specific product, the bigger the order they can make, which drives down the price of the item. Small and mid-cap retailers purchase these items in quantities that meet the customer demand in their stores. This also allows them to be more price-competitive with larger retailers. Most wholesalers deal with retailers all over the U.S. and, in some cases, worldwide. Therefore, having a system in place where they can obtain the merchandise, box it, and ship it to the retailer in a minimal amount of time and at the lowest cost possible is crucial. And fence wholesalers such as Alpha Trading take advantage of this system.

Likewise, the location of the legitimate wholesaler is just as important as what it offers retailers. If a wholesaler isn't located near a main transportation hub, such as an interstate, railway station, or seaport, it becomes difficult and expensive to get merchandise into the warehouse and out to customers. Every year a plethora of wholesalers go out of business because the costs of running a large warehouse and shipping become so great.

This issue came to an apex in 2007.

Profile of a Purchaser

As the world acknowledged that a global recession was upon us, gas prices started to rise, the real estate bubble began to burst, and interest rates increased the cost to own, rent, and finance real estate, especially big buildings. Consumer confidence faltered, and retailers as well as established wholesalers felt the pinch to their margins. Seeing an opportunity in the market, shell warehouses fronting as legitimate wholesale warehouses started to pop up all over the country. They promised heavy discounts on items and transportation costs that were a fraction of what most real wholesalers charged. What's more, because these shells run their businesses in the most technologically advanced way possible, they were able to move merchandise around the country as quickly as, if not more quickly than, their legitimate wholesale counterparts. The shell warehouses' low capital overhead allowed them to advertise and market themselves online with ease. Discount web sites and illegitimate warehouses started to outprice legitimate warehouses, and potential buyers who wanted to keep their costs down caught on quickly.

In 2007 the U.S. Census Bureau reported the number of retailers going through wholesalers (which includes warehouses) had gradually increased since 2002. Manufacturers and merchant wholesalers relied more heavily on e-commerce than retailers (ranking second with e-commerce) accounting for 21.2% ($1.226 billion) of total sales.[3]

What this means is wholesale businesses did most of their business and transactions online versus regular retailers.

Alpha Trading (a shell warehouse), for example, would get deliveries from boosters on Mondays and Fridays, with 450 boxes on average being delivered on those days. Boxes had everything from over-the-counter drugs, makeup, diabetes test strips, and baby formula to clothing from department stores such as The Limited and The Gap. The deep discount on merchandise became a major incentive for buyers from domestic and international stores to purchase from these warehouses, thinking they were getting a deal. But they didn't realize the merchandise they were purchasing was stolen.

It's easy to mistake a shell warehouse for something that is legitimate. When you pull up to the building, everything seems normal. Guards at the front gate asked for my identification as I drove in for an undercover visit. They record your name, time of arrival, and who you are visiting. At the front of the warehouse, someone carrying an official-looking clipboard comes out to greet you and take you inside.

Once you are through the glass doors, the warehouse greeter shuffles you into a larger room filled with rows of boxes similar to that in a warehouse retailer such as Costco. On the shelves, boxes are arranged by what they contain and cards that say how many items are in the boxes, as well as their price. One row is labeled detergent and is organized by brand name. Tide, according to the warehouse guide, is the best seller, followed by Cheer and Gain. All are sorted in boxes of 50 to 60 per bin and are priced between $30 and $40 a bin. In the adjoining row, over-the-counter medicines ranging from Tylenol to cough suppressant are stacked neatly in rows. According to my tour guide, a box of Tums EX 750 Antacid Calcium Extra Strength in Assorted Berries flavor, 200 count, has been one of the best sellers for more than three years. It may retail for $9.99 at Walgreens, Walmart, or Target. However, the warehouse's price is $3. The buyer (either legitimate or not) will mark it up 100% to 200%, pricing it between

$6 and $8. This is still a discounted retail price compared to Walgreens' price but is priced according to market demand.

But over-the-counter drugs for colds and indigestion aren't the only items in stock at these warehouses. They comprise about 60% of the stock. Many warehouses also include hard-line items, such as electronics, and soft-line items, such as clothing, handbags, perfume, and lingerie. Soft-line items make up 30% of the warehouse, while 10% is allocated to hard-line items.

Keeping Shelves Stocked Through Cargo Theft

As shell warehouses started sprouting up and demand for product increased, the incidence of cargo theft (swiping tractor-trailers filled with goods) also grew. It is estimated that cargo crime in the U.S. results in losses of $10 billion to $25 billion a year.[4] It continues to increase as thieves get more sophisticated and flexible and take advantage that U.S. law enforcement rarely shares information across agencies and companies. Similar to boosting stores, thieves work quickly, without discriminating against companies or people. Nothing is off limits.

"They will steal from anyone, anytime, and anywhere," said Joe Wehrle, co-chairman of the National Cargo Theft Task Force and president of the National Insurance Crime Bureau (NICB), at the National Cargo Theft Summit in 2009. "Cargo theft is also providing the seed money for all kinds of nefarious activities, including funding terrorism. That's why we need to break down all barriers to win this battle. Americans deserve our best effort."[5]

Cargo theft rings (also known as cargo theft gangs) are made up of several low-level boosters and fencers organized into crews that are ethnically based and usually not well educated.[6] Part of their strategy is to obtain a lot of items in a short amount of time. In south Florida, the average age of a crew member is 20. They are usually from Cuba and are unemployed new U.S. citizens. They are recruited by ORC rings to work as part of the group because they have knowledge of how trucking operations operate. Although most of the cargo theft rings are made up of males, female members are used as a diversion to give these groups access to areas they may not be permitted to enter.

In 2009, there were on average 72 cargo theft incidents per month and 859 cargo theft incidents in total, a 12% increase from 2008.[7] The majority of these thefts were full truckload thefts, and 36 were warehouse burglaries. Thirteen of the truckload thefts were hijackings. Electronics, including TVs, computers, and cell phones, was the hardest hit industry when it came to cargo theft, increasing from 174 cargo thefts in 2008 to 196 in 2009, representing 23% of all cargo thefts. The second group was food and beverage, making up 20% of all thefts, with home and garden items coming in third at 10%. In addition, the states that had the most cargo theft correlated to where the most ORC happened between 2007 and 2009. California, Florida, and Texas saw the most cargo theft in 2008. Georgia, Illinois, and New Jersey were identified as being at the next tier of risk.[8]

Coveted Items: Over-the-Counter Drugs

Although electronics (specifically, cell phones, whose average loss value was $2.05 million per incident) were the items most stolen, in terms of value the average pharmaceutical theft was valued at $4 million in 2009.[9] In total, there were 46 drug thefts, which were valued at $184 million, up from 35 thefts at $41 million in 2007.[10] Of course, the thought of purchasing contraband over-the-counter medicine when you are trying to remedy a cold, cough, stomachache, or heartburn is enough to make me sick. But for those who have chronic illnesses and who depend on medicine such as insulin, Copaxone for multiple sclerosis, or liquid antibiotics, ending up with contraband medicines can be deadly. This is particularly true of medicines that need to be refrigerated; these are especially affected by cargo theft because the stolen boxes are rarely handled properly. Chuck Forsaith, corporate director of supply chain security for Purdue Pharma Technologies, Inc., acknowledges that although the street value of his company's drug Oxycontin makes it more of a target for cargo theft, other drugs that need to be handled properly can and will do serious harm to people who need them when mishandled.

"If something like Copaxone or certain antibiotics are heated above a certain temperature, when injected they could potentially cause lethal damage," explains Forsaith. "Drugs like these need to be handled very carefully by everyone in the supply chain, and the last thing cargo thieves are thinking is to keep these drugs safe during transport."[11]

On March 16, 2010, Eli Lilly & Co. experienced one of the largest pharmaceutical cargo thefts in history. The well-planned scheme resulted in the loss of $75 million worth of drugs, including antidepressants such as Cymbalta and the antipsychotic Zyprexa. The theft was orchestrated by thieves who cut a hole in a warehouse roof and lifted the merchandise through it. Pharmaceutical companies are widely known for diligently protecting their supply chain, compared to other industries, because when a cargo theft happens, it not only affects their bottom line (Eli Lilly had $21.8 billion in sales in 2009) but also becomes a matter of public health.[12]

The level of sophistication at which these thieves operate is the stuff that spy movies are made of. Most cargo thieves start out as truck or bus drivers or as common thieves in their homeland countries and are then recruited to be cargo thieves in the United States. According to Jared Palmer, Cuban crime syndicates actively recruit new members in Cuba who have the proper background or training to commit these crimes and then smuggle them into the U.S. by way of Florida. Thieves get jobs working at warehouses or as truck drivers for the warehouses around the country. They steal and ship merchandise back to warehouses and ports near Miami, where the merchandise is loaded into container boxes. These boxes are shipped to countries such as Paraguay, Venezuela, Colombia, Brazil, Argentina, and the Dominican Republic and then are sold through black market distribution channels.[13] The Cuban crime rings aren't the only ones who have adopted this model. Organizations such as the MS-13 in El Salvador, which recruit boosters, also recruit potential cargo thieves.

Profile of a Cargo Thief

Julio Gomez, 32, a former truck driver for B. Rosen and Sons meat company, didn't realize part of his meat delivery (which included beef and pork) was being stolen from the back of his truck until it was too late.[14] While sitting at a stoplight, Gomez heard a faint noise coming from the back of his truck. He disregarded it until he caught a glimpse in his rearview mirror of three young men carrying away three boxes of meat. The men vanished in less than a minute, taking almost $1,000 in prime-grade beef—meat that is usually sold to fine hotels and restaurants in the New York area. "My stomach was in knots when I pulled in [to the market] and saw the lock had been smashed and the doors completely unlocked," said Gomez in an interview in the Hunts Point Meat Market in the Bronx. "It seemed like they were moving at the speed of light. I didn't even see them coming."

Gomez may have been transporting meat at the time, but the methodology cargo thieves use across the board is the same. The amount of research, observation, and coordination that cargo thieves engage in is unprecedented. First, the thieves must figure out where the merchandise is being bought, sold, and shipped to outside the U.S. The Internet is an indispensable tool for such thieves. They search for information on industrial parks and the locations of warehouses and distribution facilities. After they have identified a couple of shipment facilities, they spend weeks conducting surveillance on the property.

They case the building and take notes on everything from when and where shipments come in, to where they are coming from, to who is driving the trucks, to when breaks are taken, to when the cargo is left unattended. The thieves set up surveillance spots around the perimeter of the facility. When the moment is right, they steal the cargo by breaking into the truck when it is left unattended and manipulate the ignition and drive off with the cargo, or they attach their own truck to a stolen trailer and drive out of the shipping site. All of this is done within five to six minutes. In some instances, thieves case rest stops or fueling stations on interstate highways and pay off truck drivers to give up their haul.[15]

Thieves know that stolen trucks or cargo may have GPS tracking devices. Therefore, they engage in a "dump," leaving the truck in an industrial park or on the side of the interstate, watching to see if law enforcement arrives to look for it. If no one comes to retrieve it, they move it to a warehouse. There they go through the merchandise and "clean" the product by stripping it from its old packaging. They relabel it or, in some cases, change or create fake documentation so that customs can move out the cargo boxes more efficiently. The "cleaning" process also ensures that product can never be tracked to its originating retailer.

"Shell Stores": A Conduit for Organized Retail Crime

Cross-border trade is facilitated by a slew of fake retailers and web sites selling the contraband products. The Coalition Against Organized Retail Crime has identified Florida, California, New York, Texas, and Michigan as the five states that have the most ORC activity. This is true because of their close proximity to U.S. borders and their large amount of tourism. Many fences who run illegitimate warehouses in the middle of the country also own or are affiliated with stores geared toward tourists who want batteries, electronics, discounted clothing items, and, in some cases, household appliances. The fastest way to identify these stores, according to Jerry Biggs, is that these retailers often have the words "sample sale" or "liquidation" in their names.

"Most of these fences target mom-and-pop stores in tourist towns, especially during peak season, when merchandise turns over quickly. With a quick turnaround time, a national recession, and an offer of merchandise well below what most legitimate warehouses are offering, this became a perfect storm for fences to make a killing on selling stolen goods," Biggs explained to me.

Ties between shell warehouses and the retailers purchasing from the shells allow the supply chain to work like clockwork. Stolen merchandise hits the shell warehouse, is "cleaned" within hours via an assembly line of people, and is back out on the street in a matter of days. Speed and agility are crucial if fences and shell warehouses want to make money. The faster the fences can get the merchandise out to the retailers, the more money they make, despite merchandise being spoiled, tainted, and harmed through the careless method of transporting the goods.

Where these fences sell items is crucial to how they are bought overseas and then resold. According to Joe LaRocca, National Retail Federation (NRF) asset protection advisor, products such as infant formula are sometimes cut with a high-grade white powder made of ground-up plastic and flour to create more product to sell. "What's most disturbing about this scenario," says LaRocca, "is that infants are ingesting this excuse for nutritious formula to help a young body grow when it's clearly not nutritional and could potentially cause brain and nerve damage, harming a baby's ability to see properly or hear properly. [Parents who] are trying to save money are potentially and unknowingly doing long-term harm to their children. The whole scenario is very upsetting."[16]

Shell Stores Move Online

Setting up shop online is also one of the most common ways fences at the warehouses get stolen merchandise into the hands of unsuspecting consumers. In 2009, the Coalition on Organized Retail Crime estimated that this process, also known as e-fencing, is a $42 million business, up from more than $5 billion in pre-recession 2007.[17] Web sites are easy to set up, relatively inexpensive to run, and can leave the seller virtually anonymous. In addition, the Internet allows criminals to easily convert stolen goods into cash. According to a study done by the NRF, 5% of products stolen in 2009 were sold on the Internet, equaling an estimated $610 million of stolen merchandise in 2009 alone. While most of the goods stolen and sold are personal items—razors, beauty products, and diabetes test strips—luxury items are also stolen and sold. More than 68% of interviewed retailers have found stolen goods on a web site.[18]

Auction sites, such as eBay and Craigslist, offer added anonymity because sellers of merchandise can use fake names and screen handles and can ship from P.O. boxes, essentially making them untraceable.

In 2009, the FBI picked up Ahmet M. Keskes, 38, in Illinois for selling stolen merchandise ranging from golf clubs made by Taylor-Made, Ping, and Callaway to electronic dog collars, Victoria's Secret perfume, and car headlights. According to FBI files, Keskes made more than $2 million in sales through online auctions and his registered web site. Even though Keskes was running his business out of a corporate office in Streamwood, Illinois, he sent merchandise through a P.O. box established under a fake name. It wasn't until an FBI informant went undercover and bought items from Keskes that he was charged with mail fraud—a felony that could carry a maximum sentence of 20 years. But he was not brought up on charges of selling stolen goods.[19]

"The problem is twofold," explains Jerry Biggs. "The first problem has to do with what constitutes a felony. In some states it's stealing just about anything. For example, in Indiana such a crime is a felony. But in states like Florida or California, only stealing merchandise totaling more than $1,000 is a felony. Secondly, the law doesn't cover people who are purchasing stolen items and selling them through legal outlets—that is, the 'gray market.' It's incredibly difficult to track. We know where the merchandise is coming from. We can try to track it internally, but once it leaves the store it's virtually impossible to tell where it is going."

In 2008, retailer Victoria's Secret reported an 80% increase, or $2.7 million, in store theft from the previous year,[20] largely because of a crime ring that spanned the country from California to Connecticut. According to a report filed by the FBI, thieves used the typical boosting method by stealing bras in bulk, often clearing out an entire shelf. In the span of four minutes, security and price tags were removed and merchandise was placed in foil bags, a common method boosters use to avoid setting off security systems. Once these boosters were out of the store, they sold the merchandise on eBay and to third parties such as George Tutaya of Rego Park, New York. He was charged with 18 counts of criminal possession of stolen property after he sold more than $80,000 worth of bras on eBay.[21] He claimed he got the merchandise from the same ring that was stealing the bras. Instead of going through a direct source or person, Tutaya went to a warehouse near New York City that housed mostly stolen merchandise from Victoria's Secret. "Unless stores start putting GPS tracking devices on their merchandise, it becomes virtually impossible to find out exactly where this merchandise is going and if it is being sold to legitimate retailers or other criminals who are using the proceeds of the sales to fund something sinister," Biggs tells me.

Similar to Keskes' case, Tutaya's scheme was uncovered when the FBI was tipped off via an online service that tracks criminal activity.

However, if this service hadn't been tracking purchases on eBay, Tutaya would have gotten away with profits of more than $200,000.

A Hotbed of Stolen Merchandise: Flea Markets

Another way contraband merchandise is disseminated is through flea markets and thrift shops. On any given Sunday, most major cities in the U.S. host one or more flea markets. Vendors sell merchandise ranging from rare vintage finds to bulk socks, hair clips, beauty products, and various knickknacks at bargain basement prices. Marketed as places where people can get a deal on merchandise that might cost them twice as much at a regular store, flea markets are hotbeds of resold items. The Aqueduct Flea Market in Queens had close to 500 vendors before the city shut it down in January of 2011—an increase of 100 vendors from 2009.[22] The best sellers were discounted makeup, Blu-ray DVDs, discounted jewelry, and ladies' clothing. However, it was discovered that expired medications such as Robitussin, Claritin, and children's medicines were being sold at heavy discounts and illegally, according to Federal Drug Administration regulations.[23]

Nabbing the Bad Guys: Classifying Organized Retail Crime as a Felony

With all that we know about the prevalence of ORC, why does this crime continue to rise? ORC increased by 8% in 2009 over 2008. With the economy in one of the worst slumps in U.S. history, 92% of retailers reported their companies were victims of ORC.[24] Retail theft is a high-profit, low-risk crime. Frank Muscato, another member of the organized retail crime division at Walgreens, says, "Ninety-nine percent of the time, people who are a part of ORC are engaged in much worse crime and realize this is a good way of funding it," explains Muscato. "They [people involved in the rings] have the understanding that if they are caught, they will only be picked up on a shoplifting charge, which is a misdemeanor and will result in a minimal jail sentence or a warning. For a professional criminal, that is music to their ears!"[25]

The problem, according to Jerry Biggs from Walgreens, comes from the way in which law enforcement perceives the crime of boosting versus shoplifting, which are two different things. He identifies and blames mainstream media for putting a lighter spin on the act of stealing from stores. Instead of being depicted as a hard-core crime in movies, TV shows, and other forms of entertainment, it's portrayed as being not that big of a deal.

"When you have starlets like Winona Ryder stealing from luxury department stores, her story gets glamorized in the newspapers and magazines. It only makes our jobs more difficult when it comes to convincing law enforcement and loss prevention executives in stores to take this problem seriously. When criminals perceive their crime isn't going to be taken seriously by the retailer they are stealing from and law enforcement, they are going to have more of an incentive to engage in that crime," Biggs tells me.[26]

Joe LaRocca of the NRF points out that 72% of the retailers surveyed for his study stated that their internal investigations identified ORC syndicates that were exporting merchandise not only across state lines but also overseas. In addition, 28% of the criminal groups under investigation have connections to street gangs with international connections.[27] "Organized retail crime rings have realized that tough economic times present new business opportunities by stealing valuable items from retailers and turning around to sell the merchandise to consumers looking for bargains," says LaRocca. "And unknown to the consumer, they are funding things like human trafficking, corruption, and, in the case of the Neira case, which involved the three businessmen in Miami, they are funding terrorist groups like the Hezbollah."[28]

Insurance Companies: The Missing Link

The USA Patriot Improvement and Reauthorization Act, passed in 2006, increased prison terms for people who are convicted of stealing cargo. It also established a national tracking system of cargo theft data through the Unified Crime Reporting System used by the FBI. But chief security officers of trucking and shipping companies are the first to acknowledge that even with the new provisions to the Patriot Act, cargo crime, especially with the downturn in the economy, still remains rampant.

As an addendum to the Act, organizations such as the NICB are trying to further bridge this gap by partnering and creating cross-border information-sharing databases, with companies such as ISO, a database software company owned by Verisk Analytics. However, compiling so much information from so many different sources has proven difficult and, most importantly, cost-prohibitive. Law enforcement efforts to install tracking devices, as well as to establish systems to screen cargo containers and trailers being imported and exported into and out of the U.S., are cost-prohibitive as well. Parvonis Research estimated that losses reach further than just stolen merchandise and include insurance claims, investigation costs, and consumer costs, all of which are estimated to climb to $50 billion annually.[29] Apart from losses, cargo theft also poses a threat to national security. The problem is not just lack of knowledge about products being smuggled out of the country and the potential for weapons of mass destruction to be smuggled in, but what the stolen merchandise funds after it leaves the country. Furthermore, most of the products developed to help curb cargo theft are mostly for recovery, not prevention.

The Gray Market: Another Retail Facilitator of ORC

By profiting from goods sold through the "gray market," thieves circumvent law enforcement. Unlike the black market, where illegal goods are channeled through illegal means, the gray market allows regulated product from a legal source to be sold to an unauthorized marketplace or channel.[30] Walk through a tourist area of any major city, and you will notice electronics stores that have TVs, DVD players, and computers all drastically underpriced. According to an NYPD source, most of those stores are selling gray market products. Products intended for a specific market are diverted and sold to a different, unauthorized marketplace through an intermediary. These diverters include shell or fake companies, fake Internet sites, or shady wholesalers and distributors that are supposed to be selling overseas but that end up selling it in the U.S. Gray market activity, while regulated by state governments[31] and the Tariff Act of 1930,[32] is not legal. However, law enforcement finds it difficult to act against such illegitimate sales. In one instance, Biggs tracked an ORC ring operating out of New York that posed as a shell warehouse selling stolen merchandise right back to Walgreens in addition to the smaller city-based unlicensed drugstores. "The ring in this case didn't immediately own up to the fact that they were selling hot merchandise, and that's what makes it is impossible to trace," says Biggs. "Sometimes they were going to steal something specific and got stuck with a different load and wanted to get it off their hands. Other times they obtained the merchandise illegally and pretended like they don't know where it was coming from." Medical merchandise, such as diabetes test strips, bandages, and, of course, over-the-counter pharmaceuticals, were some of the top-selling goods. In another case Biggs was investigating, he found that the ORC ring made nearly $12 million by selling test strips. But top brands across all categories remain huge sellers.

Laws Have Been Passed, But Are They Helping?

In February of 2009, the Combating Organized Retail Crime Act of 2009, also known as S. 470, was introduced to Congress in an effort to curb the illegal activity taking place in flea markets, pawn stores, and online marketplaces such as Craigslist and eBay. Several other bills, including the E-fencing Enforcement Act of 2009 and the Organized Retail Crime Prevention and Enforcement Act of 2009, were introduced to Congress, but all have yet to pass. S. 470 calls upon law enforcement to crack down on thieves who steal, sell, or transport more than $5,000 in stolen merchandise over a 12-month period. Although that aspect of the bill could be very effective for regulating one-shot criminals, it doesn't take into consideration that professional ORC members often steal well below that amount as individuals. In Maria's case, her ring was stealing between $500,000 and $600,000 retail value each year; however, she would steal well under $500 worth of goods every time she would hit a store. In addition, with the economic downturn, RILA estimates that the level of retail crime rose despite partial economic recovery in 2010. Sixty-five percent of retailers surveyed saw an increase in ORC, and 74% saw an increase in stolen items being found in online marketplaces.[33]

Clearly there is nothing "white collar" about ORC, although the proceeds fund high-profile criminal activities. While the likes of Bernie Madoff won't be coming to a flea market near you to sell stolen items, the mind-set of retail crime rings isn't much different from Madoff. Both fund a fix or try to make money so that they can fund their version of the American Dream. But this is to the detriment of hundreds of thousands of people and costs retailers as well as state and local governments billions.

5

Profile of a Booster and a Fence

In most organizations, from The Coca-Cola Company to an ant farm to a beehive, it's the underlings, the worker bees, who make the organizations run at maximum efficiency. It is no different for an organized retail crime ring. Boosters (the people who steal merchandise from stores) and fences (those who purchase the items and sell them on the black and gray markets) have varying degrees of importance within the ORC. A person's importance is based on his level of experience, how long he has been associated with the organization, and his skill set.

For someone like Maria, the former MS-13 member who traveled all over the Midwest and the West Coast, boosting was a means to an end. She was recruited to work for her boss, an MS-13 kingpin, when she was just 16. Now, at 35, she's been doing this for almost 20 years and has recruited others. She had plans to continue working for the MS-13 prior to getting arrested.

"This is something I know very well and, most importantly, make money doing it," she said in an interview tape obtained by the Walgreens organized retail crime division. "For as long as I've been working the same route, nothing changes. We have lifted the same merchandise, over the same amount of time, and when we get caught it's the same punishment. As boosters, the question isn't 'Why do we do this?' it's 'Why wouldn't we still do this?'"

Maria was from East Los Angeles and quickly got swept up in gang life. Like many women who are part of an ORC ring affiliated with a gang, Maria, along with four other women, started stealing from stores such as Walgreens and Target and sold stolen merchandise to support her drug habit and others in the gang.

According to Jerry Biggs of Walgreens, there are three different levels of boosters and fences. This distinction is important for legal reasons. Level 1 boosters and fences are often categorized as "petty thieves" (what Maria started out as). When caught, they are charged with a misdemeanor and are released, regardless of whether they are stealing to fund their drug habits, to ease their emotional issues, or if they are working for a larger organization.

A Level 1 booster fits everyone's image of a typical shoplifter—an emotionally needy starlet, the little old lady across the hall, the neighborhood heroin addict. The person usually has a drug, gambling, or alcohol addiction and steals to fund fixes. The Level 1 booster may commit theft on his own or in a group of other potential addicts.

"I did it for the drugs," says Nick Jojola, a scruffy skateboarder who for years was the bane of the Albuquerque Police Department's existence. He managed an ORC ring that consisted of 20 people much older than he was (and who also were drug addicts). At just 15, he was the youngest Level 1 booster to be convicted in Albuquerque.

Jojola was, for the most part, like any typical teenager growing up in New Mexico. On the weekends, you could find him at the Los Altos skate park doing tricks on his board and hanging out with a crew of eight other guys who called themselves "Feey Town."

Jojola used his talent as a skateboarder to his advantage. While most kids saw skateboarding as a hobby, Jojola quickly developed it into a potential way to make money. At age 13 he was sponsored by a skating marketing company that gave him free skateboards and clothing. By the time he was 16, he was making nearly $2 million.

But it wasn't from skateboarding.

When Jojola was just 14, he realized he could make more money by reselling stolen items than through sponsorships. Reaching out to his sources and his friends from the skate park, Jojola started putting together an ORC ring that primarily engaged in "smash and grab" theft. They stole cars, drove them into store windows, and lifted as much as $10,000 worth of merchandise within minutes. Every couple of days Jojola gathered his workforce to plot out which stores they would hit next. He would dispatch his ring members to stores such as Kmart, Best Buy, Hastings, and a handful of mom-and-pop stores (50 in total). He said that stores selling "Christian-themed merchandise" had the highest resale value.

"What shocked us the most was that he was so young to have so many people working under him," says Albuquerque Police Department detective Harold Prudencio, who was familiar with the case. "No one would think a kid that age would be able to have the sense to run such a large ORC ring on his own. It was as if he was running a corporation."[1]

According to the APD and published reports, Jojola's ORC underlings were mostly ex-convicts and drug addicts. Jojola faced more than 82 counts for his scheme, including burglary, larceny, and racketeering. In 2007, despite the numerous crimes he had committed and the amount of merchandise he had stolen, Jojola was sentenced to just one year in a juvenile detention center. His accomplices were brought up on larceny charges. However, putting away this group for racketeering (a charge that would come with a stricter penalty and longer jail sentence) wasn't going to help.

"These people do not care whether or not they get caught," says Biggs. "They are focused on one thing, and that is how they are going to make their next dollar on what they are selling. They know if they are ever caught, they are facing a maximum of a couple days in jail. Likewise, they also know law enforcement doesn't want to take the time to book them. With those factors in mind, this is a crime that is tailor-made for these types of criminals."

Moving the Merchandise: The Role of a Fence

Although the role of a booster is important, the role that the fence plays in an ORC ring is equally vital. Fences and fencing operations are the point people who sell stolen merchandise to consumers at flea markets, swap meets, pawn shops, and online auction sites (also known as e-fencing). Fences often operate legitimate businesses in conjunction with illegitimate enterprises.[2] Fences fall into two categories: commercial and residential. Level 1 fences usually are in the residential category, operating out of their homes and selling merchandise to friends, family, and neighbors, and can be broken down further into six categories or subsections when describing their business. The highest level is the professional fence, who treats her fencing operation as a legitimate business (also categorized as commercial). Other levels include part-time fences, associational fences, neighborhood hustlers, drug dealers who barter drugs for stolen property, and amateur fences.[3] Most Level 1 boosters take the merchandise and sell it to a fence, who then resells the merchandise at the local level at a flea market, street fair, or pawn shop, or sells it back to the retailer.

At the Los Angeles Police Department's annual LEAPS conference in August of 2010, Joe LaRocca from the National Retail Federation showed a couple of pictures in his presentation that were hugely disturbing. The first was of a haul of clothing, merchandise, and equipment uncovered in a $3 million bust where seven residents were arrested for selling stolen merchandise out of their home. What was shocking about the image was that the home was set up just like a store, complete with racks, shelving, and areas to try on merchandise. When I looked closely at the product, I couldn't help but think, "If the merchandise looks this good, why *not* purchase it from your neighbor?" Then I realized I was talking about a criminal enterprise! The next picture was of three semi-tractor trailers filled with piles of Levi's jeans. According to LaRocca, these jeans were part of a sting authorized by a search warrant; the LAPD uncovered $3 million worth of denim lifted by a South American booster crew targeting Levi's. That day I wandered around downtown Los Angeles and visited a local weekend flea market and checked out the stacks of unworn, fully tagged jeans and the cartons of beauty products. I wondered how much of the merchandise had been delivered by Level 1 boosters, and if I purchased this merchandise, whose fix (either drugs or something more sinister) was I funding?

Being Convicted as a Level 1 Fence: More Like a Slap on the Wrist Than a Slap in the Face

A Level 1 booster or fence arrested in California might face different charges than if he is arrested in Illinois, Florida, or New Mexico. For example, in California, "petty theft" involves taking property valued at less than $400. The penalty can be a sentence of up to six months in jail and a fine ranging from $50 to $1,000. If the property is worth less than $50, the booster might only be charged with an infraction, with a fine of $250 or less. Grand theft applies to stolen merchandise that has a value of $400 or more. If a booster is convicted, the crime can be classified as a misdemeanor or felony, based on what the prosecution decides is the proper penalty.

"The laws are very gray around it, and they're usually dealt with at the local level," said loss prevention expert Paul Jones in an interview with NBC News. "There is no consistent law across the board that invokes a sense of fear in Level 1 boosters. Because the laws are so loose, they think they can get away with it, and, most of the time, they can."[4]

In Florida, the law is more complicated. For example, the shoplifting laws have several sections with nearly 16 different subsections for laws pertaining to retail and farm theft, transit fare evasion, detention and arrest, exemption from liability for false arrest, resisting arrest, and penalties. Sorting through the laws to figure out exactly what law pertains to someone who has just lifted $400 worth of merchandise took me half a night. I can't imagine what law enforcement and prosecutors must be thinking. No wonder Level 1 boosters are turned out as quickly as they can say "shoplifter."

The laws in Illinois are not much better. Article 16A of the Illinois statutes has 13 different sections, all of which have different definitions of what "to conceal" merchandise means, as well as what a "peace officer" is, all the way down to the definition of what a "person" is. And what constitutes a felony is much more complicated. For example, if someone commits the offense of "retail theft," as defined in Section 16A-3, paragraphs (a), (b), and (c) of Article 16A on Retail Theft, [the person] shall be civilly liable to the merchant of the merchandise in the amount consisting of (i) actual damages equal to the full retail value of the merchandise as defined herein, plus (ii) an amount not less than $100 nor more than $1,000, as well as (iii) attorney's fees and court costs. For minors accused of a committing retail theft, the parent or guardian is responsible and civilly liable for the minor. To be convicted for a Class 4 felony (which, according to Illinois law, can mean one to three years in prison), the amount of the item stolen cannot exceed $150. You also would have to have been convicted of any type of theft, robbery, armed robbery, burglary, residential burglary, possession of burglary tools, or engaged in a home invasion.

In New Mexico, not only are the values of the merchandise shoplifted different for petty misdemeanors (the amount must be under $250), but the definitions of "merchant," "store," and "merchandise" also differ compared to how they are defined in Illinois and California. One thing that all local shoplifting and theft laws do have in common is that they are filled with confusing language, definitions, and loopholes that vary from state to state. This makes retail theft a perfect crime for those who want to finance something quickly with virtually no legal ramifications.

"In most cases, as long as the boosters keep theft under $1,000, it is just a misdemeanor [depending on the state]," says Frank Muscato, an executive in the organized retail crime division at Walgreens. "They have not created a federal offense unless they cross state lines into, for example, Indiana or Pennsylvania, where it is a felony to transport stolen merchandise of any value across state borders. I'm telling you, it's really a bad problem."[5]

According to the CRISP (Connecting Research in Security to Practice) Report on organized retail crime, put out by the ASIS Foundation, the absence of criminal statutes that address the unique nature of ORC contributes to the crime's growth. Many state and federal laws are applicable and directed toward two criminal statutes: shoplifting or the Interstate Transportation of Stolen Property Act. Currently no federal criminal statutes are used to prosecute organized retail criminals.[6] In addition, the report outlines how shoplifting penalties fail to recognize the aggregated impact and the number of individual shoplifting acts committed against multiple retailers in multiple jurisdictions, as well as penalties for selling and distributing merchandise both online and offline. The lack of criminal statutes also applies to the Level 1 fence, who by law can be apprehended for knowingly selling stolen merchandise. However, because these fences operate at such a low level, fences who are apprehended rarely have enough information to help law enforcement in larger ORC cases. On the rare occasions when those arrested do have information about the larger ORC ring, the law enforcement involved uses them as potential sources rather than arresting them on the spot.

Tracking the stolen merchandise is equally difficult. Once the product is taken out of the store and sold on the black market, it pretty much doesn't exist anymore. While stores take into account costs for shrinkage, stolen products valued at $100 or less are just written off as a loss, says Muscato. Although it might seem like a petty crime, the result is nearly $30 billion in lost revenues for the retail industry—a major and expensive issue when you look at the big picture.

The Level 2 Booster: Inside the Mind of a Potentially Dangerous Criminal

The difference between a Level 1 booster and a Level 2 booster is subtle, yet significant. Many Level 2 boosters suffer from the same addictions and "survival mode" mentality as a Level 1 booster. However, the Level 2 booster is more organized, tends to travel to different states, and takes an entrepreneurial approach to boosting by creating a small business out of it.

A typical day for Samuel Elias, a Level 2 booster well-known by the Walgreens Loss Prevention group, started out like this: He got up, read the paper, and checked in with his children before they went to school. After his morning ritual, he got ready for work. His workplace wasn't in an office park, tall building, or downtown metropolis. His work space was a garage filled from floor to ceiling with stolen merchandise that he and his team of boosters took from stores such as Target, Walgreens, and Walmart. Around mid-morning, Elias would call some potential fences needing product for their stores. He filled orders based on what he had in his office-turned-warehouse. Then he went out for a couple of hours to case stores or sometimes boost, depending on the day. On a typical outing, he took as much as $5,000 to $7,000 in merchandise, mainly in OTC drugs, razors, diabetic test strips, and baby formula. The OTC drugs with the highest value on the market are Prilosec and Sudafed, both of which Elias boosted often. (When Immigration and Customs Enforcement [ICE] operatives, as well as the organized retail crime team at Walgreens, raided Elias's home, they found well over 400 boxes filled with stolen OTC medication.) At some point during the day, Elias would also figure out a route for a boosting spree. The M.O. of a typical Level 2 booster is to occasionally travel to different states to boost from other retail stores. Elias would go out for five or six days once a month, traveling through northern Kentucky and southern Indiana, according to Biggs. During his week-long trips, Elias would pick up close to $41,000 worth of merchandise from one state alone. His total haul usually equaled $200,000 to $300,000.

"Elias was such a seasoned professional booster he had a three-ring binder that kept track of the merchandise he would sell to another Level 2 fence called Alpha Trading. This wholesale business would clean the merchandise, repackage it, sell it to another, higher-level fence, who would then turn around and sometimes sell it back to the stores," says Biggs.[7]

Elias grew up in Iran. When the Shah fell, his close-knit family decided to stay in Iran despite an oppressive government and even worse living conditions. Elias made his way to the U.S when he was in his 20s. A chronic gambler, Elias started out boosting to supplement his addiction. The money he made selling the merchandise would ultimately be spent at the blackjack table or roulette wheel in Las Vegas or Reno, Nevada or Indiana. He spent at least four or five days out of the month at these gambling locations, where he might win up to $200,000. This money was used to make mortgage payments for a 5,000-square-foot home and two luxury cars. To say Elias was living well off the profits of stolen merchandise would be an understatement. On the radar of many local authorities, Elias was apprehended and arrested often. Sometimes he would be jailed for a couple of months. However, due to different state laws and penalties, Elias continued to boost for almost a decade, working with a group of three or four recruits who were immigrants from Mexico and South America before he was ever convicted of a felony and put in jail for 15 years.

The psychology behind being a booster isn't as complicated as you might imagine. Level 2 boosters work in groups of two or three people made up of a man and two women or all women. They coordinate a hit on a store that takes them at most three to four minutes. In this short amount of time, they may steal a couple of items to a hundred items—if they are lifting OTC drugs. Because Level 2 boosters operate in a group, their mission is to be able to pull as many products as possible in a short amount of time and then turn around and sell them for profit. Because boosters don't resell the merchandise on their own at a flea market or online (they merely obtain it and then give it to their fences), they usually receive 15% to 25% of the total worth of the items sold (or returned, in the case of receipt fraud). In some cases, if the Level 2 booster is a severe drug addict, he will ask for payment in the form of drugs.

Other Forms of Theft from a Level 2 Booster

Level 2 boosters and fences also engage in "retail returns fraud," in which a booster returns merchandise and presents receipts that have been falsified, stolen, or reused. In 2009, the National Retail Federation reported that 93.1% of retailers said stolen merchandise had been returned to their stores, up from 88.9% in 2008. In addition, three-quarters of the retailers surveyed said they had experienced returns using counterfeit receipts.[8]

"Criminals have been fond of using a 'woe is me' mantra because of the economy, but the truth remains that most return fraud is more 'greed' than 'need,'" says Joe LaRocca in an NRF press release. "In many cases, return fraud is committed by people who use technology to produce counterfeit receipts or take advantage of lenient return policies by stealing large quantities of merchandise and returning it to dozens of stores without a receipt."[9]

In November 2009, Miami-Dade authorities arrested four men who lifted $4,600 worth of hair-care products from a CVS drugstore. As authorities later found out, David Nil-Jose Arostequi, Julian Rivera Cruz, and brothers Anthony and Harry Aponte worked together to steal hundreds of hair-care products from the store. They also hit as many as eight different CVS stores in the area within two weeks. Arostequi told authorities that he was the one driving the getaway car while the other three went inside to take the merchandise. Video evidence taken during one of the heists shows the men taking the merchandise, throwing it into white bags, and running out.[10] Like an engineer, surgeon, or mechanic, tools are essential for the skilled Level 2 booster to steal hundreds of boxes and bottles of product within minutes. One common tool that Level 2 and Level 3 boosters use is a "booster bag," which is lined with aluminum foil or cellophane. These bags are made from actual store bags taken from a prior boosting hit, or possibly obtained through a legitimate purchase. They are lined with several layers of sensor-eclipsing material, which masks security tags on clothing, CDs, and DVDs and prevents the security detection systems at the front of the store from going off. Security companies have taken measures to improve their systems to detect booster bags and merchandise within them. However, web sites such as www.rotteneggs.com and www.wonderhowto.com constantly update their criminal information on how to create better bags and deter security systems.

Level 2 and 3 boosters also use baby strollers. They create a fake bottom for the stroller and use blankets, toys, and, at times, even the baby to conceal the merchandise being stolen. Sometimes they drop merchandise into an umbrella hooked on their arm. Other boosters wear baggy clothes. Sometimes the women line their own handbags with foil or cellophane similar to a booster bag to carry out merchandise undetected.[11]

At LAPD headquarters, James Hooper, a private investigator who who has worked with the LAPD on a number of major cases, shows me surveillance tape of a woman carrying around a large brown shopping bag with "Bloomingdale's" written on it. There is nothing particularly alarming about this woman. She has dirty blond hair, is average height and weight, and looks like a legitimate customer—but there is nothing legitimate about her. When she thinks no one is looking, the cameras catch her swiping a stack of shirts into her bag. This takes her no longer than ten seconds. As the surveillance cameras follow her around the store, her bag is getting noticeably fuller. Within ten minutes of being in the store, the woman leaves with a full bag, walking through the sensors without setting anything off.

Next, Hooper shows me another tape of the same woman with the same bag going into a store. This time, she takes merchandise to try on into the dressing room. A couple minutes later, her shopping bag is again noticeably fuller, but she isn't carrying any of the clothes back out with her. James shakes his head as he shows me the hundreds of digitized videos he has on this woman, all from different stores—and always carrying the same shopping bag.

"She was a booster who had been on our watch list for a long time," Hooper explains. "In five months she has stolen $700,000 worth of clothing from different stores around the area."

Level 3 Boosters and Fences: A High-Level Organization Equals High Profits

Level 3 boosters and fences have more in common with Fortune 500 company executives than they do with their Level 2 and 1 cohorts. The Level 3 booster is tactical and strategic. Having boosted for many years, now he runs a larger organization that recruits Level 1 and Level 2 boosters. Most Level 3 fences make profits of $2.5 million to $18 million, according to the NRF. A RILA report identifies Level 3 fences and boosters as including all races and involving international organized criminals, gangs, Nigerian criminal enterprises, Irish travelers, and traditional mobsters such as La Cosa Nostra. The Level 3 boosters organize at a high level, have a very tight and organized network, and tend to send much of their profits from items they've stolen to support overseas terrorist groups in Latin America, Africa, the Middle East, Ireland, or Italy.

Carlos Espinoza Gonzalez was a 38-year-old native of Chile who had also been on Hooper's radar for a long time. Hooper started seeing him in California retail stores in 2000 and 2001 working with groups of 10 to 20 individuals (most of them Chileans) to boost department stores. According to Hooper, who had watched Gonzalez for more than ten years, he would steal mostly apparel and sell it to garment district fences in Los Angeles. The fences that Gonzalez and his team worked with were of Middle Eastern descent and ran several warehouses that sold merchandise to smaller apparel shops and off-price stores. The money these Middle Eastern warehouses made was sent back to Hamas-supported groups, according to Hooper, who said that the men who owned the warehouses had been on FBI watch lists since 2005.

In a surveillance tape shown to me by Hooper, Gonzalez, a relatively average-looking man of medium height, with dark hair and a nice smile, enters a store with an accomplice. He makes his way to the apparel section. He loiters around the men's jeans section, while his lookout watches for salespeople suspiciously eyeing him. In one quick movement, Gonzalez takes a stack of pants and places them in a shopping bag. He then signals to the lookout, and they both walk out of the store and into a getaway car driven by another accomplice. In a different surveillance tape, Gonzalez took the same type of pants in a different store, walked into a dressing room, and then a couple minutes later walked out with nothing in his hands. Yet the clothing he was originally wearing looked bulkier, indicating that he stuffed his original clothing with the stolen pieces. Per his usual pattern, Gonzalez walked out of the store with the merchandise, hopped into a getaway car, and sped to another location.

"Since Gonzalez was part of a larger Level 3 boosting and fencing operation, law enforcement saw him more of an asset in busting a larger ring as opposed to worrying about the 20 items that were stolen from the store. The problem with that strategy is people like Gonzalez learn that they can get away with boosting for years and not be penalized for it," says Hooper, who calls Gonzalez a "super-booster" due to the large number of fencing operations that he supplies. Because Gonzalez supplies so many fencing operations, the traditional strategy for combating ORC of targeting the fence or "going after the head of the snake" would be ineffective since it would be like "cutting off the first head of the mythical Hydra," with "more heads just sprout[ing] up in its place," Hooper says. Gonzalez didn't concentrate on stores just on the West Coast. He traveled up and down the East Coast as well, visiting Florida, Washington, D.C., and New York. Saks Fifth Avenue and Neiman Marcus were also retailers he and his team of boosters hit, according to Hooper.

Since the incident depicted in the surveillance tape I watched, Hooper worked closely with the LAPD and the FBI to disseminate Gonzalez's photo and information to retailers across the country. Gonzalez became one of the most recognized professional boosters in the U.S., and his newfound notoriety made it much harder for him to escape without consequences. Gonzalez has served jail terms of 6 months to 2 years in several different jurisdictions where he was arrested, enabling Hooper and his team to be more effective at contacting local police departments around the country to make them aware of Gonzalez's criminal history.

In addition to Level 3 boosters such as Gonzalez, the FBI closely watches South American theft groups involved in jewelry and diamond heists. Like Gonzalez, these groups operate with 10 to 20 people, hitting stores in the diamond districts of major cities, such as Los Angeles, New York, and Miami. When dealing with theft of items that have a high retail value, Level 3 boosters and fences are very careful to execute the heist in the stealthiest way possible. In another surveillance tape, Hooper showed me two boosters—both well-dressed, seemingly wealthy men, wearing crisp button-down shirts and driving moccasins—walk into a watch store in Las Vegas. The salesperson approaches them and asks if they have any questions or want to see a couple of items. When the salesperson turns his back, the boosters go into action, cutting the seal of the glass case with a special tool, lifting the top, and swiping the Rolex watches. The theft is over within 90 seconds. By the time the salesperson turns around, the two men are walking out of the store carrying nearly $100,000 worth of watches. The only people who noticed were those watching the surveillance video after the incident.

One way Level 3 boosters, as well as fences, circumvent Department of Homeland Security (DHS) or ICE investigation is by creating and using fake Puerto Rican driver's licenses and presenting them at the time of their arrest. Not only was Gonzalez found to be carrying one, but his team of boosters carried them as well. The South American theft groups are known to carry fake licenses, passports, and, in some cases, birth certificates, according to LAPD Detective Amaury Guevara.

Like most Level 3 ORC groups, cargo theft gangs operate on a hierarchical system, where several people assume different roles. One person may take on the role of leader, truck driver, warehouse worker, booster, fence, broker, and buyer. All of these people work in tandem to get the merchandise and sell it to overseas buyers in South American countries, such as Colombia, Paraguay, Brazil, and Argentina.

This is exemplified by Ulises Talavera, owner of Transamerica Express of Miami, the third component of the Miami Sony PlayStation 2 ring used to ship stolen Sony PS2s, cameras, and stereo equipment to Paraguay to be sold in the Galeria Page mall. According to a study done by FreightWatch, buyers and distributors have ties to the countries that are receiving the stolen items. Talavera was working in conjunction with Samer Mehdi—his business partner, who also owned a shipping company—to get millions of dollars worth of merchandise into his stores. Level 3 boosters are highly sophisticated and will fly to a location where the product is being delivered, stay at a nearby hotel, and rent a car under an alias so that they remain untraceable. They case the property or port where the goods are being delivered to ensure a seamless execution of the theft outlined in the FreightWatch study. Level 3 boosters either work for the freight company that delivers the goods, work within the warehouse that stores the product, or have close ties within the freight company or warehouse. This helps them easily lift the merchandise while remaining off everyone's radar. Sticking to the plan is critical. One sloppy move or miscommunication, and millions of dollars worth of product could slip through their hands. Even worse, the Level 3 booster and their team could get caught. If the Level 3 booster doesn't have contacts at a freight company or product warehouse, another method of theft they might engage in is stealing directly from the back of the truck at a terminal yard. Based on gathered intelligence through GPS systems and a detailed map, a Level 3 booster might follow a truck carrying a load of merchandise and wait until the driver stops, or go to a truck terminal yard and break into a truck there. Because most states do not allow rigs to be parked in residential areas, truck drivers often leave their trucks overnight and sometimes over the weekend in unmanned terminal yards. This gives Level 3 boosters the perfect opportunity to steal.

Level 3 Boosters: Frequently Lifted Merchandise

In 2003, the Tactical Operations Multi-Agency Cargo Anti-Theft Squad (TOMCATS) raided a Miami warehouse, where they uncovered $1.3 million in stolen merchandise from trailer heists. Out of the stash, $1 million worth of cigarettes stolen from Boca Raton was recovered. With the help of false identifications and paperwork, the five men associated with the heist were able to pick up the containers left at railroad yards and export the stolen cigarettes overseas. In an interview with the Associated Press, Marc Zavala, a Senior Detective with the LAPD cargo-theft squad called BAD-CATS, said the majority of the cargo stolen in the Miami-Dade county area ends up in Los Angeles. "Especially when it comes to cigarettes, we are seeing more and more loads ending up here," said Zavala, who has been a member of the Burglary Auto Division Criminal Apprehension Team since about 1990.[12]

In the first six months of 2010, recorded cargo theft increased by 5% over the same time period in 2009. Products that were most likely to be stolen included food and drink, pharmaceuticals, consumer care products, and tobacco, which increased from an average loss of $751,000 in 2009 to $1.6 million in 2010.[13] Next to cigarettes and pharmaceuticals, the most frequently boosted product when it comes to cargo theft is auto parts.

But auto theft-related organized retail crime doesn't always happen on a large-scale level.

Autotheft Gone Rampant

Back in Albuquerque, Commander Harold Prudencio was about to let me in on a little secret. Leaning in close, he said: "If you want to see where most of the ORC happens in New Mexico, look at the stolen car reports for the week, then drive over the border. A lot of the ORC rings steal automobiles and sell the parts in border towns." It's hard to believe, but with statistics that say the amount of cargo theft that involved auto parts went from 19 thefts in the first six months of 2009 to 30 during the same time period in 2010, it seemed Prudencio was right. To see for myself, I drove to the border town of Palomas, Mexico. Now, if you are thinking that Palomas is anything like Cabo San Lucas, Acapulco, or Mazatlan, think again. Palomas borders Columbus, New Mexico, the place where Mexican revolutionary general Pancho Villa launched his attack on the U.S. in 1916. It's also famous for cheap dental procedures, prescription drugs, and its drug wars involving the Juarez Cartel. Ten days before I started my trek south, I read that three people were beheaded. Their heads were found separated from their bodies in the town square by a priest. A couple of days later their bodies were found charred in a car just outside of town. This was definitely not a safe town.

Soon, amid blistering desert sun and yucca plants, my luxury car (full disclosure—it was my mother's SUV and, no, I wasn't on the registration or insurance and didn't have permission to drive it to Mexico, but I did it anyway) and I were sailing across the border between the U.S. and Mexico to test how easy it is to get a stolen car across the border. I was feeling uneasy. At customs, the nonchalant border agent on the Mexican side took a swig of his Coca-Cola and asked me in Spanish if I had anything to declare. He briefly looked at the car and into my tinted windows, and then let me drive across. He had no questions about my registration or identification. Neither did he check to see whether there was anything in my SUV that I could potentially be smuggling into Mexico. The whole process took less than 45 seconds.

I parked the car on a dusty road just a few feet south of the customs checkpoint. I made sure to park on the main street. I didn't know which would be worse—if the car was stolen, or if an auto parts smuggler realized I was in Palomas doing undercover investigative work and decided to seek vengeance. I figured my mom's wrath would be far worse. As I wandered around the town's main street, I found several auto parts stores selling what looked like used hubcaps, rims, bumpers, mufflers, and tires, cleaned and on display for less than market value. "Most of these come in every couple of days," said Arturo, the owner of the store, in Spanish, as he pointed to a long row of shiny rims selling for just $10 apiece. (If I wanted to buy a set of four, the price would be $35.) He explained there were more styles in the back if I wanted to see them, or I could wait until Friday and see the new rims come in. A couple doors down from Arturo's store was another auto parts store. The prices were less expensive, but they sold the same merchandise.

But Arturo's store wasn't the only one in Palomas selling stolen auto parts. During my afternoon trip, I counted 11 different storefronts with shiny hubcaps, fenders, and wheels lining the chain-link fence in front of the store. Walking along the dusty streets of Palomas, I was reminded of a story Commander Prudencio told me about Anjun Tahir, a Pakistani native who was arrested in August 2009 for committing bank fraud by way of stolen vehicles. His scheme was simple. According to Prudencio, Tahir would apply for a loan and then purchase a salvaged luxury vehicle. He would steal the exact same model and then swap the VINs. Then he would drive the stolen model with the swapped VIN to Palomas. Tahir claimed he was sending the money back to his home country (although it was unclear exactly which method he was using—hawalas or stored value cards), but he was brought up on charges of loan fraud. Tahir's scheme was just another example of how the proceeds of stolen vehicles are laundered through various means (in this case, committing loan fraud).

The FBI estimates that 794,616 motor vehicles were stolen in 2009, a rate of 258.8 vehicles stolen per 100,000 residents. Nationwide, nearly $5.2 billion was lost because of motor vehicle theft.[14] ICE estimates that 30% of the cars stolen in the U.S. are taken apart and sold across the border. And what was the most-stolen car in New Mexico? Definitely not my mother's Lexus, but a 1994 Honda Accord. Good thing I didn't opt to take my sister's car instead.

Crossing back into the U.S. was a much different story. The line of cars was long, and it took 45 minutes to move just a few yards. When I finally got to the station, the border patrol agent on the U.S. side inspected the trunk, backseat, and undercarriage in meticulous detail. He asked my name, my age, why I had been in Mexico, and how long I had stayed. He asked me for my passport. When I didn't produce it (I didn't even think to bring it!), he took a long look at me and then asked to see my driver's license, which he ran through the system. Now I was intimidated and hoping that nothing from my teenage past could sneak up and get me into trouble. After I went through the wringer of questions, I asked the agent why the same due diligence wasn't taken going into Mexico. His reply was deadpan but honest: "That's Mexico for you. We can't tell them what to do."

Curbing Boosters and Fences: What Does and Doesn't Work

Detective Amaury Guevara from the LAPD makes an effective suggestion for curbing boosters and fences, which is pretty much shared by everyone in the loss prevention industry: For shippers, forwarders, and carriers to help combat ORC and cargo theft, they must first learn how these groups operate. "I tell all of my men when we are investigating a case to do their homework and learn how to steal," says Guevara. "Once you know and understand how to bilk the system, you will have more of an understanding of how these criminals think and therefore be five steps ahead of them."

The difference between the LAPD and most retail employees and private security is the lack of employee training needed to keep them ahead of criminal tactics. This is exemplified by my former colleague the handbag bandit, who explained that the handbags he was trying to sell me came directly from warehouse employees at Barneys. In a warehouse, whether it's for a luxury retailer or grocery store, staff members are less than diligent about checking all paperwork when freight is picked up and delivered. Giving fictitious pickup times is a common practice for these groups. Members of these gangs typically are careless when it comes to producing official documents, so simple mistakes can signal that something criminal may be happening. For example, photos on fake IDs often are doctored snapshots, or the person pictured might be wearing inappropriate attire, such as a sombrero, which would not be allowed by a government licensing agency. Also, on shipping documents, gangs often include misspelled words—or even revert to Spanish—when making the forgeries, according to a FreightWatch study. Managers can take steps to fortify their supply chain security systems just by taking a few minutes to really examine a document. It's an easy step that could save a company hundreds of thousands of dollars in losses.

When I asked Barneys for a response regarding their warehouse policies, the head of loss prevention declined with "No comment."

Although Congress has made a significant effort to introduce boosting laws, these will barely make an impact. HR 6713, the E-fencing Enforcement Act of 2008, was introduced to do the following:

- Toughen the criminal code's treatment of ORC "by refining certain offenses to capture conduct that is currently being committed by individuals engaged in organized retail crime and requiring the U.S. Sentencing Commission to consider relevant sentencing guideline enhancements."

- Require physical retail marketplaces, such as flea markets and online auction sites, to review the account of a seller and file a suspicious activity report with the Justice Department when presented with evidence showing that the seller was selling items that were illegally obtained.

- Require high-volume sellers on online auction sites to display a physical address, P.O. box, or private e-mail box registered with a commercial mail-receiving agency to help online buyers get in touch with sellers and help law enforcement agents identify people who may be selling stolen goods online. In addition, the bill requires retailers to halt the sale of online goods if they find evidence that the goods were stolen.[15]

This law does not protect the consumer from internal employees (employees who work within the store) selling items on sites such as eBay and Amazon, nor shield potential employers from hiring people who have previously been involved in an incident at one or more of a retailer's stores, nor prevent the creation of "multiple identities" on an auction web site who shop at these stores, nor does it identify relationships between incident victims and employee eyewitnesses.

In general, the proposed law might address weaknesses in federal laws that help facilitate growing ORC rings. This law also calls on retailers to take responsibility for curbing ORC on their web sites by collecting information about their customers who are involved in fencing goods on their web sites. Retailers are then required to give that information to the government so that law enforcement officials can use it to prosecute fences. The problem arises when retailers don't collect the information or inquire about certain sellers on the site, in the store, or on another auction site and then synthesize that information to obtain a multichannel overview of loss and fraud. In addition, retailers are noticing that fences and boosters have less fear of getting caught, are engaging more in smash-and-grab activities, and are becoming more violent.[16]

The E-fencing Enforcement Act of 2008 also doesn't include the sale of gift cards. What's more, the only ORC bills that have been passed have been at the local and state level. Therefore, they are inconsistent with other states in respect to how they define ORC and measures that should be taken in prosecuting ORC members and fences.

"ORC criminals are ten steps ahead of law enforcement," says Detective Guevara. "Identity theft and gift card fraud is just scratching the surface. These criminals spend their days on social networking sites, or sites such as Second Life, and figure out ways to mine information from people's data that they mindlessly mention online. Banks used to prevent fraud by having real people in place who checked for signatures and saw the person making a $100,000 deposit. Now, with Internet growth, those types of checks and balances are quickly being eclipsed by online banking, fast deposits, and even faster monetary transactions. The worst part is that federal laws aren't moving fast enough to keep up with changing technology. By the time Congress introduces a new bill and it gets voted on, technology changes, and they have to revise a law that hasn't even been passed yet. The system is very inefficient and is causing retailers to lose money at a rapid rate."[17]

Like most organized groups, boosters and fences often work with people they know and trust—people they consider "family." But this is not the type of family you would want to have Sunday dinner with. This is an altogether different type of family—and not a very nice one, as we'll explore next.

6

Family Ties

In 2007, the concept of "family" was the topic of conversation *du jour*. With the economy on the decline and a heated presidential election gaining momentum, everyone from conservative Republicans to pop singers were redefining what "family" meant. For ORC rings that function domestically and internationally, "family" takes on several definitions.

In the Tri-Border Area (TBA) of South America (which includes Paraguay, Brazil, and Argentina), ORC groups have indigenous and nonindigenous roots. "Families," such as the Morel family based in Paraguay, had ties to international mafias and smuggling rings that have garnered them influence and political power within the country. The Morels functioned similar to the Italian mafia, complete with family members and a boss to whom they reported. They ran one of the largest smuggling rings in South America, smuggling arms, drugs, cars, and stolen car parts.[1]

Nonindigenous families have existed in areas such as the Tri-Border Area for generations. Many of these crime syndicates come from China, Colombia, Corsica, Japan, Lebanon, Mexico, Nigeria, and Russia.[2] The three main ethnic communities within Ciudad del Este (located in Paraguay) are Chinese, South Asian, and Korean. In 2003, Ciudad del Este counted 30,000 people of Chinese descent in its community. However, only 9,000 are legally registered as residents.[3] The Lebanese and Arabic ethnic communities also have a strong presence. Portuguese is spoken fluently in this area, although Arabic is spoken with the same frequency as Portuguese (if not more so).

Brazil is home to 1 million Muslims who have citizenship. Of that 1 million, the second-largest concentration of Muslims, after Sao Paulo, is in Foz do Iguacu, about 283 miles from Paraguay. The Muslim population within the city is of Lebanese and Palestinian descent, and they maintain commercial outlets in Ciudad del Este.[4] Hezbollah Lebanese merchants are tied to the Shia in both Paraguay and Brazil. But the Hezbollah in the Tri-Border Area is a political movement that engages in terrorism, explains Larry Johnson, a former analyst at the U.S. Central Intelligence Agency and co-owner and chief executive of BERG Associates.[5] Tiered multicountry terrorist organization allows them to create and gain leverage against local governments and this leverage benefits them when it comes to negotiating on a larger level. Sticking to their own ethnic group is one way ORC rings can ensure that information doesn't leave the circle.

One of the main conduits for smuggling stolen merchandise is the Sindhis in western India and Panama, commonly referred to as the "Hindu brokers," according to Johnson. "They literally have catalogs of knockoff items; you can buy everything from a coffee pot to Sony PS2 consoles. In addition to counterfeiting, these Sindhis buy and sell stolen items by acting as 'the brokers.' Counterfeit items come from countries such as China and Malaysia, then are sent to free trade zone countries, such as Colombia, Panama, Aruba, and Chile. In Panama there is a walled city of shops and banks in one of the largest shopping malls in the world, mostly run by these brokers, who buy, sell, and trade counterfeit and stolen merchandise." Wholesale distributors are the merchant classes, with strong Jewish, Arab, Hindu, and Chinese contingents. About 80% of them are legitimate businesspeople representing companies such as Samsung and Nike, but the remaining 20% purchase, produce, and sell counterfeit items using names that are slightly different from legitimate brands. On one of his most recent trips to Panama, Johnson discovered "Sidney," the counterfeit brand for "Disney." Counterfeit PlayStations are called "Polystations."

"This also happens with cigarettes, perfumes, and liquor. Companies don't do much to stop it," says Johnson. "It's cost-prohibitive [to fight], and even if they get some counterfeit merchandise out of there, it is free advertising [for the product counterfeiters]." Johnson described how he found a 19-year-old boy working in his uncle's store selling counterfeit coffee makers. His uncle, says Johnson, was teaching him the trade of the business.

When Family Funds Support Terrorism

Like the Sindhis, the Arabic community also has a large contingent in the Tri-Border Area. The Lebanese population makes up 90% of the city (Ciudad del Este), and the estimated size of the Lebanese community ranges from 20,000 to 30,000. The group is tight-knit, with their own schools and clubs, making it incredibly difficult to infiltrate unless you are "a member of the family." In the bordering city of Foz do Iguacu in Brazil, most Arabic immigrants live in gated condominiums,[6] making it easy for extremists to congregate, brainstorm plans of action, and execute those plans without any repercussions from their community. According to a Library of Congress study,[7] al Qaeda sympathizers have been active in the Tri-Border Area for these reasons. In Argentina the Muslim population outnumbers the Jewish population by almost 500,000. The number of Jews living in Argentina totals 250,000 compared to the 700,000 to 900,000 Muslims, with nearly 80% living in Buenos Aires.

In addition to the estimated $60 million to $100 million per year the Hezbollah receives from Iran, it also gets funding from the Shi'ite Lebanese diaspora in West Africa from sources in the U.S. and the Tri-Border Area.[8] Islamic money laundering in the Tri-Border Area is concealed by the common practice of the local Arab community of remitting funds to relatives in the Middle East. In late 2002, Argentine officials linked Lebanese terrorists in the Tri-Border Area to money laundering, counterfeiting of U.S. money, and other illicit financial activities. As evidence, they cited "thousands of U.S. dollars bearing stamps from Lebanese currency exchange banks, tens of thousands of dollars in phony bills, and receipts from wire transfers made between the Tri-Border Area and the Middle East." What's more, Brazilian authorities have estimated that more than $6 billion a year in illegal funds are being laundered in the Tri-Border Area. According to John Moynihan, partner at BERG Associates, armored trucks loaded with laundered money leave Ciudad del Este for Fox do Iguacu, the Brazilian town on the other side of the border. Paraguay's Finance Ministry issued an order in January of 2003 to suspend sending dollars abroad, but a report found this order was apparently not being applied to armored vans or trucks leaving the Tri-Border Area. One van known to be carrying reais and dollars was observed crossing the Friendship Bridge into Brazil on January 20, 2003.[9]

Islamic fundamentalist groups in the Tri-Border Area and similar areas in Latin America also send to radical Islamic groups in the Middle East between $300 million and $500 million a year in profits from drug trafficking, arms dealing, and other illegal activities, including money laundering, contraband, and product piracy.[10] Hezbollah derived a substantial amount of its income from various illicit activities in the Tri-Border Area, in addition to financial support from the government of Iran. Media reports also indicated an al Qaeda presence in the Tri-Border Area as well as cooperation between Hezbollah and al Qaeda. Conventional thinking suggests the Sunni-minded al Qaeda would never collaborate with the Shi'ite-minded Hezbollah, but the reported strategic alliance was indicative of a larger collaboration.[11] For example, one report suggested an Islamic terrorist summit was held in the Tri-Border Area in late 2002 to plan terrorist attacks against U.S. and Israeli diplomatic facilities in South America. In 1996, a Tri-Border Area-based terrorist plan by Hezbollah and al Qaeda intended to blow up the U.S. Embassy in Asuncion. Attacking targets would appear to be a high priority for al Qaeda, Hezbollah, and other Islamic terrorist groups that may have a presence in the Tri-Border Area. According to the report, targets could also include hotels, tourism centers, airports, or multinational companies, especially those of Israeli, German, French, or U.S. origin.

Assad Muhammad Barakat and His "Family"

In June 2002, Brazilian authorities arrested Assad Muhammad Barakat, a 37-year-old Lebanese national. At the age of 17, Barakat emigrated from Lebanon to Paraguay with his father. Prosecutors believed he was a major player in the 1992 bombing of the Israeli embassy in Buenos Aires and the 1994 bombing of the Jewish Community Center in the Argentine capital.[12] Barakat started out as a street peddler, selling trinkets and items to locals and tourists. As he built his business, he created an import-export store in the Galeria Page shopping gallery called Apollo Import Export. It was here that he accumulated most of his wealth and then started acquiring companies such as the Mundial (World) Engineering and Construction company, as well as several other properties and businesses in Paraguay, Chile, New York, and Miami. He became co-owner of the Galeria Page shortly after he started his business. Barakat was identified as the Hezbollah's military operations chief as well as the chief fund-raising officer in the Southern Cone (the areas of South America south of the Tropic of Capricorn, encompassing Argentina, Chile, Paraguay, and Uruguay). In addition to being heavily involved in fund-raising operations in the Tri-Border Area, the U.S. State Department has identified him as being connected to the al-Gama'a al-Islamiyya (Egyptian Islamic Group).

Located in Ciudad del Este, the Galeria Page mall was described by Argentine police as the regional command post for the Hezbollah and home to many businesses selling stolen, smuggled, or counter-feit items. Law enforcement raided a store owned by Assad Ahmad Barakat and confiscated more than 60 hours of video and CD-ROMs of military marches and attacks with explosives in various parts of the world. They also confiscated material for professional training courses for suicide bombers. Boxes were found containing financial statements totaling $250,000 in monthly transfers to the Middle East and descriptions of at least 20 recent attacks in Israel and Israeli-occupied territories. According to the U.S. Department of the Treasury, Barakat used two of his businesses, Casa Apollo and Barakat Import Export Ltda, as a cover for Hezbollah fund-raising activities. These shell companies sold stolen and counterfeit merchandise. As part of a bank fraud scheme, Barakat used Barakat Import Export Ltda to raise money for the Hezbollah in Lebanon by mortgaging the company to borrow money.

But Barakat didn't work alone. His network included two of his brothers and several confidants who used management positions at the mall to shroud what they were really doing. His brother Hamzi Barakat was a member of the Hezbollah in the Tri-Border Area and was suspected of trafficking counterfeit U.S. dollars, arms, explosives, and stolen merchandise to fill his stores. According to a study done by the U.S. Treasury Department,[13] he has owned and held the position of general manager of Casa Hamze, a store in the Galeria Page that has employed Hezbollah members and has served as a source of fund-raising for the terrorist organization. Assad Ahmad Barakat was a longstanding partner in Casa Hamze.

Hatim Ahmad Barakat was one of the only members of the Barakat network who was allowed to share information with his brother Assad Ahmad Barakat. Hatim would travel from Chile to Paraguay to raise and collect funds for the Hezbollah. He was a shareholder in two Chilean businesses believed to fund Hezbollah activities in Paraguay. Hatim acted as Assad's primary confidant when it came to financial matters. Functioning like a first-stage venture capitalist,

Hatim not only went out to raise money, he was also deeply involved in Assad's business dealings and finances. He offered his brother advice on how to expand the two businesses he co-owned with him, such as SDGT Casa Apollo and he offered advice on how to raise capital for additional funding. "He was known as the numbers guy," says an FBI source on the case. "He had a photographic memory and knew every detail of what was going on within the mall and with the businesses they co-owned. Nothing would slip past him. If he were running a legitimate business, it would be a Fortune 500 company by now."[14]

Muhammad Fayez Barakat, a cousin of Assad's, played a special role in the Tri-Border Area network: He was in charge of transferring funds from South America to the Middle East. In July of 2006, Fayez collected funds on behalf of the Hezbollah Tri-Border Area by hosting black-tie dinners and fund-raisers for Hezbollah sympathizers. After the event, the money was gathered and sent back to Lebanon via a hawala. A numbers whiz, Fayez would often provide financial assistance, floating Assad millions of U.S. dollars to keep his businesses afloat when times were tough.

Sobhi Mahmoud Fayad, a "personal secretary," was also known to be a military leader in the Tri-Border Area, a high-ranking Hezbollah member in Lebanon in the 1980s, and a weapons expert. He is said to have supported terrorist efforts in the Tri-Border Area prior to his arrest and conviction in 2003 for tax evasion. During his trial, Fayad admitted to transferring money to a Hezbollah-controlled charity in Lebanon. The name of the charity was not identified at the time.

Back in the U.S., an entirely different ORC scheme that funded terrorism was taking place. Khaled T. Safadi, Ulises Talavera, and Emilio Gonzalez-Neira of Miami, Florida were trying to figure out the best way to sell Sony PlayStation 2s (PS2s) to the Galeria Page in Paraguay. The elaborate scheme went on for almost three years before they were arrested. The men worked with Samer Mehdi, 37 years old and owner of Jomana Import Export, an electronics store in the mall. With the help of two distribution companies located in

Miami, the men were able to easily sell and move stolen Sony electronic items for profit in Paraguay with the help of Hatim Ahmad Barakat and by recruiting people from Lebanon as well as South America to join them.

Setting up fictitious trucking companies (like the fictitious distribution companies in Miami) is common practice, especially for ORC rings shipping stolen merchandise overseas. And they are usually run by contacts made through family connections. The recruiting process for the trucking industry, as well as many ORC rings, is very ethnically based. They stick to a common bond.

The fake trucking companies accept shipments from another company that ships the merchandise. After the funds have been transferred, the shipping company learns that the trucking company doesn't exist. In a federal prosecution case in California, a company was accepting money for shipments but didn't fulfill deliveries.

According to the indictment filed in a Dade County court on January 11, 2008, Gonzalez-Neira, under his company Jumbo Cargo, filed a falsified Shipper's Export Declarations (SED) listing the ultimate consignee name and address for the 400 PS2s as Atlantic International, S.A., Monsenor Rodriguez y Pampliega, Ciudad del Este, Paraguay. The following day, Gonzalez-Neira fictitiously listed Dally Center (Jo) Shopping Vendome, Ciudad del Este, Paraguay as the ultimate consignee on the export documentation. A year and a half prior, Talavera provided fraudulent invoices to law enforcement corresponding to 1,000 PS2s exported on June 8, 2007 as well as 2,070 PS2s he attempted to export on August 27, 2007.[15]

Ninety percent of America's non-North American trade arrives by sea in containers. Almost 25% of the American GDP, some $2.4 trillion worth, comes from international trade through imports and exports. More than $8.8 billion worth of goods is processed daily at U.S. entry points nationwide, of which $1.4 billion is processed at domestic major ports.[16] The volume of U.S. international trade, measured in terms of dollars and containers, has doubled since 1990. Depending on how well the global economy recovers, the volume could double again in the next decade, which would materially contribute to the lives and economic prosperity of this nation. Yet the border agencies do not have the resources to examine more than 2% of the cargo that comes into this country.

Illegal Entry into the U.S. Is Not Difficult—if You Have Money

"Terrorism is cheap," says Professor Ibrahim Warde of Tufts University. "There has been a shift in the cost of terrorism post-9/11. There was a time when terrorism was state-sponsored and involved large amounts of money. In the 1970s and 1980s, the Soviet Union was a significant sponsor of terrorist organizations. With the collapse of the Soviet Union, Libya became one of the main financiers of terrorism activity. In those days, terrorist plots were very costly. This was before the Internet and social networks, which significantly dropped the price of terrorist funding, because communicating became so much easier. To fund the September 11 attacks, al Qaeda spent $500,000 over two years for 20 people to put together the terrorist plot. Later, as many financial controls were put in place, terrorists adapted to the new environment. Almost every terrorist act thereafter, including the 2005 London bombings, cost under $20,000."[17]

Making Fake Documents

One thread (albeit, an expensive one) that all terrorist and ORC groups have in common is producing and using fake documents to conceal their illegal activities. This includes using fake passports, travel documents, company credentials, and driver's licenses. However, the cost of getting people into the U.S. since 9/11 has tripled, and with insufficient border control, it's become easier to get illegals into the country. Most of the cost has to do with fake green card costs. U.S. residents and naturalized citizens by the hundreds send their Social Security cards, "green cards," stripped-out visas, or passports to their former countries, where people pay thousands of dollars for one with a photo that matches their features and age.

Specialists may superimpose a razor-thin image over the passport photo to retain a new picture.[18] Says Detective Amaury Guevara of the LAPD, "There has been a trend with violent criminals to pursue nonviolent ways to make and raise money. They are getting older and are less inclined to shoot people for payment. Therefore, making connections within prison and creating fake official documents is another very lucrative revenue stream."[19]

In a letter to Secretary of Homeland Security Janet Napolitano in June 2010, Representative Sue Myrick (R-NC) warned that the Hezbollah might be colluding with drug cartels along the U.S.-Mexican border. She called on Homeland Security to establish a task force to clamp down on the national security threat.[20] She noted that Iranian agents and members of the Hezbollah were learning Spanish in Hugo Chavez-run Venezuela before trying to obtain false documents to enter the U.S. as purported Mexicans.

In the events leading up to 9/11, many of the terrorists, including Mohammad Atta and Khalid Sheikh Mohammed, had United Arab Emirates IDs that allowed them entry into the U.S. However, as with many potential terrorists brought in from overseas, their documents were forged and created based on legitimate (and legal) documents obtained through family members.

When Atta applied for a U.S. visa, however, his application was denied. Earlier in 1999, Osama bin Laden had sent Khalid Sheikh Mohammed to Yemen to help Rahim al-Nashiri obtain explosives for the planned ship bombings (the USS *The Sullivans* and the USS *Cole* in January and October 2000) and to obtain a visa to visit the U.S. so that he could participate in an operation there. Atta applied under another name, using the cover story that he would be visiting a medical clinic to obtain a new prosthesis for his leg. Another al Qaeda operative gave Atta the name of someone living in the U.S. whom Khalid Sheikh Mohammed could use as a point of contact on a visa application. Atta contacted this individual to help him get an appointment at a U.S. clinic.[21]

Atta and Abu Zubaydah each played key roles in facilitating travel for al Qaeda operatives. In addition, al Qaeda had an "office of passports," located in host countries such as Saudi Arabia, Yemen, and Afghanistan and overseen by its security committee. One of the offices was located at the Kandahar airport and was managed by Mohammed Atef (another al Qaeda operative and alleged military chief of al Qaeda). The committee altered papers including passports, visas, and identification cards.[22] Moreover, certain al Qaeda members were charged with organizing passport collection schemes to keep the pipeline of fraudulent documents flowing. To this end, al Qaeda requires jihadists to turn in their passports before going to the front lines in Afghanistan. In the ultimate in identity swapping, if the operatives are killed, their passports are recycled for use.[23] The operational mission training course taught operatives how to forge documents. Certain passport alteration methods also were taught, including substituting photos and erasing and adding travel cachets. Manuals demonstrating the technique of "cleaning" visas were reportedly circulated among operatives. Atta and Zakariya Essabar were reported to have been trained in passport alteration.[24]

Getting into the U.S. by Way of Fake Passports and Human Smuggling

"The terrorists are smart about which passports they use," says David Simcox, director of migration demographics and chairman of the board of the Center for Immigration Studies, in an interview for PBS's *Frontline*. "At least two of the September 11th attackers used stolen Saudi Arabian passports. Saudi Arabia is a friend of the U.S., so using their passport makes it easier to get in at the border." Many times terrorists work in conjunction with corrupt government officials who allow them to purchase a legitimate passport issued in the terrorists' own names, or using an alias, for several thousand dollars. Or the terrorist can purchase the passport off the black market from countries that have "visa-free" relationships with the U.S., such as Japan and Sweden. Speaking of paying people off, terrorists have recently started working with human traffickers. For all intents and purposes, they are fake document and passport experts and have ready documents used to smuggle scores of people over the border. The average cost to get a fake passport from a smuggler is upwards of $50,000. As a bonus, the human smugglers can help smuggle terrorists over the border. Most of the time these smugglers work in conjunction with drug cartels and gangs, such as the MS-13, to ensure a smooth journey and law enforcement-free routes. (This means that law enforcement was paid off using ORC funds and sales from pirated merchandise.)

To find out if this theory was in fact true, I spoke to a Department of Homeland Security officer while I was leaving Palomas, Mexico. He was stationed at the second checkpoint going back into the U.S. "Everyone knows the Mexican side of the border is corrupt," he said. "Let's say you had ten bags filled with $100,000 of cash each. Even if they inquired about it, you could make a deal with them by giving them a bag, and they will let you through, no questions asked."

Making or obtaining a counterfeit passport isn't that difficult, according to Detective Guevara. Blank British passports have been known to be sold at premium cost through dishonest employees at passport offices. In addition to forging official documents from exchange-friendly countries, terrorists create fake Puerto Rican driver's licenses because they are valid in the U.S. Furthermore, law enforcement officials in states in the middle of the country and the West probably don't know what one looks like. "It comes down to training, and unfortunately for law enforcement, it's hard for them to tell the difference between a fake Puerto Rican driver's license and a legitimate one. You have one or two lazy guys who don't feel like doing the research, and all of a sudden millions of dollars of merchandise is moving across the border, no questions asked." Guevara says the Immigration and Naturalization Service (INS), while trained in identifying fake passports by checking them against a database, can barely tell the difference anymore, because the quality is getting so good.

The Hammoud brothers from North Carolina knew what it was like to be a part of an identity theft scheme. They operated a Hezbollah support cell out of Charlotte, which included cigarette smuggling, money laundering, and immigration fraud. Mohamad Hammoud became involved with the Hezbollah when he joined the group's militia at the age of 15 in Beirut, Lebanon. Many of the members of the theft group he was working with out of North Carolina were tied to the same neighborhood in Beirut and knew each other long before they immigrated to the U.S.[25] The bond between Hammoud and his brothers was facilitated by family ties, religion, criminal activities, and an association with and sympathy for the Hezbollah.[26] In the case of the cigarette smuggling scheme in North Carolina, financial investigations linked more than 800 bank accounts to the Hammoud brothers cell. They also had multiple identities adopted from departing international students who had acquired driver's licenses, Social Security cards, credit histories, and the necessary immigrant documents. Harb was a friend of the family who worked with the brothers and was recruited to deliver $3,500 to a Hezbollah military commander in Lebanon. He became part of the state's evidence and testified against the brothers. He admitted that he would max out credit cards he obtained with a particular identity, declare bankruptcy, and then refrain from using the identity of a departing student for another seven years. He made at least $150,000 per contraband identity card.[27]

According to the *Identity Theft Handbook: Detection, Prevention and Security* by Martin T. Biegelman, travel documents are as important as weapons. Terrorists must travel clandestinely to meet, train, plan, case targets, and gain access to attack. The Internet has been a gateway for easy access to fraudulent documents. Biegelman notes in his book that many web sites offer fake IDs. One site, now closed pending a criminal prosecution, was www.fakeidsite.com. Another site, also shut down, was www.sob-ids.com. It allowed customers to come to their physical location if they happened to be in Mexico. The site allegedly had to relocate to avoid U.S. government investigation and prosecution. But before the site was shut down, one customer noted, "The holograms were flawless, and the bar code and magnetic strips work."

The Great Entrepreneurs: Terrorists

The new terrorists are much better financed than their predecessors, who relied mainly on crime or the funds of antigovernment state-based groups. Today's terrorists have income streams from legal and illegal sources and are not accountable to state sponsors or anybody else.[28] Terrorist organizations are run much like corporations, employing personal assistants, chief financial officers, and spokesmen.

According to Horacio Calderon, an expert on international affairs and terrorism, "ghost" companies are established by criminal and terrorist front men to conduct their operations and businesses even on a small scale. The al Qaeda networks and prime transnational crime organizations are always looking for new state-of-the-art technologies to hide their assets. They conduct their business using sophisticated measures and countermeasures to avoid detection and monitor punitive actions from enemy intelligence as well as law enforcement agencies.[29]

The Hezbollah as Entrepreneurs

The Galeria Page mall is well known as a main source of fundraising for the Hezbollah in Paraguay. It also is a front for the central headquarters for members in the Tri-Border Area. The mall was established in 2001 and houses many shell businesses, including electronic and import/export stores.

Executive Order 13224 empowers the U.S. Secretary of State to designate certain individuals or entities as having committed or as posing a significant risk of committing acts of terrorism that threaten national security.[30] The Galeria Page mall has been considered a Specially Designated Global Terrorist (SDGT) since December 6, 2006.[31] Jomana Import Export, owned by Samer Mehdi, was identified as an entity providing support (in this case, financial support) to foreign terrorists. It was aided by Cedar Distributors, an electronics distributor and exporter based in Miami, Florida (owned by Khaled T. Safadi) with operations throughout the U.S. It was distributing and selling, among other items, Sony PlayStation 2 consoles, gaming equipment, and cameras. The company was incorporated in 1997 and is still active.

Transamerica Express of Miami is a freight-forwarding business owned by Ulises Talavera. Talavera knew Mehdi for years, but it was only after Jomana Import Export was designated as an SDGT that they started doing business together on March 30, 2007. Mehdi asked Safadi and Cedar to forward 200 Sony brand digital cameras to defendants Talavera and Transamerica to export to Jomana in the Galeria Page. Jumbo Cargo Inc. is another freight-forwarding company owned by Emilio Gonzalez-Neira, a Paraguayan national who legally resided in the U.S. Although this business had other legitimate business going on, Gonzalez-Neira acted as the go-between for Mehdi and Talavera by taking and forwarding orders, transferring funds, and falsifying documents. This was a violation of Title 31, Code of Federal Regulations, Section 594.201; Executive Order 13224; Title 50, United States Code, Section 1705; and Title 18, United States Code, Section 2.

In addition to working with his close allies, Mehdi wanted to expand his business by joining Business to Business (B2B) sites like tradeboss.com, which allowed him to buy imported merchandise from around the world and sell it in his store.

Raising Money Like Venture Capitalists

Al Qaeda has become the most well-known terrorist organization in the world because of the 9/11 attacks. Osama bin Laden, who was trained in Afghanistan to fight the Russian occupation, decided to create his own extremist group, which would later become al Qaeda. By August 1988, bin Laden was clearly its leader (emir). This organization's structure included in its operating arms an intelligence component, a military committee, a financial committee, a political committee, and a committee in charge of media affairs and propaganda. It also had an advisory council (shura) made up of bin Laden's inner circle.[32]

Bin Laden's vast number of offices located around the world covertly provided financial support for terrorist activities. The network included a major business enterprise in Cyprus; a services brand in Zagret; an office of the Benevolence International Foundation in Sarajevo, which supported the Bosnian Muslims in their conflict with Serbia and Croatia; and a nongovernmental organization (NGO) in Baku, Azerbaijan. The Egyptian Islamic Jihad used it as a source and consultant for finances and as a support center for the Muslim rebels in Chechnya. Bin Laden also made use of the already-established Third World Relief Agency (TWRA) headquartered in Vienna, whose branch office locations included Zagreb and Budapest. (Bin Laden later set up an NGO in Nairobi as a cover for operatives there.[33])

This pattern of expansion through building alliances extended to the U.S. A Muslim organization called al Khifa had numerous branch offices, the largest of which was in the Farouq mosque in Brooklyn. In the mid-1980s, it had been set up as one of the first outposts of Abdullah Yusuf Azzam and bin Laden's Maktab al-Khidamat. (This organization raised money to recruit foreign *mujahideen* to fight the war against the Soviets in Afghanistan and became the main fundraising organization for al Qaeda.) Other cities with branches of al

Khifa included Chicago, Pittsburgh, Tucson, Atlanta, and Boston. Al Khifa recruited American Muslims to fight in Afghanistan. Some of them participated in terrorist actions in the U.S. in the early 1990s and in al Qaeda operations elsewhere, including the 1998 attacks on U.S. embassies in East Africa.

Bin Laden wasn't the only head of a terrorist group to employ a corporate strategy to raise dwindling funds. Hatim Ahmad Barakat, also known as the "face of fund-raising" for his Hezbollah cell in Paraguay, would raise funds from different sympathizers and merchants. In one case, he used "strong-arm" tactics to coerce business owners at the Galeria Page mall to donate a percentage of their profits to the Hezbollah or risk getting their businesses shut down. In addition, links have been made between Assad Muhammad Barakat and bin Laden. A report in a Paraguayan newspaper in 2002 pointed out that Hatim, who owned the Mundial (World) Engineering and Construction company, with offices in Ciudad del Este and Beirut, was suspected of making contributions to al Qaeda. He obtained money via real estate fraud by purchasing apartments in Beirut and wire-transferring the money to al Qaeda in amounts upwards of $120,000.[34] Barakat also channeled money to al Qaeda by using charitable donations to orphanages as a monetary guise.

Says professor William Martel, "The Hezbollah, like al Qaeda and Taliban, incorporate many factors that make the organization complicated. With very dynamic evolving networks, subgroups of these larger organizations are popping up all over the world less, and instead of physical recruitment you would see maybe through a mosque, foundation, or community center, these organizers and recruiters are going on the Internet. They are trying to find niches and chinks in the armor in order to get the funding they need without being detected, which inevitably leads to a higher frequency of bank account and currency manipulation and fraud, smuggling, document alteration, and eventually funding of terrorist plots."[35]

The Trust Factor: The Basis of Any Organized Retail Crime Ring

Funding terrorism takes a lot of coordination, planning, and strategizing on behalf of the members, the subgroups, and the leaders running the organization. Because most fund-raising is done through illegal means, trusted sources are imperative, and having the same mission is crucial. However, the mission statement isn't written down in a business plan or formally discussed. It's a state of mind.[36] Most ORC fences are of Middle Eastern descent.[37] Through a series of interviews with law enforcement, ORC fence suspects admit to being sponsored by other fences to come into the U.S. Upon arrival, the sponsoring fence bankrolls them into a business, creating an arrangement similar to indentured servitude. Newly arrived immigrants must conform to the organization's methods or risk loss of financial support or, worse, deportation.

Burglary rings are well planned and organized, employing rooftop entries, destruction of surveillance systems, and disabling of alarm systems. These groups have a team leader who plans, coordinates, and executes the theft. Most of these teams are made up of illegal immigrants from Central America. In 2001, Pasadena, California police apprehended two teams stealing nearly $20 million, linking the group to a family of Middle Eastern fences to whom they would sell the merchandise. These burglaries took place not just in Pasadena but in other states, including Texas.

ORC rings operate across the nation and internationally, but the "foot soldiers" in this crime are professional shoplifters—the boosters. When ORC rings recruit boosters from within, their families add a layer of protection from being reported to law enforcement. In some cases, boosters as well as fences share the same ideologies. But in most cases longtime members and family organizations strong-arm recruits into supporting the cause.

Keeping track of the money is a job that falls to someone who has the complete trust of the ORC ringleader or terrorist group. Trust permeates not only organized groups who steal, but also the fences who purchase and resell the merchandise. According to Randy Merritt, a detective in the Pasadena Police Department, many Middle Eastern fences use the same bookkeeping firm, one also invested and participating in the fences' illegal activity.[38] Fences usually engage in layering schemes that can work effectively only if fences agree to operate together. One fence might own a company that sells merchandise to another company that is owned and operated by the same family or group. To eliminate any paper trail, these fences create separate invoices where the company selling the merchandise has records of items being purchased, but the company buying has no proof of the transaction.

Counterfeiting rings also function within the family. As Chris from the Congo explained to me, the Senegalese and most West Africans create their own counterfeit rings when they come to the U.S., based on a recommendation from "family" friends back in Senegal. "When you come here, you know you have to make money quickly, and this is the way you do it," he explains. Chris got hooked up with another buyer of counterfeit handbags within a couple days of arriving in New York. Instead of working for a larger business owner, he decided to go out on his own using his "mentor's" contacts and by establishing a good relationship with Chinese suppliers. While Chris doesn't send his money overseas, many of the Senegalese vendors do to ensure that family members are taken care of and live well above the poverty line. Chris also explains that a portion of the money that is sent overseas from donations goes to fund "benevolent organizations." He notes that some people bring in so much money that they feel they have no choice but to stay in this industry. "You know those big houses in Senegal? Who do you think finances them? It's these guys! And guess who comes to them when they need financing? It's the 'organizations' who use that money to spread the word about Islam."

"These cases take a lot of people, a lot of investigation, a lot of stakeouts, and all this is resource-intensive," explains Robert C. Scott, Congressional Representative from Virginia and chairman of the Subcommittee on Crime, Terrorism, and Homeland Security. Even with razor-sharp scrutiny, it's nearly impossible to permeate "family" bonds.[39]

The act of moving money around to finance a large-scale terrorist attack also benefits from family relationships. In some cases, money laundering can be equally dangerous to homeland security and retail stores. This is what we will examine next.

7

Money Laundering 2.0

As Faisal Shahzad sits in a cell in the Metropolitan Correctional Center in New York City awaiting trial, he passes the time by reading and eating specially prepared kosher meals in lieu of halal meals.[1] Pir and Aftab Khan, his accomplices in connection with the Times Square bombing, sit in a jail 400 miles away in Massachusetts. Pir, who is being held in the Plymouth County House of Correction in Massachusetts, maintains that he has never met Shahzad and has never had any contact with him. Aftab, a former gas station attendant in Brookline, also maintains his innocence by claiming he has never met Shahzad. He sits alone in his holding cell in the Suffolk County House of Correction in Boston. He receives few visits from friends or family. When authorities searched Aftab's apartment on May 18, 2010, they found an envelope with Shahzad's name scribbled on it and a phone number beginning with the 203 area code. It was Shahzad's cell phone number.

"It's possible both Shahzad and the Khans tapped into the informal banking network also known as a 'hawala' to transfer the funds from one place to another," said an authority working on the case. "[Aftab] Khan claims he doesn't know what is going on or why he is in jail, and that may be true, but the fact of the matter is, the money that was transferred was used to potentially harm the citizens of the United States, and that is a federal offense."[2]

Historically, terrorist groups funded their operations through money laundering. The most popular means of raising money were drug trafficking, smuggling and selling illegal weapons, selling narcotics and gold, and conducting kidnappings.

Terrorist organizations have a primary mission: to fly under the radar while executing a plan to further their political objectives and staying well funded. That is why historically, terrorist groups such as Avanguardia Nazional (otherwise known as the National Guard in Italy), the Ordine Nuovo (New Order), the Red Brigade (another neofascist group out of Italy), and the Irish Republican Army (IRA) all obtained funding by laundered methods through shady sales of product. Terrorist cells were not immune to the global recession of 2007–2009 that wreaked havoc on U.S., European, Asian, and Russian markets. Al Qaeda, Hamas, and Hezbollah in the Middle East were major organizations affected by funds running out more quickly than had been anticipated. Raising capital and, more importantly, obtaining cash became crucial.[3]

The most talked-about and seemingly best-known method of terrorist financing is the opium trade or "poppy fields" of Afghanistan. The Taliban used it to finance kidnappings, the theft of contraband weapons, and the recruitment and training of al Qaeda members. But as the post-9/11 world started to evolve, these once strong terrorist organizations became less in control and less centralized, allowing subgroups to pop up in countries all over the world, says Bill Martel, a professor at the Fletcher School of Law and Diplomacy at Tufts University and an expert in terrorist financing. This meant the splinter groups were independently operated and had to find their own way of financing, similar to how a fast-food franchise operates. Financing for jihad comes from various sympathizer means, especially when dealing with smaller cells in different parts of the country where the cell may have roots. There are the donors (whom we'll talk about in later chapters) and the "passive sympathizers," who provide material support by giving funding through the sale and resale of stolen merchandise.[4]

"The global network for terrorism, and especially al Qaeda if you look at it, is ubiquitous, resilient, adaptive, and evasive. Using illegal funds is their bloodline to train, recruit, and attack, and most of this funding comes from money laundering. And we, as people who monitor this activity, need to be extra careful. Our experience is that they are very adaptive, and they pop up somewhere else and generate funding," says Martel.

Prior to 9/11, laundering funds through the American banking system was considered fairly simple. Terrorist organizations with recruits in the U.S. and Canada relied on the passive approach of bankers when it came to transferring large sums of money from one account to another. But as banks cracked down, terrorists and their organizations were forced to get creative when it came to laundering money. If going through a bank would set off a red flag, other means had to be found.

The Three Stages of Money Laundering

The International Monetary Fund (IMF) estimated that between $600 billion and $1.5 trillion is laundered every year globally.[5] Out of that amount, 20–30% is funding terrorism.[6] According to John A. Cassara, formerly detailed to the Department of the Treasury's Office of Terrorism Finance and Financial Intelligence and author of *Hide & Seek: Intelligence, Law Enforcement, and the Stalled War on Terrorist Finance*, money is laundered from the U.S. to other countries in three stages. The first is placement, in which dirty money must be deposited into a financial institution. Criminals risk getting flagged by depositing large sums of money into accounts or by purchasing monetary instruments with illegitimate funds. Therefore, they try to distance themselves from the money by "layering" the cash. They move it around via wire transfers in multiple accounts in different jurisdictions, or through money orders; this is the second stage. The third and final stage is integrating the laundered funds back into the system. Here criminal organizations create an air of legitimacy by reinvesting laundered funds into a "tangible good" such as a business or property.[7]

Hawalas: An Ancient System Posing a Global Threat

Even with the most sophisticated of money-laundering schemes, transferring funds to remote areas of the world is not easy, especially if you do not have a Social Security number to open a legitimate bank account, or if you want to transfer money rapidly. Faisal Shahzad, also known as the "Times Square Bomber," used hawalas (a way to transfer money overseas between two people without creating a money trail) to finance his plot. This prompted U.S. Representative Stephen F. Lynch to call for a congressional probe on the use of Islamic informal banking networks.

Shahzad became an American citizen by marrying a woman from Colorado. He came from an educated family (his father was a retired vice air marshal in Pakistan). He owned his own home and had a master's degree from an American university. But to get money to fund his foiled plot, he dodged the banking system and used an informal way of transferring money to go unnoticed. To execute the money transfer, Shahzad enlisted the help of Pir and Aftab Khan, said to be distant relatives of Shahzad, both located in Watertown, a small town outside of Boston. According to court documents, the transfer was for a minimal amount, a couple thousand dollars. However, what it was funding could have had devastating consequences.

The rise of underground and parallel banking systems and hawalas and the use of large institutional banking systems became a way criminals could stay ahead of banking regulations. They began to be used more frequently, and their schemes came under scrutiny by the authorities.

Inside Job: How a Hawala Is Run

Hawalas (an Islamic term that means "word of mouth") exist in 50 different countries, primarily in areas where people don't have access to a large bank. They are found predominantly in Islamic nations but are cropping up in the Middle East, the Indian subcontinent, Southeast Asia, and Africa.[8] The fee to transfer funds varies between 2% and 5% when the money is transferred, but in most cases the fee is much less, if anything. This makes a hawala an appealing way to transfer money for those who don't have much money to begin with. When someone needs to transfer money, he contacts his local hawaladar, or hawala operator, who then contacts his counterpart hawaladar in the corresponding country. The hawaladar comes from the same family or tribe, creating a net of trust and eliminating the possibility of fraud, misuse of funds, or stealing. If the amount of money is available, a password known only to the two hawaladars is given, and the transfer is carried out. The transaction happens quickly. In most cases, people using a hawala can receive funds just hours after making a few phone calls, as opposed to the 24 to 48 hours it takes for bank or money order wire transfers to go through. The hawaladar delivers the money taken from local funds to the recipient's business or office.

With a hawala, money never changes hands. No paper trail is left behind, other than scribbled notes on a piece of paper. No electronic ledger tracks funds being transferred. These facts make the auditing and investigating process next to impossible. The U.S. Department of the Treasury estimates that $7 billion in funds circulates between hawalas in Pakistan and a staggering $608 billion in India—an amount roughly the size of Switzerland's gross domestic product (GDP) and 40% of India's GDP.[9]

Despite the vast amount of untraceable funds going between hawalas, they are not illegal and have been used for centuries, according to Ibrahim Warde, a professor of international business at the Fletcher School of Law and Diplomacy at Tufts University. The U.S. requires hawalas to register. However, illegal hawalas are extremely difficult to identify, and the penalties for running one are not severe. Countries such as the United Arab Emirates (UAE) and Afghanistan require hawalas to register with each country's central bank. However, the UAE had only 220 registered hawalas in 2007, and Afghanistan had 300. But the World Bank estimates that there are between 500 and 2,000 unregistered hawalas in Kabul and major city hubs in Afghanistan. Loose laws and regulations prevent the UAE from cracking down on unregistered hawalas. Therefore, terrorist organizations have been known to use hawalas to bypass the Bank Secrecy Act (BSA) of 1970 and other instruments established by financial institutions to help combat money laundering.

For example, the 9/11 attacks cost from $300,000 to $500,000 and were financed though wire transfers, travelers checks, and cash. The 9/11 Commission's *Monograph on Terrorist Financing* acknowledged the use of hawalas to move cash within and outside of the U.S.[10] Likewise, 60% of the funds generated from the drug trade in Afghanistan come from hawalas in the Kandahar and Helmand provinces. An estimated $800 million was believed to have been circulated in the Helmand province hawala system, much of which went to fund the Taliban, which in turn used the money to finance kidnappings, the theft of contraband weapons, and the recruitment and training of al Qaeda members. Many of the most recent terrorist attacks in South Asia, especially Pakistan and India in the Kashimir region, were financed entirely through the exchange of cash in these informal banking systems.[11]

In November 2001, the U.S. government froze the assets of two hawalas: the Al Barakaat (a financial, telecommunications, and construction group headquartered in Dubai that operates largely out of Somalia) and the Al Taqwa. Both were believed to be funneling nearly $10 million a year to al Qaeda by skimming money off transfer fees. The FBI and U.S. Customs agents raided the two networks' offices in Alexandria and Falls Church, Virginia; Minneapolis, Minnesota; Boston, Massachusetts; Seattle, Washington; and Columbus, Ohio. The founder of Al Barakaat, Shaykh Ahmed Nur Jimale, is believed to be an associate of Osama bin Laden.[12]

Fighting The Enemy: U.S. Banks Try to Combat Money Laundering and Fail

The Bank Secrecy Act of 1970 was the first law passed that dealt with money laundering concerns and that tried make banking transactions more transparent. However, compliance within U.S. financial institutions remained weak. For example, under the BSA, banks were required to file a currency transaction report (CTR) with the Treasury Department for any currency transactions of more than $10,000. However, as criminals became aware of this new law, they started to think outside the box by moving funds through the purchase of gold, which was often thought of as an international currency. Likewise, terrorist operatives used financial instruments such as unregulated hawalas, profits made from stolen merchandise, and contraband sales of weapons to outfox BSA rules. Operation Polar Cap was an investigation that uncovered the laundering of more than $1.2 million in currency generated by the sale of cocaine in the U.S.[13] It was masked by the purchase and sale of gold by way of Switzerland and through the collusion of jewelry and gold dealers in the U.S.

More recently, Farooque Ahmed, a Virginia native who was sentenced to 23 years in prison with an additional 50 years of law enforcement supervision upon being released, pled guilty to providing material support to members of al Qaeda. According to an FBI affidavit, Farooque sent money totaling $10,000 to foreign terrorists in $1,000 increments so as not to raise red flags.[14]

"Banks knew they were losing leverage, but they didn't know what or how to combat it," says a source in JP Morgan Chase's Global Risk department. "Criminals were getting savvier and coming up with instruments to transfer funds that were ten steps ahead of the banks. Not until 9/11 did banks have a collective 'wise up' and implement more stringent regulations along with proper training of their staffs."[15]

Following the Money Trail: The U.S. Department of the Treasury

Regulating hawalas has been a thorn in the side of the U.S. Treasury. Security issues that arise because of money laundering through hawalas pose a potential threat to the U.S. On the other hand, heavily regulating hawalas cuts off a large amount of money that is circulated in the financial system by low-wage workers and that makes up a large percentage of the GDP in other countries. In 1994, Congress passed a law to regulate informal financial enterprises such as hawalas and check-cashing businesses by requiring them to register with the government and report transactions greater than $3,000. Yet regulations for the statute were never published, outlining what legal ramifications businesses would encounter, so many informal banking institutions continue to operate unregulated. A few years later, the United Nations adopted the International Convention on the Suppression of the Financing of Terrorism. Article 2(1) of the convention reads as follows:

> Any person commits an offence within the meaning of this Convention if that person by any means, directly or indirectly, unlawfully and willfully, provides or collects funds with the intention that they should be used or in the knowledge that they are to be used in full or in part, in order to carry out:
>
> (a) An act which constitutes an offence within the scope of and as defined in one of the treaties listed in the annex...[16]

The issue is that the U.S. and other countries have been grappling with the definition of "terrorism." Because no universal definition of terrorism and terrorist act exists, regulations have yet to be set.

The Financial Action Task Force (FATF) is an intergovernmental body whose purpose is to develop and promote national and international policies to combat money laundering and terrorist financing. In 2003 the FATF established a list of "best practices" for countries that defined the term "money or value transfer service" and anti-money-laundering regulations. These involve customer identification, record-keeping requirements, suspicious transaction reporting, compliance monitoring, and, most importantly, sanctions if informal financial institutions violate these clauses.[17] Regulations may be in place in countries such as Germany, Iran, Iraq, Afghanistan, Thailand, UAE, UK, Qatar, Saudi Arabia, Singapore, and Syria that are not being enforced and thus allow terrorist funding to occur. India became the 34th country to join the FATF by requiring national banks to create suspicious activity reports (SARs) to generate evidence that shady activity was going on within their banking system. According to my source who has consulted for India's top state-owned banks, the government called top bank executives at the Canara Bank, one of the oldest banks in India, with close to $50 billion in assets. The executives were asked to submit false SARs to indicate potential terrorist transactions and accounts that had ties in India as well as overseas.

"While it's a good thing India wanted to be a part of the FATF, the flip side is that they had to have banks like Canara create a false paper trail, because a legitimate one didn't exist," says my source. "If one of the biggest banks in India had to falsify transactions happening in their bank, could you imagine what the nationalized and cooperative banks are doing?"[18]

Banking Regulations: Still Behind the Eight Ball

Immediately after 9/11, the world and the U.S. devised an entirely new strategy when it came to banking systems. In an effort to halt terrorists in their tracks and go for the proverbial jugular of these terrorist organizations, the Bush Administration in conjunction with the U.S. Department of the Treasury decided to aim U.S. policy at "starving the terrorists of funding and shutting down the institutions that support or facilitate terrorism."[19] Months after the attacks, the Treasury Department was on a mission to freeze all terrorist assets within banks.

To crack down further on terrorist financing, the U.S. Department of State implemented an anti-money-laundering counter-narcotics/

counterterrorist financing strategy.[20] It sought to disrupt terrorist financiers through "investigations, diplomatic relations, and criminal prosecutions." The State Department decided to build programs to improve domestic financial, legal, and regulatory institutions of U.S. allies outside domestic borders. It also would implement a global effort including intelligence gathering, financial regulation, and law enforcement. By doing so, the State Department would create a foolproof web of checks and balances that would make money laundering difficult. As well-orchestrated as these efforts were, organized and technologically savvy terrorist organizations continue to slip through the cracks. The most pertinent law implemented, when it comes to terrorist financing, is Title III of the Patriot Act, which was passed shortly after 9/11. The premise of this revamped law was to establish that laundering "dirty money" through shell stores; selling stolen products on auction web sites; or funneling money to organizations through illegal means such as drug sales, theft, or kidnapping is considered an offense for money laundering prosecution under Section 1956, Title 18, of the U.S. Code [38]. Such a person also could be charged with providing terrorist organizations with material support. Specifically, this law compels financial institutions to take extra steps past the BSA and the Currency and Foreign Transaction Reporting Act (CFTRA), established in 1970 under the Anti-Money Laundering Act. In addition to requiring banks to file a CTR and SAR for transactions of more than $5,000, banks can obtain information through correspondent accounts. Under the Patriot Act, financial institutions are prohibited from establishing other corresponding accounts in "shell" banks overseas—meaning banks that do not have a physical presence in the corresponding country. Banks are subject to a $1 million fine if they do establish such accounts.

Even though banks have established and taken extra measures to ensure that laundered funds can't move through the system, the process is not automated. It relies on bank and fund managers as well as executive regulators to communicate if they see suspicious activity. The "If you see something, say something" mantra indoctrinated into the American public after 9/11 still has not resonated with bank managers, despite their extensive training on how to identify and flag a suspicious account. Section 312 of the Patriot Act outlines how banks should do special "due diligence" when they encounter suspicious accounts. This includes procedures to identify bank owners and account security and enhanced "scrutiny" of senior political figures' accounts.[21] However, banks never implemented set standards for global regulation; individual banks must come up with their own arbitrary, individual procedures. The result is that human error allows suspicious and potentially dangerous accounts to slip through.

"I cannot tell you how much training we've had, and there are still problems [such as] false positives or accounts that go undetected," says a source in global risk management at JP Morgan Chase. "While the Patriot Act and all the regulations that came with it have definitely helped, it's an imperfect system, and the only way it will ever be regulated is if communication within the banks, both domestically and internationally, are working in tandem—and that won't happen."

Another way in which banks sought to step up their game when regulating their accounts (but that was seemingly unsuccessful) was through the use of interbank transmittal letters that accompany checks or cash instruments sent from one bank to another internationally. This also was regulated not by an automated system, but by humans. Cash letters often contain hundreds or thousands of bundled checks as they are sent to the correspondent bank for collection. Banks require all deposits greater than $10,000 to be flagged as potential money laundering. However, when cash letters include money orders and checks less than that amount, they aren't flagged. Crime groups and terrorist organizations move money in bulk amounts of check and cash letters into foreign accounts unregulated by the U.S. government.[22]

Banks might have their problems regulating accounts, but another issue comes from how criminals are prosecuted under the Patriot Act. According to Kevin Tyrrell, a special agent at Immigration and

Customs Enforcement, loopholes in the act impeded prosecution. "Closing the Patriot Act loopholes was crucial for us in terms of prosecuting criminals to the fullest extent of the law," says Tyrrell. "Banking regulations can only go so far, and due to the nature of the way they are written, there are bound to be loopholes. Modifications such as the MSV Title 18-US 1960 Section 359 (a) and Section 373 have allowed us to regulate further when it comes to transferring money [under a certain amount] in accounts, but criminals and terrorists are constantly creating new tactics that are smarter, better, and faster ways of moving money. Unfortunately, U.S. banking system regulations aren't changing fast enough to keep up."[23]

A blatant example of this, Tyrrell points out, is stored value or gift cards used by retailers. In the U.S. last year, more than $1 billion in fraudulent gift cards was used, and 30% were transferring money overseas to places like Pakistan, Afghanistan, and Latin America. Criminals transferring money through these means cannot be prosecuted under the Patriot Act. Tyrrell explains that "Bulk cash smuggling is covered under 31, US Code 5332, a statute which makes it a crime not to declare currency greater than $10,000 if you are coming in or out of the United States. But this statute does not cover money cards or gift cards. In some cases, terrorists are smuggling millions of dollars on these gift cards overseas, and we cannot prosecute them because what they are doing is not covered by the law, even though they are essentially acting as a financial services provider, with the cards being money instruments."

Likewise, the 1986 Money Laundering Control Act (an amendment to the Bank Secrecy Act of 1970) does not cover wire transfers or digital e-cash that is not FDIC insured. Title III of the Patriot Act was implemented by President George W. Bush on October 26, 2001, a month and a half after 9/11. Its intent is to keep criminals from bypassing the $100,000 deposit limit. But it does not include potential "cyber-laundering" regulations on wire transfers, digital e-cash, or online accounts that aren't FDIC insured.[24]

Organized Retail Crime and Latin America

In the past, terrorist financing usually came from the proceeds of drug sales, among other illicit transactions such as diamond sales, often utilized by Hezbollah. In the tri-border region between Paraguay, Argentina, and Brazil, terrorist organizations often sell cigarettes and pirated DVDs to finance their operations. The term "narcoterrorism" in the Latin American context describes drug trafficking organizations that use terror tactics, such as detonating a grenade in a packed public plaza, as a method to spread fear. The most notable was the drug war waged in Medellin, Colombia, which involved Pablo Escobar. He ran the Medellin drug cartel, making an estimated $30 billion annually.[25] He waged war against the Colombian government through a series of hijackings, kidnappings, assassinations, and bombings. He wanted to change the extradition policies the government had put in place because of pressure from the U.S. government. The Medellin cartel eventually came tumbling down after Escobar's much-celebrated assassination. However, organizations such as the FARC (Fuerzas Armadas Revolucionarias de Colombia) began attacking Colombian soldiers on a larger scale in 1982 as their income from the coca harvest increased. They also were able to fund the training of FARC fighters in Vietnam and Russia. The FARC's primary source of income was drug trafficking until recently, when stringent international laws on drug traffickers began to be enforced.[26] The result was a shift in fund-raising where FARC operatives work in conjunction with members of Mexican gangs, such as the Arellano-Felix organization and the Sinaloa Federation. The MS-13 has geographic roots in the Rampart Park area of Los Angeles, CA and cultural roots in Salvadoran culture due to the deportation of many of its members to El Salvador. MS-13 has an estimated 16 factions or "cliques" in the U.S. alone. Internationally the MS-13 has an estimated 36,000 members in seven countries. In the U.S. these cliques are located mostly in California,

Maryland, and Texas, although MS-13 is present in all 50 states and in over 2,000 American cities, according to the FBI.

This is how it works: Profits from illegally sold merchandise are split into different funding sections. About 60% of the funds sent to the group's country of origin goes to fund bribes to get members of the MS-13 out of prison in El Salvador, Colombia, Paraguay, or Mexico. In El Salvador, for example, judges make decisions based on written arguments, not oral. Therefore, there is very little accountability, and money talks, according to Samuel Logan, author of *This Is for the Mara Salvatrucha* and a Latin American security expert.[27] Fifteen percent of the funds goes toward the operational costs of getting members of terrorist organizations, such as al Qaeda, into the country. This includes making fake passports and documents, for which al Qaeda members will pay double. They also need cash for hotel rooms, funds, and so on.[28] Yet another 15% of the money is used to support families of MS-13 members who are imprisoned in the U.S. The remaining 10% is used to pay MS-13 mules, boosters, and fences.

"Groups like the MS-13 and the FARC use funds from stolen merchandise as well as sales of drugs for funding their operations," says Larry C. Johnson, CEO and co-founder of BERG Associates, an international consulting firm with expertise in combating terrorism. "The money, especially if it is being used to fund overseas operations, was being laundered through Swiss and Luxembourg accounts. While selling drugs was one of the main income sources for them, selling items on the black market is more beneficial for the potential terrorists than selling drugs or contraband weapons. If they get caught, the ramifications are not as severe."[29]

Funneling Money Through the Black Market Peso Exchange

The MS-13 (as well as many South American terrorist groups) funded the Hezbollah through the Black Market Peso Exchange, another form of money laundering that allows cash to go relatively undetected.

This system is operated through brokers who purchase narcotics and stolen merchandise in the U.S. from the cartels and transfer pesos to the cartels from within Colombia, Panama, or Mexico. These dollars are laundered into the U.S. financial system by the peso broker without attracting attention. The dollars are then "sold" by the brokers to businessmen in Colombia who need dollars to purchase U.S. goods for export. Goods ready for export are often paid for by the peso broker using purchased "stolen goods" dollars on behalf of the importer.[30] For example, an MS-13 member may either sell drugs or steal $2 to $3 million worth of merchandise a year, which includes merchandise that is difficult to track—baby formula, OTC drugs, razor blades. This merchandise is sold within the U.S. via the Internet, flea markets, or pawn shops. Those dollars are exchanged into pesos through a broker who sells the dollars for pesos to either Colombian or other Latin American businesses and business owners. The laundered funds are deposited into U.S. domestic banking accounts, which are then used to purchase merchandise for businesses. (In some cases, small business owners who own fence stores use the funds to purchase merchandise for their "stores" or pay off debt.) The merchandise that is bought is usually from another illegitimate source, such as a fake warehouse or an ORC ring that happens to have ties to the MS-13 or another gang. Then the merchandise is shipped back to Colombia, El Salvador, or Paraguay and is used to stock stores in the country. Pesos made from the sale of this stolen merchandise are given to the peso broker, who pays the trafficker, who in this case is an MS-13 member. Because the larger amounts of money are converted into pesos, they go undetected by banking systems.

Black Market Peso Exchange, ORC, and Cartels

The very notion of a "cartel" conjures images of a well-run yet sinister ring operating more like a corporation than a gang of low-level guys buying and selling drugs. The Mexican Zetas are no different. The Zetas are a sophisticated and well-run organized crime ring with a strong paramilitary background. The gang was started by El Lasca, "The Executioner," who was once a special forces soldier in the Mexican army, trained in the art of psychological warfare. The Zetas are one of the most ruthless Mexican drug cartels. Much of the Zetas' funding comes from drug sales. They smuggle potential terrorists from the Hezbollah and Hamas and illegal aliens across the border into America. They traffic large quantities of cocaine and chemicals to make methamphetamines in Europe by way of Western Africa from the FARC. They also sell stolen merchandise on the black market. Like most large organizations, the Zetas are allies with other gang-related groups, such as the MS-13 in El Salvador, to stream-line their operations in porous U.S. border towns in Arizona, Texas, California, and New Mexico, as well as in Latin America.[31] As part of a plea for more antidrug aid from the U.S., in April 2010, Mauricio Funes, president of El Salvador, announced that the Zetas had been "exploring opportunities" in his country while strengthening ties with local gangs. The Zetas, he said, are using Central and South American countries as a transit hub to transport drugs into the U.S. and Europe.

But the drug trade isn't the only moneymaker for drug cartels such as the Zetas. Car theft is one of the most common practices and is an easy way to make quick money. According to a report by the National Insurance Crime Bureau (NICB), many cities that border Mexico are within easy access of drug cartels that use stolen cars to finance and transport drugs, weapons, and, in some cases, people into and out of Mexico.[32] In McAllen, Texas, a border town similar to Columbus, New Mexico, five people were arrested in 2007 for alleg-edly being part of an auto theft ring that gave stolen cars to the Zetas in Mexico. According to McAllen police, the auto theft ring crossed illegally and would use the cars for "alien smuggling and transporting drugs."[33]

In a National Drug Intelligence Center report titled "Accomplishments of Fiscal Year 2007," four major Mexican drug cartels were identified as being "associates" of Islamic fundamentalist groups, mostly in Argentina, Brazil, and Paraguay. The document, which was put together with information from the Central Intelligence Agency (CIA), the Drug Enforcement Administration (DEA), and the Federal Bureau of Investigation (FBI), outlines the nature of the relationship between the Mexican cartels. It describes which terrorist organizations they are associated with and the specific contracts they have set up, which total hundreds of millions of dollars, to sell weapons to these cartels. It says, "The results of 74 investigations of narcoterrorism that have been carried out by the Special Operations Division of the DEA indicate that Islamic groups present on the common border of Argentina, Brazil, and Paraguay launder money, sell arms, and traffic drugs in Mexican criminal organizations." The document also goes on to identify the groups as being in South America and having ties to the Hezbollah, Palestinian Liberation Organization (PLO), Palestinian Liberation Front (PLF), and Hamas.

Although the cartels aren't directly identified in the document, a source at the FBI noted the Sinaloa, the Arellano Felix, the Gulf, and the Mexican Zetas (also known as "Los Zetas") were the main cartels that had connections to the Islamic groups.[34]

The South American, Mexican, and African Connection

South American drug cartels and Mexican cartels use the same African route to traffic illegal substances to the U.S. and Europe. The Mexican cartels—specifically, the Mexican Zetas—import chemicals used to make methamphetamines, according to Jay Bergman, DEA director for the Andean region of South America. "In order to get around ever-changing law enforcement efforts, these cartels use West Africa as the alternative," he says. "When sea interdictions stepped up, we saw traffickers using aircraft taking off from Venezuela, which shares a border with Colombia. Geography is the key reason why Venezuela has become a springboard location."[35]

In January 2010, it was reported that the FARC were employing the help of al Qaeda to smuggle cocaine into Europe by way of Africa.[36] Sanctions imposed by both the U.S. and Europe make it difficult for Andean drug producers to send their product directly to each country. To circumvent these laws, FARC worked in conjunction with a large drug trafficking network. It moved the product from South America, through western Africa, and into Europe. In December 2009, Oumar Issa, Harouna Toure, and Idriss Abelrahman, three Malian men in their 30s, were extradited to the U.S. while they were in Ghana. They are currently being held on drug trafficking and terrorism charges in New York. They are said to have ties to the al Qaeda in the Islamic Maghreb (AQIM), a West African cell of al Qaeda. Issa told an informant posing as someone with Hezbollah connections that he worked for Toure, a well-known Songhai smuggler of hashish as well as humans who was from the village of Bamba on the Niger River. Toure's route was through Morocco, a common route once used for the Toudenni salt trade. The area surrounding Bamba had a reputation for petty crime, smuggling, and ethnic violence.[37] What's more, Abelrahman was identified as an AQIM leader, commanding a group of 11 men. Abelrahman's connections were to the Brazilian drug trade, with plans to take cocaine through Togo, Mali, and Niger and then over to Algeria, Morocco, and up the coast to the Canary Islands.

The Department of Homeland Security reported a 41% increase in immigrants from countries known to have large populations of terrorists from al Qaeda and other terrorist groups after 9/11. In March 2010 it was reported that 23 Somali illegal immigrants who had been apprehended in Mexico and then released in January had ties to the terrorist organization al Shabaab, which has direct ties to al Qaeda.

Many African nations including Somalia are becoming hotbeds of terrorist activity, especially cells that are connected to al Qaeda. What the consumer doesn't realize is how many everyday products, from discount handbags to clothing to soap, come through these terrorist-mandated channels and into the hands of unsuspecting Americans—until something sets off a news frenzy and makes the threat a global issue.

8 ————————————————————

The Political Agenda

High above the dense jungles of Somalia, in an area known as the "highlands" just west of Mogadishu, sits a row of mansion-type custom-built homes. They were recently built and have every comfort—a modern washer and dryer, flat-screen TVs, and a gym and spa for those who like to work out. Outside, armed guards watch over the homes. At first sight, they look as if they belong to government officials.

In reality, the houses belong to Somalians who reside in the U.S. They make millions by selling counterfeit handbags and channeling the profits back to their homeland through a hawala located in a mosque. Chris from the Congo introduces me to his handbag-selling colleague, who shows me a picture of his new home on his cell phone. "We are putting in a swimming pool next month!" exclaims the man as he scrolls through construction pictures. "Praise Allah for all these successes. Nothing would happen without him."

Historically, fringe groups pursued their political agendas through criminal activities such as kidnapping, extortion, and drug sales. But as retail theft rings became more prevalent and easy to form, criminals have realized that ORC can be a virtually penalty-free enterprise. In late 2007, law enforcement as well as financial crime units started to see an increase in the proceeds of sales from stolen merchandise going directly to fund terrorist organizations.[1]

Why the sudden spike?

"Most fringe groups are notoriously two steps ahead of the law," explains John Tobon, Unit Chief, Financial Programs at the Cornerstone Unit, a division of Immigration and Customs Enforcement (ICE). Such groups are constantly adapting their business models by exploiting loopholes in the system. Global monetary and charitable institutions are riddled with inefficiencies. Local organizations and charities have become the perfect way for fringe and terrorist groups to capitalize on the sympathies of potential donors. Likewise, the monetary systems tend to be less strict when it comes to charitable giving. Armed with this knowledge, terrorist groups have shielded their illegal transfer of funds by claiming it is for legitimate purposes. The U.S. Tax and Finance Department estimates that 10–20% of dollars funneled out of the U.S. and into charities are on the State Department's list of illegitimate charities. Globally, billions are funneled to these organizations. And, as fringe groups and terrorist organizations become more technologically savvy and adapt their fund-raising accordingly, the problem is bound to get worse.

Homegrown Terrorism: How Retail Theft and Piracy Has Funded Terrorist Operations

There's no question that the world has become a more politically charged place after 9/11. Just as homegrown terrorism has gained momentum in federal and state prisons as well as small communities in New Jersey, Brooklyn, and Los Angeles, political extremism has gained momentum and is being more prominently displayed on the Internet. Online extremist web sites such as www.revolutionmuslim.com, www.alminbar.com, and www.islamicawakening.com claim to be portals for Muslims to share information about Islam. However, these free information exchange platforms often call for and promote jihad and denounce anyone who doesn't follow the Islamic path, all while claiming to help Muslims develop themselves spiritually and reach the level of Ishaan (a level of giving), all in the name of Allah.[2] What's more, most of these sites get their money from selling stolen merchandise as well as from donations generated by illegally stolen and illegally sold merchandise.

While attending Columbia University, Yousef al-Khattab and Younous Abdullah Mohammed actively preached the notion of having Islamic law in the U.S., the destruction of Israel, and taking al Qaeda's messages to the masses. From their group, www.revolutionmuslim. com was established, in addition to a YouTube channel that had 2,500 people checking out their content. Although it started out as an open, albeit extreme, group, the organization was guided by spiritual leader Abdullah Faisal, a 46-year-old convert to Islam by way of Jamaica. He had been imprisoned for five years for inciting young Muslims to kill Hindus and Jews in England. His powerful sermons (which were broadcast on Revolution Muslim's web site, YouTube, and another web site dedicated to Faisal's teachings called www.islamicjihad.com) instructed people to drive "terror into the hearts of [infidels] with the best of our abilities with power."[3] Faisal is also rumored to have recruited potential "soldiers" for the al Shabaab in Somalia, according to Jamaican authorities.

Al-Khattab (who used to go by the name of Joey Cohen, grew up in Brooklyn, and is the son of Jewish parents) noted in an interview with National Public Radio (NPR) that the group was supposed to promote the idea of having one united world of Islam, where the *kaffirs* (Muslim nonbelievers) would leave the land of Mohammad.[4]

In July 2010, Khattab left the blog, prompted by an incident involving online blogger and Revolution Muslim member Zack Chesser. The American-turned-extremist was arrested by the FBI when they realized Chesser was on his way to Somalia to join the al Qaeda-affiliated and ORC-funded al Shabaab.

"In Islam, we have a principle of loving and hating for the sake of Allah," said Khattab in an interview with NPR. "They focus on the hating all the time. When you see youth only talking about the hate, that's a warning sign."[5]

Revolution Muslim's blog has clearly written disclaimers on the site. One reads as follows:

> The views presented in this article/video do not reflect the views of the RevolutionMuslim.com (RM); rather this article/video is posted only for educational and informational purposes. The blogger [meaning the writer of the blog entry] and RevolutionMuslim.com is not affiliated with any terrorist states or organizations and condemns all forms of terrorism carried out in the name of freedom and democracy.

The disclaimers after every extremist post are included to proclaim that the web site is for informational purposes only (so that the site is protected under the First Amendment and does not get shut down, according to Khattab). Younous Abdullah Mohammed, current editor of the web site, denies that the site fosters and instigates extremist behavior. However, people on the FBI's "homegrown terrorist" list have been linked to or are members of Revolution Muslim. A week before the Times Square bombing, a contributor by the name of Abu Talhah Al-Amirikee on the blog called out the creators of the TV series *South Park* for depicting the prophet Mohammed in a bear costume:

> We have to warn Matt (Stone) and Trey (Parker) that what they are doing is stupid, and they will probably wind up like Theo van Gogh for airing this show. This is not a threat, but a warning of the reality of what will likely happen to them.

A week later, Faisal Shahzad attempted to detonate a bomb in Times Square.

While Abdullah Mohammed ardently denied that the web site had any connection to the bombing, Shahzad did mention at his trial that he was influenced by the teachings of Abdullah Faisal. (The NYPD and news outlets initially speculated that the bomb was aimed at Viacom and the producers of *South Park* but later announced that the web site's anti-*South Park* cyber rant and Shahzad's attempt were not connected.)

"I neither condone [terrorism] nor condemn it," said Mohammed in a radio interview with ABC News shortly after Shahzad's attempted attack. "I think it's possible that there was retaliation for what your government was doing overseas. The Mujahideen could have very well planted a bomb in Times Square and they are suffering [from] your [U.S.] drone attacks right now in Pakistan [and] if you want to continue bombing villagers in Pakistan and Afghanistan and Yemen, and continue killing the civilians, then you are going to get many incidents that resemble what happened [in Times Square]. That has nothing to do with us."[6]

The actions of Shahzad, as well as suspected New Jersey terrorists Mohamed Mahmood Alessa and Carlos Eduardo Almonte (apprehended before boarding a flight to Somalia by way of Egypt), aren't as uncommon as people might think. All three men were influenced by extremist web sites and decided to take matters into their own hands when it came to their own religion and waging war against the U.S.

Rebel Kids: Extremist Ideas Financed Through International ORC

"I grew up in a home with hippie parents who didn't care about anything, especially religion," said Younas Abdullah Mohammed in a candid conversation with me outside of the arraignment for Alessa and Almonte. "My parents were very hands-off. They didn't give a shit at all. I think that's what pushed me to convert to Islam." When asked why he was at the trial of Alessa and Almonte, who were suspected of heading to Somalia to allegedly join the al Shabaab, Mohammed said he was there to support his "brothers in faith."

He had never met the two defendants.

The "homegrown terrorism" movement in the U.S. is not unlike most cults. The movement capitalizes on two human vulnerabilities: the yearning to be included in a group, and the ability not to question or see the truth if it's coming from an "authoritative" source. Much like the two cofounders of Revolution Muslim, Shahzad as well as Alessa and Almonte were no different from those who chose to watch a particular political pundit on television, were brainwashed by serial killer Charles Manson, followed the hippie movement of the 1960s, or become a black-makeup-wearing, vampire-movie-watching goth fangirl. And Muslim extremist groups understand that tapping into a vulnerable person's need to fit in is a way to garner funding through donations as well as potential recruits for jihad.

"Other countries have seen a similar pattern. First the fringe joins. When it gets dicier is when college-educated, ordinary, white-collar people start taking up the cause," says a law enforcement source. "They are attractive recruits because they are harder to spot and move about more easily."[7]

The same could be said for Shahzad. By all accounts he looked and acted like a regular 30-something man. Friends and family thought of him as religious but not fanatical. Not until he was in his late 20s did he decide to embrace the extremist view of Islam.

When Things Went Awry

According to court documents, Shahzad's finances were on the brink of collapse. He received close to $10,000 via a source in Pakistan to fund his attempted attack on Times Square, which included paying $1,300 in cash for the Nissan Pathfinder that contained home-made explosives.[8] Shahzad also worked in conjunction with 44-year-old Mohammad Younis, convicted in September 2010 for running an illegal money transfer business between the U.S. and Pakistan.

Court documents stated that Younis met with Shahzad in Long Island three weeks before the attempted Times Square bombing.

He helped Shahzad obtain $5,000 in funding via an unnamed co-conspirator in Pakistan who Shahzad believed to be with the Tehreek-e-Taliban (TTP). The TTP is known to get its funding from the smuggling of cigarettes, electronics, counterfeit clothing, handbags, CDs, and DVDs by colluding with the Afghan Trade and Transit (ATT) association. The ATT is known to allow smuggled products into Pakistan by way of Afghanistan[9] and take a fee in exchange for the service. Shahzad also received $7,000 from the same source through another money transfer agent in Long Island—Younis. While both men denied the charges, it was the facilitation of this funding that helped Shahzad collect the necessary tools to create and attempt to detonate a bomb in Times Square.

ORC Funding by Way of Somalia: A Tale of Two Misguided Kids

Ahmed Monsoor, a 30-year-old fellow Muslim who was also at the trial to support Alessa and Almonte, remembers meeting the two at the Dar-ul-Islah Mosque in Teaneck, New Jersey. "The two seemed like badly behaved kids instead of actual religious extremists," says Monsoor. "I knew Alessa when he was younger, and while he always had behavioral problems, I think they were exacerbated by Almonte." Monsoor, who converted to Islam almost ten years ago, explains that Alessa had talked about going abroad to Jordan in 2007 and most recently talked about going to Somalia to join the jihad there. "I didn't take him seriously when he would say things like that. It seemed as if he was trying to make himself sound more important, but no one took him seriously."[10]

The two men allegedly watched numerous videos, lectures, and recordings online about jihad provided by American-born cleric and fugitive Anwar al-Awlaki, which showed attacks by the al Shabaab in Somalia. The men also showed recordings of an undercover NYPD officer and described how Americans were their enemies and how everybody other than Islamic followers are their enemies and must all be killed. Awlaki was not the only one bringing funds and donations from sympathetic donors to the Somalian cause. Almonte and Alessa were funded by the same means.

This is corroborated by Chris from the Congo, who admits that most of his fellow vendors take the money they make and send it home to the Congo, Somalia, or Senegal because they feel it's their religious duty. "To be honest, I don't know where exactly the money is going," Chris tells me. "I don't have time to do my research, and I trust since it's a charity they are doing good things with my money. But just because I don't know where my charitable donations are going doesn't mean my fellow vendors don't know either. I am the first person to admit that our governments are corrupt and it wouldn't be the first time 'charitable funds' were used to fund something para-military. It doesn't make me that angry. I know I did the right thing by giving my money away, and that's what matters."

Kris Buckner, a scruffy surfer type who looks more like he hangs out on the beaches of Kauai instead of being the owner of Investigative Services in Los Angeles, has been tracking piracy groups who engage in selling counterfeit products. Through his extensive network of sources, he has uncovered how funds from the sale of counterfeit items are sent back to specific terrorist groups in their countries of origin.

"We've been looking at the Somalians, the Senegalese, and the Ghanaians. As a private investigator familiar with these cases, there is no doubt in my mind money is going back to those organizations," he says one afternoon in his southern California office. "Not only have I been told that by sources, I've had a source call me at 4 a.m. to tell me $120,000 is going back to Hezbollah by way of unmarked bags through the Los Angeles International Airport. When I let the authorities know this transaction was about to take place, they intercepted the transporter and seized the cash."[11]

In other cases, Buckner, who has posed as an undercover buyer of counterfeit items, has witnessed how his sellers pay homage to Hezbollah in their homes and warehouses.

"The minute I walked into their home, I saw the Hezbollah flags and New Warrior tattoos and knew exactly what was going on," he says. "I not only knew they were engaging in the buying and selling of counterfeit apparel and handbags, they were raising money for their cause by selling counterfeit goods. They funnel money back to the cause in cash, with the money going back in small amounts through wire transfers, hawalas, and Western Union-type stuff. Sources within that community gave me information that the people I was doing a deal with undercover were giving the money back to the Hezbollah. Their whole mission is money, and America is the cash cow. The money they raise here by selling counterfeit goods helps support suicide bombers and logistical support on the ground in these countries, and they are not about to let that slip away."

In the his piece "44 Ways to Support Jihad," Anwar al-Awlaki calls for the support of jihad with wealth. "The financial Jihad has preceded the physical Jihad in every verse except one," he states. "The most important thing to the Jihad is wealth because Jihad depends on it. In other words, no money, no Jihad, and Jihad needs lots of it. That is why, according to Al Qurtubi, that the personal reward for money given as Sadaqah is multiplied by ten, but the reward for money spent in Jihad is multiplied by 700!"

Awlaki also notes that jihad can be supported by fund-raising for and financing the mujahideen (Muslim fighters). "In addition to paying from your own money, you should encourage others to do the same." Awlaki quotes Rasulullah: "The one who guides others toward a good deed would receive rewards equal to those who practice it. By fund-raising for the Mujahideen you are also fulfilling a sunnah of Rasulullah (saaws) (in a nutshell, this means a Muslim's religious obligations to Allah and practicing of Islamic law) which he would often practice before going out for a battle."

As Local as Down the Street

Jack Gee is a retired Florida-based cop of 31 years and former president of the Florida Law Enforcement Property Recovery Unit. These days he spends his time as the founder of the Coalition of Law Enforcement and Retail (CLEAR), where he interfaces with retailers and law enforcement to help build better systems to fight ORC. In his years of fighting ORC, Gee still remembers the exact moment when he realized how much of what he recovered from a sting of a local mom-and-pop deli was funding a terrorist attack.

Gee explains that out of all the mom-and-pop deli ORC stings he's been involved in, almost half are being watched by the FBI task force or were on their terrorist list even before 9/11.

"There is a huge correlation between ORC and terrorism, especially on the grassroots level," says Gee. "They get brainwashed for whatever reason into believing this is the way to support their faith, people, and country and that their God wants them to do this."

Funding Evil Under the Guise of Charitable Contributions: The Mosques

In 2003, the Al Farooq Mosque in Brooklyn came under scrutiny when it was discovered that several Brooklyn businessmen and a cleric from Yemen, according to prosecutors, funneled more than $20 million to al Qaeda.[12]

According to NYPD police commissioner Raymond W. Kelly, "They [al Qaeda] did fund-raising right here in our own backyard." Although the money trail is unclear in the affidavit, Abderahman Mohamed, the Imam of the Al Farooq mosque, said in an interview that one of the functions of the mosque is to serve as a go-between for donors and charities. "The mosque had never knowingly steered donations to terrorists," he said. "It would be hard for a mosque like us to control a large organization once the money leaves us." In other words, although they require worshipers to donate a portion of their earnings to charity, they have no idea what the charity might be funding or where the funds go after they are donated.[13]

On the first floor of the mosque is a man who started an unlicensed money transferring business out of a rented storefront. The hawala is where many members of the mosque would transfer funds back to their homelands.

Muslim Charities: Capitalizing on Natural Disaster and Religious Empathy

In addition to mosques, many Muslim charities and organizations are fronts for illegal activity. Terrorist groups take advantage of the notion that Muslims are required by their religion to donate a portion of their earnings to charitable causes. One way they engage in fundraising is by taking advantage of "the business of national disaster." Jihadists capitalize on the global sentiment of wanting to help out the country (in this case, the Pakistani earthquakes of 2005 and the floods of 2010) by taking a percentage of the money given by people within the country. Once the funds are in their pockets, they use the money for weapons procurement, the financing of training camps, and logistical support.[14]

Many "shadowy donations" flow into Pakistan through both normal and illegal banking channels, according to an official with the Federal Investigation Agency crime department in Pakistan.[15] Donations come from the Middle East and Europe and are funneled into Islamic charities, which act as a front for militant organizations. The Holy Land Foundation (originally known as the

Occupied Land Fund) was established in California in 1989 as a tax-exempt charity and moved to Texas in 1992. The organization's main offices were in California, New Jersey, and Illinois, but it had representatives across the U.S., the West Bank, and Gaza.[16] In 2006, The Holy Land Foundation and many of its directors were indicted on criminal charges for providing millions of dollars of material and logistical support to Hamas offices in the West Bank and Gaza, as well as other charitable organizations that were part of or controlled by Hamas.

Other groups pretend they are collecting funds for charity but are actually funding a terrorist group. A nonprofit identified by the Financial Action Task Force on Money Laundering falsely asserted that it was collecting funds for orphans and widows. The finance chief of the nonprofit was head of organized fund-raising for Osama bin Laden, and the money collected on behalf of the charities was actually being turned over to al Qaeda operatives.[17]

In most cases, extremist organizations have welfare wings, such as the Jamaat-ud-Dawa, which collects money for schools and medical clinics and is also a front for Lashkar-e-Taiba (LeT),[18] the same terrorist organization that took responsibility for the Mumbai attacks in 2008. "At least 800 million rupees [$940,000] have been allocated for the institutions [linked to the Jamaat-ud-Dawa] during the current fiscal year,"[19] said Rana Sanaullah, a senior Punjab minister, in an interview with the BBC.[20]

During the Pakistani earthquake in 2005 and the flooding in 2010, global sentiment expressed through donations gave terrorists an opportunity to exploit the influx of cash.[21]

Talat Masood, a retired army general from Pakistan, admits the Jamaat-ud-Dawa was quicker and more efficient in responding with disaster relief, especially during the 2010 floods and the 2005 earthquake. With that said, he does not believe the Jamaat-ud-Dawa's charitable help is altruistic; he thinks they are being helpful to try to recruit potential members. "They have a grassroots network which operates in several parts of the country. And so they're the first ones to respond to disasters, because the government takes much longer to respond," said Masood.[22]

Wealthy international donors are also a main source of income for fringe terrorist organizations because of their sympathetic ties. Abu Abdul Aziz, an Indian Muslim donor from Saudi Arabia, invested millions of dollars in LeT, Lashkar-e-Jhangvi (LeJ), and various jihadi organizations, even donating 10 million rupees to build a mosque at Markaz-e-Dawa's headquarters. He has been credited with organizing a jihad in Bosnia as well as helping the Kashmiris fight the government of India.[23]

Idara Khidmat-e-Khalq (once the Markaz-e-Dawa Irshad) was designated by the U.S. Treasury department as a terrorist organization and a front for the LeT. As of 2009, the IKK ran 200 schools, 11 madrassas, two science colleges, an ambulance service, mobile clinics, and blood banks.[24] The IKK received donations from wealthy overseas businessmen involved in the buying and selling of stolen and counterfeit DVDs, CDs, and apparel items. It also received the benefits of a "call to action" on behalf of the Jamaat-ud-Dawa (one of the terrorist organizations linked to the Mumbai attacks in November 2008).

According to the *Wall Street Journal*, the Jamaat had been asking its Pakistani, U.S., and European supporters to also give money to the IKK by depositing funds in an Alfalah Ltd. bank account in the name of a separate charity.[25] What's more, U.S. supporters were allegedly asked to make donations via wire transfers through the Bank of New York. A Bank of New York spokesperson said that no donations were ever transmitted through the account. However, in the same interview with the *Wall Street Journal*, Rehman Malik, Pakistan's interior minister, said despite investigations that are under way regarding the Jamaat funding and assets, "The government is not tracking everyone's accounts, frankly speaking."[26] After the Mumbai attacks, Pakistan shut down all but one account of the Jamaat, where they were still receiving donations weeks after the government supposedly announced that all assets were frozen. The IKK played an integral role in giving funds to the Markaz-ud-Dawa-wal-Irshad (a Sunni anti-American missionary organization formed in the 1980s to oppose the Soviets in Afghanistan)[27] to help victims of the 2005 Pakistan earthquake as well as other natural disasters.

Terrorist Fund-Raising Via Charities Finds Roots in the U.S.

Fund-raising also occurs on American soil through recruitment. In August 2010, 14 people from Minneapolis, Minnesota; Mobile, Alabama; San Diego, California; and Rochester, Michigan were indicted for helping support the al Shabaab by fund-raising. The al Shabaab is a conservative insurgent faction similar to the Taliban, with ties to al Qaeda.

Amina Farah Ali is a 33-year-old "go-to woman" when it comes to donating items and money to help the needy in Somalia. She and Hawo Mohamed Hassan, a 63-year-old with a kind face and gentle dark features, were accused of going door to door raising money under false pretenses by claiming it was for the poor. Both women were living in Rochester, a small town in southern Michigan, and were known to preach to the community about the virtues of donation and giving.

Ali, like any typical American, had a stable job and by all accounts was a productive member of the community. Working as a home health care provider, and a longtime resident of Rochester, she never had any issues with the law. Likewise, Hassan was self-employed and ran a daycare center. While Ali insists she is innocent, the indictment states that after the FBI raided her home in 2009, she placed a call to Somalia, stating, "I was questioned by the enemy here... they took all of my stuff and are investigating it... do not accept calls from anyone."[28] Abdifatah Abdinur, a community leader in Rochester, told the AP in an interview, "I know a lot of people might send money or goods, without knowing the consequences of what they are doing. I was surprised, as almost everybody was, [to learn] that she was sending clothes to the al Shabaab."[29]

Abdirizak Bihi, a community leader in Minneapolis, helped with the investigation by convincing the Somali community to work with officials and not against them. This included telling FBI agents if they suspected suspicious activity, if they were coerced or intimidated by local mosques into not talking about charitable donations going to fund jihad, or if the mosque encouraged parents to encourage their children to return to Somalia to join forces with the al Shabaab. Bihi explains in an interview with the Investigative Project on Terrorism that Somalis were approached in mosques and in their homes by women like Ali and Hassan holding up pictures of sick people in Somalia and asking for donations to help them. Playing the "victim card" is a common tactic for operatives living stateside and trying to raise funds.

"Somali community members have a tradition of volunteerism and are leery of giving money to charity," says Bihi. "That's why it's so difficult to comprehend how these two women manipulated a community. These women claim they were soliciting funds 'for Allah' or for purposes like building mosques in Somalia [not to fund jihad]."[30]

Charitable Donation Loopholes: How the IRS and Banking Systems Failed to Prevent Fraudulent ORC Funds from Financing Terrorist Groups

Executive Order 13224 was passed by President George W. Bush in 2001. Its intent was to freeze assets controlled by or in the possession of individuals or organizations deemed by the Executive Branch to be associated with terrorism and those who are associated with and support them, including charities and nonprofit organizations.[31]

Between 2001 and 2004, the Bush Administration reported that $131 million in terrorist-related assets had been frozen and seized by authorities worldwide, including $35.7 million in the U.S. and an additional $64 million globally.

According to the Department of Justice, al Qaeda received 30% of its financial resources from donations solicited in the U.S. and abroad.[32] Terrorist financing through charitable donations can be categorized in two ways: direct and indirect charitable abuse. Direct refers to people like Ali and Hassan, who engage in deceptive fundraising practices and funnel money to nonexempt purposes.[33] Indirect refers to nonprofit organizations that mistakenly raise funds for and unknowingly direct their profits to terrorist organizations.

An example of direct charitable abuse would be The Holy Land Foundation (an organization that Samuel Elias was donating money to).[34] Although they are subjected to a series of Internal Revenue Service (IRS) checks and balances, nonprofits can fly under the radar due to their tax-exempt status. Likewise, donations solicited from the U.S. are more easily sent overseas to terrorist organizations because the law exempts numerous categories of recipients and services. Recipients of the donations can bypass the Anti-Terrorism Clause (ATC), which states that organizations receiving U.S. funding and that sign the clause agree not to support or promote terror.

"[Channeling funds through a charitable organization] is a very attractive method for terrorist organizations to get funding, especially through the United States," says John Tobon. "Charities act as a legitimate front where most donors won't question the purpose of the charity or, worse, automatically assume the monies are going to a good cause. And with minimal penalties and lighter regulation of nonprofits in the U.S., terrorist organizations will exploit the opportunity. It's an issue that exists."[35]

According to Department of Justice (DOJ) court documents, the Global Relief Foundation, an Illinois-based charity, sent more than 90% of its donations abroad. It has connections to and has supported and helped individuals associated with Osama bin Laden, the al Qaeda network, and other known terrorist groups. The Global Relief Foundation has also been linked to financial transactions with the Holy Land Foundation. Similarly, the DOJ asserts that the Illinois-based Benevolence International Foundation moved charitable contributions that were fraudulently solicited from donors in the U.S. to locations abroad to support terrorist activities. The foundation has offices worldwide through which it facilitates the global movement of its funds.[36]

Charities Turn to a Cyber Audience

Raising money for terrorist organizations has evolved in the 21st century, especially by charities being used as fronts. Just like Revolution Muslim raised awareness and recruited members online, shell charities use the Internet and social media sites such as MySpace, Twitter, and Facebook to solicit donations worldwide by capitalizing on people's sympathy and shrouding the funds' real purpose.

"We are starting to see that, in a recent cases with financial fraud, there is a loose confederation of very bright young men who got together every six to eight months," says Tobon. "The group was defrauding thousands of people and making $20 to $25 million just from their ability to manipulate social media technology. As law enforcement, we need to embrace and get comfortable with new technology. At this point, we only have a couple more years before this really becomes an issue."[37]

Why the Government Can't Regulate Charities

Competing priorities slowed IRS plans to take advantage of a law enabling greater information sharing with the states. Although the

IRS said in February 2002 that it had begun to develop a system to share data with the states for the oversight of charities, as allowed by law, the IRS has not made this initiative a priority and therefore has not developed and implemented this system. Although deterring terrorism is not a primary goal for the IRS or the states, using data-sharing systems is even more important now, when feasible, in light of the charities cases involving terrorist financing. States have an important role in combating terrorist financing because they share oversight responsibility for charities with the IRS. Furthermore, according to state officials, questionable charities tend to move from state to state to avoid detection.[38]

In 2000, the president of The Holy Land Foundation received a letter from the United States Agency for International Development (USAID) proposing to terminate HLF's registration as a private and voluntary organization with USAID. The reasons included the State Department's designation that HLF's registration or a financial relationship between USAID and the organization was contrary to the national defense, national security, or foreign policy interests of the U.S.[39]

Seven years later, USAID still didn't have a plan for dealing with charities potentially funding terrorist organizations.

Based on the Audit of Adequacy of USAID's Antiterrorism Vetting Procedures conducted in November of 2007, eight recommendations were made to get USAID on board to accurately and efficiently vet potentially dishonest charities. These recommendations focused on the lack of a substantial plan for how USAID deals with terrorist financing. It had no real guidance for an approved vetting program, no unification of antiterrorism procedures between USAID worldwide offices, and no developed database to track and vet charities worldwide. Likewise, the audit singled out the management of USAID, stating, "Management needs to design and implement effective management controls to help ensure that directives are being carried out."[40] USAID did use an Office of Acquisition (OAA)-implemented database. However, the database was incomplete because information about the awards was not entered into the system.[41]

In February 2005, a USAID partner pled guilty to lying to law enforcement officials about his involvement with and support of one of the disciples of Osama bin Laden in a terrorism-related investigation. In August 2005, a U.S. District Court in Louisiana sentenced the former USAID partner to 48 months' imprisonment and a fine for making false statements to federal agents in connection with counter-terrorism investigations. Before the indictment, USAID officials had provided the partner with approximately $108,000 (of an estimated $1 million) from July 2004 to January 2005 for a program funded out of USAID/Pakistan. Initially, the U.S. Embassy in Pakistan notified USAID about the partner's arrest in October 2004 pursuant to the indictment. Of the $108,000, USAID paid the partner an additional $25,000 as a termination settlement for the grant that was awarded in July 2004.[42]

Just as some charities aren't what they seem, many multinational corporations also find themselves working (whether by force or by their own choice) with terrorist organizations on the macro- and micro-levels. Just when you thought it was safe to purchase your favorite DVD, CD, television set, or bananas, it isn't. Next, we'll expose the ties that some well-known corporations have to terrorism.

9

Strange Bedfellows

On a warm June morning in 1969, two unassuming policemen on motorcycles made their way to a General Motors plant located in the suburban neighborhood of Sayago in Montevideo, Uruguay. The watchmen of the plant were unfazed upon seeing them drive up; extra security had been commissioned by the government in anticipation of New York Governor Nelson Rockefeller's visit and press conference.

The men, however, were not law enforcement. They were members of the urban guerrilla group known as the Tupamaro. The group notoriously used tactics such as kidnapping and sabotage to communicate their disdain for the Uruguayan government and their pro-Marxist ideology. As they approached the building, the two men detonated two packages that looked like bombs. Within 15 minutes, a fire in the General Motors plant destroyed the facility's files, fuel tanks, jets, and five cars parked in the patio. Overall, the attack caused $1 million in damages, but what was more costly (specifically, to the Uruguayan government) was the damage done by the underlying diplomatic message the rebels wanted the world to hear. TV screens in American homes showed a shocked U.S. governor arriving at a smoldering pyre instead of a thriving plant. Two scrawled words summed up the attack's mission: "Out Rockefeller."

"This was the work of an Uruguayan urban guerrilla group," said an American news anchor. "The Tupas."[1]

And it wouldn't be the last.

Targeting American symbols such as embassies and multinational corporations was part of a greater strategic operation called Plan Satan. The Tupamaro sought to provoke a ministerial crisis in foreign intervention that would lead to the downfall of the government.[2]

When the world thinks of multinational companies and their involvement in terrorism, the image of what took place in Uruguay that June day comes to mind—small yet powerful rebel groups kidnapping and maiming, bombing buildings, and alarming customers and executives of multinational companies, clearly making the companies and anyone associated with them the target. What doesn't come to mind is those same people who were once the target working with, paying off, or funding rebel leaders and terrorist groups in countries all over the world.

But that's exactly what R.J. Reynolds (RJR), Sony Corp., Dole Foods, and Chiquita International Brands did unknowingly or knowingly. As much as these multinationals tried to distance themselves from terrorism plots, these Fortune 500 companies acted as financial facilitators of extortions, kidnappings, bombings, and the smuggling of people and products across borders. The terrorists used profits made from selling these companies' goods, according to court documents— the same goods consumers were purchasing in grocery stores, delis, and big-box retailers all around the world.[3]

How Banned TVs Funded Bombings

In the mountains of Afghanistan, the drug route on which illegal substances normally were transported—across the Pakistani border by way of the Khyber Pass—was being used to transport another product just as illegal and dangerous as the poppies used for heroin.

It was Sony television sets.

In 1996, a survey conducted by the Pakistan Electronics Manufacturers Association found that 500,000 TVs were smuggled into the country that year, and 75% of them were Sonys.[4] And in 2010, the National Assembly's Standing Committee on Finance was told that the Afghan Transit Trade was the main source of smuggling into Pakistan, banking $4 to $5 billion annually and subjecting the country to $2.5 billion in lost taxes and tariffs.[5]

The Taliban allowed contraband Sony television sets to be imported through Iran and into Pakistan. Smugglers would obtain the product after it shipped to the Iranian port of Baider Abbas, and from there go past the Afghan border to southeast Kandahar, into Jalalabad, and into Pakistan through Peshawar. The Taliban would let the smugglers use these routes and in return would take fees from them. The Taliban also made it easier for the smugglers to avoid paying stiff taxes and duties levied on these goods going into Pakistan through agreement deals they had with border patrol.

But Sony wasn't oblivious to what was happening. In his book *At Home in the World*, Daniel Pearl reported that Sony Gulf FZE (a wholly owned subsidiary and sales office headquartered in Dubai) sold few TVs through the proper legal channels into Pakistan and didn't assemble sets locally.[6] I corroborated this fact with my source at Sony Gulf in March 2010. According to its web site and a source at Sony Gulf FZE, the television sets were manufactured in Dubai and the United Arab Emirates. In fact, Sony Gulf FZE (similar to RJR Corp.) allegedly used smuggling as a marketing and distribution strategy for the Middle East region to gain market share over other television and electronics manufacturers. Managers of Sony Gulf FZE would actively seek out and recruit potential traders and then sell them the merchandise. They would then ship the merchandise to Iran. In one instance, Sony Gulf approached Abdul Haq, an Afghani and ex-mujahideen, about distributing TVs in Afghanistan. He began sending them to his family in Afghanistan by way of Dubai. In his book, Pearl also notes how Khalid Khan, manager of Sony Gulf, often visited the Karkhano market (known for selling smuggled goods) in Pakistan and admitted that "all of the TVs were smuggled into Pakistan from Afghanistan."[7] Wrote Pearl before he was kidnapped and killed by the Jaish-I-Mohammed (Army of Mohammed, which also goes by the alias "The National Movement for the Restoration of Pakistani Sovereignty") in 2002: "Smuggling offers employment to people in the tribal areas of the Afghan border. Smuggling is an industry, and it's the largest entry in the terror balance of payments."

Sony Gulf's involvement with smuggling televisions wasn't the first or last time Sony would be accused of supporting terrorism efforts. After years of surveillance, in October 2010 Khaled T. Safadi pled guilty to exporting Sony PlayStation 2 consoles to the Galeria Page mall in Paraguay, which is on the U.S. blacklist of businesses that fund terrorist organizations. Safadi and his two co-conspirators, Ulises Talavera and Emilio Gonzalez-Neira, allegedly sold thousands of Sony PlayStation 2s and digital cameras during 2007 and 2008.[8] Sony gaming consoles and cameras also were being smuggled into Venezuela by Hassan Hodroj, a Hezbollah official, and his son-in-law Dib Hani Harb. They were eventually arrested in November 2009 in Philadelphia for smuggling 1,200 machine guns to the Hezbollah through Syria.[9] Both men are from Beirut but were living an upper-middle-class life in the U.S. (According to court documents, the government seized more than $500,000 in U.S. currency, property in Dearborn, Michigan, and Staten Island, New York, and a BMW X5 and a Land Rover Range Rover Sport.) The men were also conspiring with Moussa Ali Hamdan, Hamze El-Najjar, Moustafa Habib Kassem, and Latif Kamel Hamzime. The four men allegedly ran a smuggling ring where they would purchase hundreds of thousands of dollars worth of Sony PlayStation 2 systems, laptops, cell phones, and automobiles from a cooperating witness.[10] Then they would send the merchandise to Margarita Island, Venezuela. Although the total value of the gaming systems was $38,997, Hamdan declared the worth on the Shippers Export Declaration of Commerce (SED) as $17,600.[11] In Venezuela, the merchandise was sold at the actual retail value. The proceeds were sent overseas to the Hezbollah by transferring funds from a TD Bank account to a Bank Audi account in Beirut, Lebanon.

"The allegations contained in this complaint demonstrate how terrorist organizations rely on a variety of underlying criminal activities to fund and arm themselves," says David Kris, Assistant Attorney General for National Security.[12]

What's more, these terrorist groups rely on consumers' desire to purchase products at the lowest possible price to keep the cash flow coming. Because bargains never go out of style, smugglers always know they have a market, and terrorist groups always have an income.

The Business of Cigarette Smuggling

Finding discounted cigarettes, as I quickly discovered, is about as easy as finding a Starbucks in a major metropolis. With a pack of cigarettes costing almost as much as my double-shot-no-foam-low-fat-in-a-small-cup latte, I channeled my addiction to coffee into finding cheaper sticks of nicotine (since I am not addicted). My search took me to Long Island, New York, to a smoke shop run by the Shinnecock Native Americans in South Hampton. This shop, which is on a Native American reservation, doesn't have to adhere to the same state tax laws imposed on cigarettes. It can sell cartons of cigarettes for $30 to $40, depending on the brand. A carton of cigarettes sold in New York state costs $120 to $140. "We have to pay 75% tax on the cigarettes. That's why they are so expensive," says an employee at The Smoke Shop in the West Village. "Even if you are purchasing the cigarettes online at a discount, you are definitely buying it from a Native American reservation."

Or was I?

As states increased taxes on cigarettes in the late 1990s and early 2000s to as much as 75% a pack, people with fierce nicotine addictions—especially in New York, Massachusetts, New Jersey, Washington, Rhode Island, and Michigan—scoured the Internet and discount smoke shops to save money. Distributors and ORC rings quickly figured out that reselling smuggled packs and cartons of cigarettes bought in lower-taxed states—such as North Carolina, Kentucky, Virginia, South Carolina, Wyoming, and Georgia—could yield them high margins when sold across state borders and online. Law enforcement officials in New York state estimate that well-organized cigarette smuggling networks generate $200,000 to $300,000 per week. A large percentage of the money is believed to be sent back to the Middle East. The money directly or indirectly finances groups such as Hezbollah, Hamas, and al Qaeda.[13]

One example was an ORC ring run out of Charlotte, North Carolina. Mohamad Hammoud smuggled cigarettes from North Carolina where the tax was 50 cents per carton and sold them in Michigan, where the tax was $7.50 per carton. Hammoud and his co-conspirators took the proceeds (he made more than $8 million, according to court documents) and sent close to $100,000 back to Lebanon to fund a Hezbollah cell. The smuggled cigarettes were not only bought by retail stores via a distributor intermediary and members of the ORC ring, but they also were available for purchase online at a fraction of the cost of regularly taxed cigarettes. As a result, smokers flocked to these outlets to purchase the discounted cigarettes, not knowing that the profits were being used to fund a terrorist organization overseas. Hammoud was arrested in 2000 and convicted in 2002.

In 2003, two women from the Seneca Nation of Indians Cattaraugus Reservation in New York were sentenced for participating in a smuggling ring. They would provide tax-free cigarettes from the Seneca reservation smoke shop to a Hezbollah-linked network in Dearborn, Michigan. Elias Mohamad Akhdar, a native of Lebanon, was the head of the smuggling ring and had direct ties to the Hezbollah.[14]

But terrorist funding through the purchase of contraband cigarettes wasn't just happening in the U.S.

In complaints filed by the European Community (EC) in 2001 and 2002, the EC accused RJR companies, including RJR Nabisco, Inc; R.J. Reynolds Tobacco Company; R.J. Reynolds Tobacco International,

Inc; RJG Acquisition Corp. (formerly known as Nabisco Holdings Corp.); RJR Nabisco Holdings Corp.; and R.J. Reynolds Tobacco Holdings, Inc., of exploiting established smuggling routes by shipping large volumes of cigarettes to shell corporations for more than ten years. According to court documents filed by the EC, RJR Corp. used fraudulent documents to facilitate organized crime by laundering funds from narcotics trafficking and the sale of its products, specifically in countries that have U.S. trade sanctions imposed on them, such as Iraq. Ultimately, the charges against RJR were dismissed.

The EC Versus R.J. Reynolds Tobacco

With the establishment of the Bank Secrecy Act of 1970, banks were required to avoid doing business with organized crime rings or known criminals or facilitating any of their transactions. Knowing this, members of organized crime rings in Italy, Russia, and Colombia had the RJR companies launder money through their own accounts in financial institutions such as The Bank of New York, Citibank N.A., and Chase Manhattan Bank, according to the court papers filed.[15]

In the 1990s The Bank of New York was known to have accounts through which Russian organized crime members would launder millions of dollars worth of funds. Accounts were set up in the name of both legitimate and fake businesses. As customers, these organized crime rings seemingly paid RJR with the laundered funds in the accounts and sold smuggled cigarettes at a discounted price within their communities and online, with RJR fully aware that it was being paid for its cigarettes with illegal funds.[16]

According to the case, to sidestep U.S. money laundering laws, top RJR executives established subsidiary companies in countries known for bank secrecy (such as Switzerland) to avoid being detected by U.S. and European law enforcement. Subsidiaries with schemes included the following organizations: The Alfred Bossert money laundering organization, the Walt money laundering conspiracy, and money laundering through The Bank of New York for a Russian organized crime ring. In addition, illegal cigarette sales in Iraq funded the terrorist organization PKK (Kurdistan Workers' Party). The EC alleged that corporate management knowingly colluded with organized crime by helping launder the proceeds of narcotics trafficking and other crimes into the purchase of cigarettes. By providing false packaging and documentation to facilitate the smuggling, RJR Corp. allowed the PKK and the Iraqi regime to profit from the illicit cigarette sales.[17]

Colombia is the primary source of cocaine in the EC according to a legal brief. Money obtained from the illegal sale of cocaine in countries including Austria, Belgium, Denmark, Finland, France, Germany, Greece, Ireland, Italy, Luxembourg, The Netherlands, Portugal, Spain, Sweden, and the United Kingdom[18] must be laundered for narcotics traffickers to use it. The complaint states that RJR Corp. helped facilitate this Black Market Peso Exchange through the purchase and sale of its cigarettes. This was also the case for heroin sales. The money laundering cycle gave participants total anonymity by passing the drug proceeds through the financial markets. This allowed them to disguise the illegal nature, source, ownership, and control of the money.[19]

The Role of Money Brokers and Money Launderers

A money broker is a crucial go-between for the drug cartels and their overseas market. In the case of the European Community versus RJR Corp., after the proceeds were made from the sale of imported cocaine, the cartel contacted the money broker and negotiated a contract to exchange pesos he controlled in Colombia for euros. After the money broker paid the agreed-upon sum in pesos, the cartel contacted its cell and instructed them to deliver the agreed-upon amount of euros to the money broker's agent. The broker then laundered the euros and converted them into dollars so that his customers could use the dollars to import and purchase RJR Corp. cigarettes in bulk.

Not only were the importers getting the laundered dollars at a substantially discounted rate, but the money broker was sometimes instructed to pay RJR Corp. directly by depositing the laundered drug money into accounts held at European banks. Accused money launderers included Gerardo Cuomo, Patrick Laurent, Gilbert Llorens, Corrado Bianchi, Werner Denz, Martin Denz, Luis Garcia, members of the Mansur family, and Patrick Monnier.[20] They worked in Europe, Asia, and Russia and acted as go-betweens for RJR and its co-conspirators. RJR would then dictate exactly how much to charge for the products, which secret Swiss bank accounts the money would be deposited into, and who would make the payments.

Another set of players in the money laundering scheme were the "cutouts." They helped bypass the direct sale by going to an illegal source interested in purchasing cigarettes. In this case, RJR Corp. allegedly selected the cutout—a group of wholesalers that, according to the court document, could "deny responsibility when the customer sells the product." That way, the manufacturer (in this case, RJR Corp.) could insulate itself from overt acts involved in the sale of the cigarettes. Because it wanted to increase its market share in the EC, RJR Corp. did whatever it took to get its product distributed—even if that meant doing business with criminals. One RJR employee based in Switzerland went so far as to instruct customers buying RJR product in bulk that the cartons should be "neutralized and decoded" by removing marks and numbers on the packaging that would allow them to be tracked and regulated within Europe.

The laundry list of illegal activity in which RJR Corp. was accused of engaging is extensive. In addition to being charged with using cutouts, RJR Corp. was charged with accepting payments from persons or entities it knew (or had reason to know) were criminals and money launderers. RJR Corp. arranged for its cigarettes to be paid for in such a way that the payments were virtually untraceable. It also established protocols for "layered transactions" that allowed for cigarettes to be paid for through multiple intermediaries (cutouts) to conceal the source and nature of the illicit funds.[21]

Despite strict trade restrictions on Iraq, RJR Corp. allegedly continued its quest for worldwide market share by selling cigarettes in the northern territories of Iraq in towns such as Dohuk and Zokho. This region was controlled by terrorist groups including the PKK,[22] which launched numerous attacks on the EC, according to court documents. The terrorist group would charge RJR Corp. a fee for every container of cigarettes allowed to pass through the territory. These fees provided a money lifeline for these terrorist groups, funding weapons purchases, ammunition, and bomb-making materials, as well as terrorist acts such as kidnapping and executions. What's more, Saddam Hussein put aside the longtime conflict between the Kurdish groups in Iraq and allowed them to import RJR cigarettes. Hussein's son Uday, who oversaw the illegal importing operation, personally profited from it. Illegal shipments of RJR cigarettes from January to April 2002 included cases of Winston (59,500), Magna (65,000), Winchester (10,909), Aspen (7,022), Doral (1,500), Barton (4,500), and Easton (1,560).[23]

The History of Cigarette Smuggling

Cigarette smuggling is not a new form of laundering money; it's been around for centuries. According to a World Bank study, what makes smuggling cigarettes convenient is the high global demand for cigarettes. Most smuggled cigarettes are well-known brands that go for $200,000 per container of 10 million cigarettes without paying taxes. Smugglers then resell the same cigarettes in the European or U.S. markets, taking into account excise duties, value-added tax (VAT), and import taxes, bumping up the value of the cigarettes to more than $1 million. The margin on the sale of the cigarettes is so high (and it's even higher if the cigarettes are stolen) that smugglers can fund not only their travel but also their illicit activities.[24] Another version of smuggling is called "round-tripping." Locally made product is exported to neighboring countries where it's exempt from duties and taxes. Then the containers in which the product was shipped make their way back into the country of origin containing tobacco products. These "ghost exports" are not subject to regular tobacco duties and taxes, thus costing the country billions of dollars a year.[25]

In the U.S. alone, a study suggests that states are losing about $5 billion annually in tax revenue because of illegal tobacco sales. In the case of cigarette schemes, authorities are seeing more organized crime and international rings supplanting mom-and-pop stores, such as corner delis and local tobacco shops.[26] Researchers estimate that 30% of internationally exported cigarettes, or about 355 billion, are lost to smuggling.[27] Globally, it's estimated that governments lose almost $40 billion to $50 billion in tax revenues annually.[28]

Cigarette Smuggling Funds Local Terrorism Around the World

RJR's alleged illicit sale of cigarettes through Europe and parts of the Middle East accounts for only a fraction of the cigarette smuggling going on worldwide that is also funding criminal acts, such as terrorism in Latin America, Africa, and Ireland. In West and North African countries, 80% of the cigarette market is illicit, meaning that most of the smoking going on in these countries profits criminals. Of that 80%, millions are used to fund terrorist groups such as al Qaeda in the Islamic Maghreb (AQIM), a group backed by Osama bin Laden. According to a document published by the United Nations Office on

Drugs and Crime (UNODC), revenue from cigarette smuggling in West Africa (around $775 million) is greater than Gambia's entire national gross domestic product.[29]

The Group of Experts, a committee within the U.N. Security Council, reported that Tibert Rujugiro Ayabatwa, a tobacco tycoon who owned Mastermind Tobacco Company, which produced Yes cigarettes, and the Congo Tobacco Company, which produced Supermatch cigarettes, pled guilty to cigarette tax evasion charges in South Africa. He was funding a Congolese Tutsi-backed rebel group called the Congress National Pour la Defence du Peuple (CNDP).[30] According to the report, The Group of Experts uncovered e-mails and gathered testimony from individuals who claimed Rujugiro had been supporting the CNDP through cash payments and supplies and that he paid the rebel group to allow the traffic of his untaxed cigarettes. What's more, authorities apprehended 97 million contraband cigarettes in Ghana in 2009. The cigarettes were manufactured in the United Arab Emirates and had "Sale in Ivory Coast" stamped on the boxes. They were destined for Mali, a country in which they were not licensed for sale.[31] The leader of the CNDP, Laurent Nkunda, was behind many serious human rights abuses, including mass murder, torture, rape and forced recruitment of children, and slavery, according to the Group of Experts report. He used the sale of illicit cigarettes to fund these atrocities.

The report also notes that Commandant Jerome, leader of the Ituri armed group Forces Armees du Peuple Congolais (FAPC), conspired with Ugandan business and political leaders to put in place a network that generates import transit tax-related revenue on both sides of the border through the sales of fuel, cigarettes, and soft drinks. In turn, he enjoys ongoing military and financial ties with Uganda.[32] The illicit trade pact between the FAPC and the Ugandan government violates Security Council resolution 1493 (2003) of July 28, 2003, imposing an arms embargo for an initial period of 12 months. The embargo requires all states, including the Democratic Republic of the Congo, to take necessary measures to prevent the direct or indirect supply, sale, or transfer of arms and any related material, and of any assistance, advice, or training related to military activities, to all foreign and Congolese armed groups and militias operating in the territory of North and South Kivu and Ituri.[33] However, the sale of and proceeds from contraband cigarettes along the well-traveled "Salt Roads of the Tuareg" (which expand across the sand plains of Niger and into the mountains of the Algerian south) is now known as the Marlboro Connection. It allows the FAPC to obtain arms despite the embargo.

Like Western Africa, Latin American drug routes also serve as cigarette smuggling routes, earning the Marxist-based insurgency known as the Revolutionary Armed Forces of Colombia (FARC) millions of dollars in revenues from cigarettes smuggled into the U.S. The FARC, whose funds mostly come from being the world's largest supplier of cocaine, also make money by imposing taxes on coca growers. In written testimony to the House Committee on the Judiciary in 2000, Ralf Mutschke revealed that "U.S.-manufactured cigarettes, especially Marlboros, Kents, and Lucky Strikes, made up a large portion of the trade goods that were smuggled into Colombia, and FARC was financed by this process."[34] Lucky Strike is a brand under the RJR Corp. umbrella.

When the IRA splintered into two different groups, funding from cigarette smuggling remained consistent. While the Provisional IRA announced in 2005 that it would use peaceful means to get its message across, the more radical Real IRA continued to use tactics including car bombings, robberies, kidnappings, and assassinations, often targeting senior British government officials and the British military police in Northern Ireland, according to globalsecurity.org.

In March 2009, an American businessman, Roman Vidal, was accused of masterminding a cigarette smuggling ring that netted the Real IRA hundreds of thousands of pounds. Vidal used a Miami-based freight company as a front to import hundreds of millions of cigarettes from Panama into Miami. Vidal would then hide the contraband cigarettes in freight bound for Dublin to avoid paying 1.5 million euros in taxes. The investigation began based on a tip to U.S. customs agents. The shipments came into Ireland by way of Panama and allegedly funded the execution of two British soldiers who were gunned down while waiting for a pizza delivery car.[35]

According to Sean Murphy, deputy chief executive of Chambers Ireland, a business organization in Ireland, cigarette smuggling costs the country at least 300 million euros in lost earnings from taxes and duty. This estimate should be multiplied by four or five to take into account income tax not collected because workers are not employed, or corporation tax decreases because of depressed profits.[36]

Drug and tobacco smuggling might be the main way insurgent groups get most of their funding, but terrorism and criminal finance investigator Larry Johnson notes in an interview that it's much easier to crack down on the flow of legal products. "You need to ensure that the products are being sold through legitimate channels through legitimate distributors—that they're not committing willful blindness," he says. "The contraband is fairly easy to deal with because it's in the power of the distributors and producers to control the process. This is actually one of those few problems that are fixable."

Chiquita International Brands: "Either You Pay Me, or I Am Going to Kill You."

Wandering through the fruit section of the grocery store, the last thing you would think would fund terrorism would be the purchase of bananas. But in 2008, buying a bunch of Chiquita or Dole Foods bananas did just that.

Deep in the jungles of Colombia and far from their Midwestern roots, the executives who oversee Chiquita Corp. in South America had to make a decision. They could either protect their employees at the banana plantation from the Colombian paramilitary groups by paying them off, or risk their lives for working there. In an interview with CBS News' *60 Minutes*, Fernando Aguirre, Chiquita's current chairman and CEO, explained that the company was forced to pay taxes to the guerrillas who controlled the territory in the late 1980s and 1990s and again to the paramilitaries known as the United Self-Defense Forces of Colombia (AUC) when they occupied the same area in 1997. "It was a dilemma of having literally a gun pointed at your head, where you have someone who says, 'Either you pay me, or I'm going to kill you, or I'm going to kill your employees.'"[37]

For more than seven years (1997 to 2004), Chiquita paid the guerillas and the AUC more than $2 million to "keep the employees safe." However, the money was also being used to fund purchases of illegal weapons that massacred thousands of people. These atrocities included the beheading of a 12-year-old boy in front of his school classmates.

In October of 2001 the U.S. government amended the law originally enacted by Secretary of State Madeleine Albright designating paramilitary groups as terrorist organizations. This made any sort of financial assistance, whether coerced or not, a felony. Chiquita continued to make payments to the AUC despite the passage of this law, claiming that it missed the government's announcement.

"What I know is all the data shows that the company, the moment it learned that these payments were illegal in the U.S., that's when it decided to self-disclose to the Department of Justice," says Aguirre.

In 2007, the Chiquita Company pled guilty to a felony and was ordered to pay $25 million in fines. The Justice Department originally planned to prosecute Chiquita executives, including former CEO Cyrus Friedheim, Jr., and board member Roderick Hill, but those charges were eventually dropped. This decision infuriated the Colombian government. The prosecutor general proclaimed he would start his own investigation that included a possible extradition of Chiquita's executives to Colombia to stand trial.

Chiquita was the first American multinational corporation convicted of financing terrorism.

But paying the U.S. government more than $25 million in fines was the least of the fruit company's worries. In April of 2010, 250 Colombians who claimed they and their relatives were victims of the violence carried out by the AUC filed a lawsuit against Chiquita. The lawsuit sought $1 billion in damages,[38] alleging that the company willingly funded a terrorist organization that regularly committed atrocities.

This case came on the heels of another lawsuit filed by the families of five missionaries who were abducted and killed in Colombia by FARC guerrillas when their mission group, The New Tribes Mission Group in Florida, refused to pay a ransom. Similar to the families victimized by the AUC, the Miami-based missionary family members sought close to $780 million in damages[39] because Chiquita knowingly gave money to the FARC after it fell under the Foreign Terrorist Organization (FTO) designation. The suit claimed that the money helped fund the group's operations at the time the killings occurred.[40] In February 2010, almost three years after the case was filed against Chiquita Brands, U.S. District Judge Kenneth Marra in West Palm Beach, Florida, ruled that the lawsuit would not be dismissed. He noted that the missionaries did not have to prove a link between money paid and each individual crime. "The factual allegations of the (lawsuit) detailing extensively coordinated secret payments and fraudulent concealment sufficiently support an inference of the conspiracy between Chiquita and (the terrorist group)," Marra said in the ruling.[41]

Judge's ruling or not, Chiquita still denied all allegations. A statement issued by Chiquita Brands spokesperson Ed Loyd said, "We [Chiquita] were clearly extorted. We don't share the same ideology of those groups. That's not the type of business we practice or we would engage in."[42]

The Chiquita case was just the tip of the iceberg according to U.S. Representative William Delahunt (D-MA), who chairs a House

Foreign Affairs subcommittee. Delahunt spearheaded a congressional investigation that involved spending four days in Colombia meeting with paramilitary bosses Salvatore Mancuso, Rodrigo Tovar ("Jorge 40"), Edgar Velosa ("HH"), Diego Fernando Murillo ("Don Berna"), and Carlos Mario Jimenez ("Macaco") to talk about other multinational American companies giving payouts to paramilitary groups and guerillas in the same area. Delahunt didn't want to disclose which companies were discussed during his conversations and therefore remained vague about other multinational involvement, but he was adamant that they were willing participants. "They [paramilitary bosses] were very specific and clear on the relationships between themselves and American companies," he said.[43]

Dole Foods' Involvement with the Colombian Paramilitary

If Delahunt wouldn't call out the other companies involved, Mancuso (the former head of the AUC) would. During the same *60 Minutes* interview, Mancuso specifically named Dole Foods and Fresh Del Monte Produce. Mancuso helped negotiate the "Justice and Peace" program, in which almost 30,000 paramilitaries were allowed to disarm, surrender, and receive reduced jail time if they confessed to all crimes. It was in this confession that Mancuso and others claimed Dole Foods involvement.

"Was Chiquita the only American company that paid you?" interviewer Steve Kroft asked Mancuso.

"All companies in the banana region paid. For instance, there was Dole and Del Monte, which I believe are U.S. companies," Mancuso said.[44] Mancuso went on to explain that both of these companies had a choice of who would protect the plantation workers, including the local police, the army, or the guerillas. But he also noted that "the police could barely protect themselves."[45]

In April 2009, 73 families of those who died at the hands of the AUC filed a wrongful death lawsuit against Dole Foods. They claimed that the 73 people were killed at the hands of the paramilitaries working as a "local police force" hired by Dole Foods in and around company-owned plantations. According to court documents, the AUC would use violent tactics on behalf of Dole Foods to allow Dole to plant banana trees. This included driving small farmers off their land, driving leftist guerillas out of banana zones, keeping unions out of Dole by murdering union leaders, and using terror tactics to discourage workers from joining the union, all while murdering thousands of innocent people in the process.

Under the "Justice and Peace" process, Jose Gregorio Mangones (alias "Carlos Tijeras"), another ex-paramilitary commander, admitted to more than half the killings cited in the lawsuit, according to Terry Collingsworth, an attorney for the families. In addition, Mangones "received 70,000 Colombian pesos per hectare per year from Dole, [which was] roughly 40% of the William Rivas Front's[46] annual budget." The court documents also state that as part of this financial arrangement, Dole allegedly asked the AUC to eliminate the leaders of the trade union in Magdelena. Mangones confessed to the murder of Pablo Perez, the former president of the union Sintrainagro in Magdelena.[47]

In addition, the lawsuit alleged that Dole hired the AUC as security forces knowing that they were designated as an FTO by the U.S State Department in September 2001. Dole Foods issued a statement denying any involvement with AUC, stating, "Dole categorically rejects the baseless allegations" and "this lawsuit is irresponsible and the allegations are blatantly false." California court threw out the case in September 2010. However, Collingsworth said he will refile it in federal court.

In an interview with Reuters, Lee Wolosky, a partner at Boies Schiller & Flexner LLP (the firm acting on behalf of the 242 plaintiffs), said, "This lawsuit and others like it will hold Chiquita—which had revenues in excess of $3.5 billion last year—accountable to those victimized by its unlawful conduct."

Whether by choice or not, the accountability will inevitably come out of consumers' pockets in the form of increased product costs. This is a high price to pay for an American multinational corporation's involvement with a terrorist group.

Many might argue that billion-dollar multinational corporations have their hands tied when it comes to negotiating locally for their product to be distributed correctly and safely while making sure their employees stay safe. Terrorist groups often rule the land, so large corporations have no choice. However, when it comes to protecting the consumer at the local level, sometimes the largest corporations can't prevent the consumer from purchasing illegitimate merchandise.

That's where the little guys with the big ideas come in.

Part III
Putting a Band-Aid
on a Broken Leg

The Failure of Preventative Measures   201

Letting the Bad Guy Get Away   219

10

The Failure of Preventative Measures

With the influx of failing security systems and preventive measures to fight organized retail crime, one chief of security took it upon himself to make his own rules. Steven Reed decided to ban people wearing hoodies and sagging pants from the Arden Fair Mall in Sacramento, California. "It was certainly controversial when I introduced it, but people were getting away with thousands of dollars worth of merchandise just by pulling the hood over their eyes and face so that no one could identify them," says Reed. "I had a $12.50 piece of clothing that was negating a $1.5 million camera system. I wasn't going to let that happen."[1]

Implemented in October of 2009, not only did the rule catch the attention of the national media, but the ACLU also got involved (but ultimately decided it had no position on the dress code). Reactions from some Sacramento locals were angry, but that didn't deter Reed. He was convinced that implementing a strict dress code was the only way to prevent theft from happening, including ORC. Customers had a choice when they decided to shop at a mall that boasted 169 retail tenants, 154 cameras, and a plethora of security officers in more than 1.2 million square feet of space. They could take off their sweatshirts and pull up their jeans or be thrown out.

Reed, who is a former teacher and vice principal and a former police officer of 20 years, would stereotypically be a likely candidate to implement such stringent dress codes in his facility. The "baggy pants and hoodie" look is associated with criminals and gangbangers. But Reed suggests it wasn't about categorizing people by their appearance and preventing them from shopping. Rather, it was about "keeping the mall safe." In addition, Reed wanted to curtail a rampant problem that most malls and retailers have yet to control despite elaborate preventive measures.

Acting Locally, Thinking Globally

The idea to implement a dress code in the mall came to Reed after he saw a kiosk robbed one Saturday morning in February 2009. When security tried to identify who was behind the heist, the culprit's hoodie prevented anyone from seeing his face, and he got away with hundreds of dollars in cash. "We needed to change the policy, and quick," says Reed. "If malls and retailers realized it's the little things that cost virtually nothing that prevent people from committing a larger crime, then they would see a significant drop in ORC and other thefts." Significant is an understatement.

After implementing the new rule, Reed saw a 70% percent decrease in ORC, car theft, and other thefts such as robberies "because [suspects] couldn't hide their faces anymore." He expected the numbers to go down even more by the end of 2010. In addition to the infamous dress code rule, Reed implemented a new license plate recognition system on each security vehicle that took pictures of license plates and kept them in a database. With a grant of $50,000 from the Department of Homeland Security in October 2006, and another grant of $50,000 from unused federal funds, Reed and his team were able to invest in a closed-circuit television system (CCTV) and license plate recognition software. Working together, the systems take pictures of license plates of vehicles in the parking lot. Then the systems communicate with a database of more than 5 million license plate numbers on file with the Sacramento Police Department (SACPD). Using Verizon Wireless technology, the inquiry is answered within seconds, and a picture of the license plate in question appears and is

GPS-stamped with the location, with information on whether the car or the license plate have been stolen. After this information on the license plate comes back to the Arden Fair Mall security officer, the officer contacts SACPD to run the license plate numbers and verify the information given by the license plate recognition system. Then the security officers quickly leave the area and review CCTV footage to pinpoint the geographic location of the suspect within the mall.

While watching the Arden Mall surveillance video, I noticed something about many of the ORC rings targeting malls. Their getaway cars are almost as crucial as ensuring that the perfect heist was being committed within the stores. Criminals committing ORC make it a point to communicate with the getaway driver, to make sure he is nearby and that the car they are using is parked close by. Criminals committing ORC typically use rental cars that they don't return, causing the cars to come up as stolen within the license plate recognition system's database and allowing the security officers to track the suspect inside the mall. They also use the car as a mobile storage facility, storing thousands of dollars of merchandise in the trunk of the car. In this particular surveillance video, Reed points out how the license plate number recognition software was able to identify a pattern with a specific car that had been stolen. After screening multiple tapes, I noticed that the car in the video had also appeared in other shopping mall parking lots and strip mall lots. When the car was identified at the Arden Fair Mall as being stolen, the security officer in the parking lot promptly notified SACPD, which verified that the car was stolen, and the security guard reviewed CCTV footage to find the suspect inside the mall. When the boosters came out of the mall, they got a law enforcement surprise—police officers surrounded the car to apprehend them. When the police officers opened up the trunk of the car, they found several thousands of dollars of stolen clothing from other malls.

"[In this area] many of these ORC rings travel in groups and come to the mall in stolen but also in rented cars," says Captain

Daniel Hahn of the SACPD. "The Arden Fair Mall has also been a target of potential terrorist activity as well. The owners of the mall are Jewish, and because of the mall's high-profile nature, we made a point to increase security and implement systems where security at the mall and local law enforcement can communicate effectively with one another."[2]

Terrorist activity? In a quaint Sacramento mall? I suddenly realized no area was safe. In a world where the suspected Underwear Bomber chose the Detroit route only because of the cheap airfare, anything—even a mall in a peaceful suburban area—could be a target.

The partnership of the Arden Fair Malls and the SACPD has proven fruitful. After just a couple years of working together, mall security and the police department not only share information, but they also attend and provide space for training sessions that include SWAT team preparations, evacuation drills, crisis management scenarios, and K-9 training. And the partnership has paid off. Within a year, the SACPD and Arden Fair Mall security have recovered 58 stolen vehicles and apprehended 43 suspects while recovering thousands of dollars of merchandise, all from the license plate recognition system.

Types of ORC Theft Prevention That Are Supposed to Work But Don't

The Arden Fair Mall might be an example of security staff, retailers, technology, and law enforcement working harmoniously, but not all retailers work like that. Stores from Walmart to Saks Fifth Avenue were plagued with the same challenge at the beginning of 2008, while facing sinking profits, a glut in inventory, and weak staffing. How does a business that once pulled in hundreds of millions of dollars in sales per quarter curb retail theft and rescue profits without inconveniencing customers and losing even more money?

Steven Reed and the Arden Fair Mall invested a couple million dollars in surveillance systems, partnerships with wireless providers, and extra staffing. But it wasn't until Reed implemented his infamous (and inexpensive) dress code policy, the license plate recognition system, and the CCTV system that he saw a 3-5% increase in traffic and a 10% increase in sales over the last 11 months. Crime incidents at Arden Fair Mall have decreased 215% from 2010 to 2011, due in large part to these crimefighting tools and Reed's eagerness to publicize these techniques via a robust relationship with the media. Although customers initially felt as if their civil rights were being compromised, Reed insists that he's "not about a Big Brother approach," and foot traffic at the mall increased instead of decreasing as customers realized that they were safer because of the security changes.

Retailers such as Target and Walgreens were placed in a difficult position because of the economy. Having to act fast, they decided to pour millions into technology upgrades, figuring this was the only way to solve the shrinkage pandemic quickly. The National Retail Federation (NRF) reported in its 2010 survey that 90% of retailers (including Target and Walgreens) indicated that their companies had been victimized by ORC. This was a drop from the 92% reported in 2009 but was higher than the 85% reported in 2008.[3] Of the retailers who responded to the survey, more than half said they were allocating additional resources to combating ORC. Staffing shortages, especially during the holidays, meant shrinkage numbers would go up. That, combined with plummeting profits, had CEOs and upper management freaking out in their corner offices.

In the 2009 Retail Information Systems (RIS) Store Systems Study, 40% of retailers reported that loss prevention is in their top ten store system priorities for 2009, up from 29% the year before.

But making loss prevention a "priority" didn't mean having endless numbers of executive meetings in board rooms; it meant retailers had to upgrade their older video cameras and recording systems.

Investing in live visible as well as hidden CCTV systems was one way in which old systems were upgraded. These improvements cost from $7,000 to $20,000 for cameras alone. That cost didn't include maintenance for the cameras, video, storage, or bandwidth if the hours of surveillance tapes were being stored on servers. And these expensive upgrades didn't necessarily guarantee protection from theft, anyway.

"Stores can install all the video cameras, security mirrors, and alarms they want, but relying on technology too much is allowing ORCs to get away with stealing millions of dollars in merchandise," says Alan Herbach, president of American Theft Prevention Products. He believes the lack of personal contact between the shop owner/ employee and potential thief allows more merchandise to be stolen. "People who are stealing items in bulk want privacy. They tend not to shoplift right in the open. If someone is looking them in the eye, thieves are more likely not to steal an item."[4]

Another way retailers upgraded their systems inefficiently was by installing electronic sensors on clothing and products and installing in-store alarm systems. Security tags and sensors can cost $10 to $20 per tag. If a moderately sized retailer with 500,000 stock-keeping units (SKUs) decides to tag all its merchandise, the cost could run as much as $5 million. It was estimated that retailers spent on average $300,000 on alarm systems that beginning boosters and experienced ORC rings could get past just by using shopping bags lined with metal. The estimated losses retailers incurred because of ORC gangs using this method was nearly $750 million per store per year.[5] Even with both of these methods of theft deterrence working in tandem, potential thieves were able to circumvent them by creating technology that was more sophisticated than what the stores were using. Loss prevention research and development were no match for these boosters, who were ten steps ahead of retailers even with their rudimentary technology.

"It's not that difficult to just put merchandise in your bag and walk out with it," says Sarah, a former department store employee turned booster. "Stores are so understaffed you can pretty much walk out with a TV set in your bag, and no one would even notice. And half the time the people they hire to 'watch' the door or conduct surveillance a) don't want to be there and so they don't care, or b) are working in conjunction with fellow employees. There is no accountability, so why should anyone care?"[6]

DigitalPersona, a biometrics company that provides retailers with biological loss prevention solutions, explains in a white paper the missing element that prevents traditional approaches to loss prevention from working: a lack of enforcing accountability for each specific transaction. "When people understand that their access to systems and resources automatically reveals who they are, their incentive to behave inappropriately is significantly reduced."[7]

A Bottom-Line Breakdown of Costs

To compensate for the decrease in profit due to an increase in ORC, shrinkage, and cargo theft combined, many retailers turned to alternative means of cutting back on the bottom line. The cost inevitably got passed on to the consumer in unbelievable ways. In a report done by the Congressional Research Service on Organized Retail Crime, shrinkage cost retailers $36.3 billion in 2008.[8] (The National Retail Security Survey (NRSS), a survey of trends in retail loss prevention measures, defined shrinkage as the reduction of physical inventory caused by shoplifting, employee and vendor theft, and administrative error.)[9] Of that amount, theft cost retailers $28.4 billion, or 78.3% of the overall number. This figure included internal and external employee theft as well as shoplifting. And of those shoplifting cases, 27.5% were executed by members of an organized crime group.

This can translate into higher price per product for the customer, or having products locked up or kept behind the register, making them more difficult for the customer to access. With an increase in store theft on both a small and large scale, there is a direct correlation between declining store traffic as well, which has fallen by 65%.

Per-Employee Theft Case Versus the Average Shoplifter

The NRSS conducted in 2008 points out that the average dollar loss per employee theft case was $1,762 compared to $265.40 for the average shoplifting incident.[10] Total shoplifter and dishonest employee apprehensions increased for the fourth consecutive year, up almost 15% from the previous year, according to analysis done by Jack L. Hayes. And with the rise of ORC during the "Great Recession," more in-store employees were colluding with or running their own rings. They believed they had a right to steal the product and felt as if the store owed them something.

"Given that the surveyed portion of the retail economy annually transacts $1.845 trillion, this percentage of loss is worth more than $32 billion," Richard Hollinger said in the NRSS. "This means that the single largest category of larceny in the United States is the crime that occurs in retail stores. This figure is larger than motor vehicle theft, bank robbery, and household burglary combined."

Labor Costs

ORC and loss prevention involve an endless cycle of costs for retailers, with labor costs taking up most of the expense. An increase in ORC has to do with the following factors:

- Making product more difficult for the consumer to access, such as by putting it behind glass or in a plastic case
- Embarrassing or awkward antitheft deterrents, such as locks that squirt ink or make it impossible to try on a piece of clothing
- Understaffing at stores

The third reason was the biggest problem retailers experienced during the "Great Recession." When consumers started spending less because they were cutting back on discretionary and nondiscretionary purchases, retailers scurried to try to figure out how to increase their sinking bottom lines and profit margins in the wake of stagnant spending. Staff was the first expense to go—but in most cases that didn't translate into an increase in profit.

In an interview with Retailwire, Derek Rodner, vice president of product strategy at Agilence Inc., a loss prevention firm in New Jersey, says the economic downturn of 2009 created a "perfect storm for retail theft." He said, "Retailers significantly scaled back expenditures and capital projects in all areas—most significantly, loss prevention. In addition, many retailers cut their loss prevention staff up to 50%. At the same time, more people were losing jobs, and otherwise-honest folks were forced to resort to theft just to get by. These two factors combined to create a dramatic increase in shrink. Retailers are doubling their efforts [all over again] to combat this trend and are being forced into updating their legacy technologies and procedures to adapt to the changing dynamics."

The NRF estimated that the average retailer spent approximately $215,000 on labor costs for loss prevention compared to $75,000 to $100,000 in 2006 and 2007, prior to the recession. But the rapid staff increases cost money not only in terms of salary, but also in terms of labor hours spent trying to find the right people after several initial misses. In terms of upper management, larger stores and big-box retailers often spend as much as $1 million to hire loss prevention executives.[11] Estimated cost of labor to staff during heavy traffic times for a department store contributes to their operating margins in a negative way. (Costco, for example, saw an increase in its 2.77% in operating margin costs.)[12] However, these costs tend to be more when there are fewer staff members or more turnover. In addition to internal staffing, retailers had to add labor expenses for setting up technology to monitor potential ORC activity to their bottom-line costs. After spending hundreds of thousands of dollars on upgrades (to establish databases, for example), partnering with wireless providers (the Arden Fair/Verizon Wireless partnership costs $1,272 a year), and investing in training their employees, labor costs were hundreds of thousands of additional dollars spent just to combat ORC.

Decrease in State Tax Revenues

When goods are stolen instead of purchased, theft, ORC, shoplifting, and cargo theft can have an adverse effect on state tax revenues. The National Retail Association estimates that nationally, shoplifting is responsible for more than $1 billion in lost sales tax revenue each year. In California alone, it is estimated that the state's losses in retail theft equal $5 billion, and $375 million is lost in annual sales tax revenue.[13] Florida loses $106 million, Texas $153 million, Illinois $77 million, and New York $74 million.[14]

Sales tax collections in the January–March 2009 quarter were down 8.3% from the same quarter in 2008, according to a report done by the Nelson A. Rockefeller Institute. This decline is far worse than the worst sales tax revenue decline in the previous recession. Using the GDP price index to adjust for inflation, Census Bureau data shows that state and local sales tax revenue declined by 9.5% in the January–March quarter of 2009—far more than in any quarter since 1963. The last time we saw such drastic declines in state and local sales tax was in the third quarter of 1991, at 6.9%.

Sales tax declines were reported in all regions of the U.S. The Western states (including California and Nevada) had the largest decline, at 14.2%, followed by the Rocky Mountain region (Colorado, Utah) at 9.7%. Forty of 45 states with broad-based sales taxes saw declines, and 11 states had double-digit declines. Georgia led the states with the largest decline at 16.3%, followed by Nevada at 16.0%.[15] In Texas, more than $1.2 billion in merchandise was stolen by ORC gangs, resulting in a loss of more than $76.8 million in sales tax revenue.[16]

This data isn't surprising. States with higher instances of retail theft also had declining state sales tax revenue. As shown in a Retail Industry Leaders Association (RILA) Crime Trends Survey, as economic pressures persisted into 2009 and 2010, amateur or opportunistic shoplifting events, financial fraud, robberies, burglaries, and large increases in ORC continued to climb across all retail segments.[17] In 2010, the RILA Crime Trends Survey reported that out of the retailers surveyed, 78% saw an increase in amateur and opportunistic shoplifting events, and 65% reported seeing an increase in ORC.[18] Los Angeles, New York, Houston, Miami, and Baltimore were some of the heaviest-hit cities.

The responsibility ultimately falls on the stores. In 2008, the NRSS reported that retailers spent only .34% of annual sales on loss prevention tools such as contract services, security equipment, and loss prevention personnel.[19] Although some experts blame the decrease in loss prevention budgets on inventory shrinkage over the years (retailers on the flip side have seen a 59% increase in ORC activity—again, a matter of how these crimes are defined), a more realistic explanation is the scaling back of budgets because of the recent economic downturn. Loss prevention measures, including loss prevention personnel, are the first to go when a store wants to cut back on costs.[20] This inevitably leads to more goods being stolen from stores.

To further put the escalating cost in perspective, according to a study done in 2006, Walmart announced plans to open 1,500 new U.S. Walmart stores over the next five years. Based on a growth rate of 300 new stores per year, and assuming that the average number of 269 reported police incidents per Walmart store remains constant, the study projected that the cost to taxpayers will rise substantially over the next five years, consistent with Walmart's growth. Extrapolating cost estimates on a national basis, the study further estimated that local police departments would respond to 6,398,165 police incidents at Walmart stores over the next five years. It also estimated that in 2010 police would respond to 1,441,033 calls at more than 5,357

U.S. Walmart stores. The estimated total cost to local taxpayers for policing U.S. Walmart stores over the next five years (2006–2010) was $495,857,788—nearly half a billion dollars.[21]

Because loss in state sales tax revenue is never about one-off petty theft or minor shoplifting cases, some states, such as Pennsylvania and Wisconsin, have introduced ORC bills that set harsher punishments if an individual is caught stealing items that are lower in value. Virginia State Representative Bobby Scott introduced the Organized Retail Theft Investigation and Prosecution Act of 2010 (H.R. 5932), passed in 2010 by the U.S. House. It establishes a new division at the Department of Justice to investigate and prosecute ORC. According to Joe LaRocca of the NRF, this bill "will work in close consultation with retailers and will be one of the keys to protecting both retailers and consumers against the massive economic costs and very real public health and safety risks posed by organized retail crime."[22] The bill (which currently is still subject to Senate approval) would also require the Attorney General to make recommendations on how merchants and law enforcement agencies can work together to combat ORC. Most importantly, it would authorize $5 million of funds per year through 2015 to support the program. As powerful as this law might be, the problem is in how people are prosecuted. Without more stringent federal, state, and local laws, ORC crews will just wander around the country, looking for the most lenient state to steal from.

Health Costs

The consumer doesn't just suffer financially when retailers are hit by ORC, shrinkage, and theft. Products that are stolen are often repackaged and sold within days, compromising the product's safety. The most common examples are items that fall into the "CRAVED" categories. (This acronym, coined by researcher Ronald V. Clarke, means goods that are concealable, removable, available, valuable, enjoyable, and disposable.) These include infant formula, ephedrine-based cold medications, smoking cessation products, steaks, coffee, OTC medications, test kits, face creams, and premium razor blades.[23] When an item is stolen and then repackaged, manufacturers cannot be certain whether their product has been contaminated, mishandled, or spoiled due to less-than-optimal storage conditions, or because expiration dates have been tampered with. FDA regulations that ensure that a product is safe for consumption become compromised the minute the product is mishandled or repackaged, putting the consumer at risk—all to save a couple dollars.

"Some of these guys have machines in their homes that cost tens of thousands of dollars, just to replicate the packaging of the merchandise they are stealing," said Detective Kent Oda in a speech given at the LEAPS conference in Los Angeles. "You would not believe the lengths these ORC rings go to just to ensure they are re-creating the exact merchandise. When it comes to turning a profit, they don't care if they are potentially putting your child, grandmother, or friend at risk. They are mostly concerned with how they are going to resell the product for what is it going for in retail."

One mother whose child was affected by contaminated formula explained the aftereffects in graphic detail: "Every two hours my child would shit right through her diaper. But not the usual six-month-old expulsion. Her crap was runny and green. It was coming out from her underneath the gatherings of her diaper, to give you an idea of how much volume there was. The minute I would change her diaper, it would start up again. Her stomach was hurting, and this went on for six days. I would have to give her water and Pedialyte to make sure she didn't dehydrate. My baby is five months old and solid, but I can't imagine if this was a three-month-old, who are much more fragile. The whole experience was frightening and devastating."[24]

Janice Ayala, Deputy Assistant Director, Office of Investigations, United States Immigration and Customs Enforcement (ICE), testified before the Subcommittee on Crime, Terrorism, and Homeland Security. She described how an ORC ring based in San Francisco was busted in 2007 for selling products stolen from larger retailers to Rosemont Wholesale, a warehouse based in Oakland, California. The warehouse sold the medicines, razor blades, and baby formula to smaller grocery stores and on Internet sites. When the Oakland Police Department and USDA uncovered the stolen merchandise in the warehouse, they seized more than 20 tractor-trailers full of products stolen from stores such as Safeway, Target, Walgreens, and Walmart. The haul included vitamins, cold medicine, and hygiene products. When law enforcement officers went through the trash bins outside the warehouse, they found thousands of security tags and bar code labels from the retailers that were discarded.[25]

Frank Muscato of the organized retail crime division at Walgreens says that Walgreens' losses due to ORC were more than $300 million in 2010. Walgreens is one of the main retailers that criminals target. Despite being a major advocate of ORC legislation and investing tens of millions of dollars in loss prevention products, such as state-of-the-art digital systems, in-store security, antitheft tagging, merchandise tracking, retail-secure devices, and employee training,[26] Walgreens merchandise is still stolen and sold to smaller stores.

In his testimony to the Subcommittee on Crime, Terrorism, and Homeland Security, Muscato described how he observed more than 52 boosters enter a small, unassuming grocery store in Chicago with stolen property and come out counting money. In an interview, an informant admitted to traveling to Wisconsin, Indiana, Michigan, and Iowa. He sold thousands of dollars worth of merchandise, which included OTC drugs, diabetes test strips, and other health aids, to the grocery store daily. The store's owner would then sell the merchandise to other businesses in Chicago and out of state. Muscato noted that because of jurisdictional issues, out-of-state cases were not pursued, and the case was eventually dropped. Another case occurred in New York City, where three mom-and-pop grocery stores were identified by an informant as purchasing stolen property. With the NYPD's help, Muscato and Walgreens were able to uncover more than $600,000 worth of stolen property, including health aid mer-chandise, that was about to be shipped to out-of-state locations.[27] However, because of limited resources and a lack of federal jurisdic-tion, the Queens County Attorney working on the case decided not to pursue it. "Again, if ORC was identified as a specific crime in a crimi-nal code, we could have pursued the case federally," says Muscato.

Legal Issues: Defining ORC Versus Shoplifting and Shrinkage

Other reasons why ORC often flies under the radar is that federal law provides no uniform definition for this type of crime, making it difficult to track. Although the size and scope of ORC are hard to pin down, 92% of respondents to an NRF survey in 2009 reported that their companies had been a victim of ORC incidents in the past 12 months.[28]

Challenges arise when a potential ORC suspect is apprehended and charged. Law enforcement defines the type of theft in differ-ent ways. For example, ORC is loosely defined as criminals fraudu-lently obtaining goods in quantities beyond what would normally be intended for personal consumption; reselling these ill-gotten goods; receiving, concealing, transporting, or disposing of these goods; or coordinating individuals to commit these retail crimes.[29] The issue involves agreeing on how law enforcement categorizes the act of ORC. For example, cargo theft, which often plays an integral role in ORC with the sheer volumes of merchandise being stolen and sold, is categorized as a completely different and separate crime. Boosters who steal a couple of items that total $250 in most cases are prose-cuted as petty thieves if the state they are stealing from doesn't have a high value threshold for felony theft. Their cases are dropped because they are small compared to the cases in the major crimes unit. Law enforcement can currently pursue these cases under the Racketeer

Influenced and Corrupt Organizations Act (RICO), but the standards can be difficult to meet in some ORC cases.

"When a criminal goes out and steals [as part of a boosting crew], he or she doesn't always meet the felony threshold per theft incident, and RICO is looking for that felony threshold," says Millie Kresevich, a senior loss prevention manager at Luxottica Retail, a luxury and sport eyewear company.[30] Because of the separate classification, law enforcement doesn't realize that all of these criminal acts are in some way associated with an ORC ring. Congress has defined ORC in terms of the following:

- Violating a state ban against shoplifting or retail merchandise theft—if the quantities of items stolen are of the amount that would not normally be purchased for personal use or consumption—and stealing for the purposes of reselling the items or re-entering them into commerce

- Receiving, possessing, concealing, bartering, selling, transporting, or disposing of any property that is known to have been taken in the violation just outlined

- Receiving, possessing, concealing, bartering, selling, transporting, or disposing of any property that is known to have been taken in the violation just outlined, or coordinating, organizing, or recruiting persons to undertake either of the two violations just outlined[31]

Regulating the Resale Market

Despite Congress's passing of legislation to create an ORC unit at the Justice Department, no federal or congressional amendments amend U.S. Code to criminalize ORC or regulate resale markets such as online retailers, auction sites, flea markets, and other resale marketplaces where fences sell their items. As a result, all the time and effort retailers expend investigating boosters, placing surveillance on potential ORC rings, and gathering evidence ends up being irrelevant if the case doesn't meet the congressional definition of ORC or does not fall under the RICO statute.

"Federal law agencies don't count the amount of investigative time, resources, and manpower a retailer spends in trying to build a case to put these guys away," says Jerry Biggs of Walgreens. "There are cases that have taken three or four years to build, gone to great lengths in order to prove what we are losing and have lost, and because it doesn't fall under the proper state statute, or there is an agent change, we have to start all over again. The only one that gets anything out of this is the government. Everyone else is losing money."[32]

With so many resources, you would think preventing ORC would be easy—that is, until retailers start looking to the government to help them put away longtime ORC rings and their kingpins for good. Federal and state laws make things much more complicated than they have to be. It starts with a little law called the RICO statute.

11

Letting the Bad Guy Get Away

The morning after Faisal Shahzad was indicted, the term *hawala* was the third most searched term on Yahoo! and brought up 214,000 results on Google. Katie Couric was talking about it on CBS. MSNBC dedicated an entire segment to the term. Even the evening news on all major networks discussed it. Why the sudden interest in a money practice that had been around for 2,000 years? And how did this unknown man create so much media buzz?

We've covered hawalas in this book. As a review, hawalas, also known as informal funds transfers (IFTs), are not illegal if they are registered with the U.S. government and used properly. But the way in which Shahzad used a hawala included secret transfers of large sums of cash (nearly $7,000 in total was transferred from Pakistan to the U.S.) among three different people, located in New York, Massachusetts, and New Jersey. There wasn't a paper trail, which made Shahzad's use highly suspicious and illegal. Suddenly the term *hawala* became synonymous with money laundering and illegal money transfers to wage terrorist acts against the U.S.

According to the United Nations International Convention for the Suppression of Financing of Terrorism, the definition of terrorist financing is "the act of providing financial support to terrorists or terrorist organizations to enable them to carry out terrorist acts." This is exactly what Shahzad was doing by transferring funds via a hawala.

Although $7,000 might not seem like much in terms of money being transferred at one time, the World Bank estimates that the annual flow of transactions through informal banking systems ranges from tens of billions to $200 billion[1] and, of that, 3–5% is used to fund terrorism.

As it turns out, Shahzad wasn't the only homegrown terrorist using IFTs to fund terrorist plots. According to Loretta Napoleoni, author of *Modern Jihad: Tracing the Dollars Behind the Terror Networks*, jihadist terrorists have a remarkable ability to mutate their funding mechanisms to sidestep U.S. antiterrorism legislation created after 9/11.[2] Policies for terror watch lists and the establishment of the Patriot Act and Financial Action Task Force (FATF) recommendations only forced potential terrorists to think outside the box—to fund their attacks using IFTs and make them less costly and more effective.

For $7,000, Shahzad and his cohorts were able to create chaos in a central part of New York City, garnering him and his jihadist cause untold publicity. Close to $2 million in city and NYPD resources was needed to close certain streets and remove the bomb. 9/11 cost al Qaeda close to $500,000 and generated billions of dollars worth of damage. Now, homegrown terrorists are spending only a couple thousand and having just as much impact. The implementation of U.S. antiterrorism policies designed to cut off large terrorist groups at their financial source has had the opposite effect and has fueled the homegrown terrorism movement.

"On one hand, tracking terrorist income, expenditures, and financial transfers is the most powerful mechanism in the intelligence arsenal for penetrating terrorist cells and organizations," says Brig. Gen. (ret.) Russell D. Howard. "But when it comes down to enforcing established statutes and acts specifically designed to cut off terrorism right at their financial sources, they end up being totally ineffective."[3]

Terror watch lists were supposed to register people and companies suspected of bankrolling terror organizations, but such lists weren't implemented globally.[4] Countries such as France, for example, didn't use the lists because their constitutions deemed them illegal. Other countries, such as Malaysia and Saudi Arabia, failed to comply with the list altogether.

Likewise, the Patriot Act did not address terrorist financing internationally because the law was established to protect banking systems using U.S. currency within the U.S. Although it made money laundering and the use of U.S. currency more difficult, it did not address money generated by legitimate businesses funding terrorism. According to Napoleoni, the fund-raising epicenter shifted from the U.S. to Europe.[5] The GDP of the "New Economy of Terror" generated by all armed terror organizations around the world was denoted in dollars ($500 billion pre-9/11). But since the attacks, the euro has been the currency of choice. This has given rise to international criminal and terror-funding schemes such as smuggling stolen merchandise overseas.[6]

Internationally, leadership in the FATF has brought the issue of IFTs to the forefront, resulting in the implementation of FATF Special Recommendation VI. It required all FATF countries to ensure that individuals and entities providing money transmission services must be licensed and registered and subject to the international standards set out by the FATF.[7]

As the U.S. government tried to apply stricter oversight of and control over banks, it ended up causing damage (both monetarily and by being a focal point of terrorist threat) to countries in Europe, South America, Africa, and South Asia without reducing the financing of global terrorism. With such stringent regulations, fees, and bureaucracy, people (especially those who didn't have the money to pay for all the extra costs) finally got fed up and reverted to old-world ways of transferring funds. In addition, statutes within the Patriot Act failed to innovatively keep up as money-transferring instruments became more sophisticated. As a result, a great number of loopholes and deflecting the terrorist financing problem off U.S. soil resulted in a mere $200 million in terrorist assets frozen out of an estimated $850 billion.[8] Even worse, as more terrorist groups turned to product smuggling and IFTs, retailers lost an estimated billions in revenues for 2007–2010.

Regulation Epic Fail: How Banking BSAs and AML Programs Let Terrorist Funding Slip Through the Cracks

In the past, the primary objective of terrorist groups was non-financial.[9] But as the recession took hold, organizations realized that they had to get funding from other means. They needed to pay for the escalating costs of recruitment, training camps and bases, housing and food, equipment, explosives, conventional and unconventional weapons, intelligence gathering, forged identity and travel documents, and day-to-day maintenance expenses. When selling counterfeit and smuggled items, they turned to money laundering to transfer their funds.

The Patriot Act, which amended the Bank Secrecy Act (BSA), required financial institutions to establish anti-money laundering (AML) programs. These included developing internal policies, procedures, and controls; designating a compliance officer; creating an ongoing employee training program; and conducting an independent audit function to test programs.[10] The types of financial organizations required by law to have AML programs included mutual funds, operators of credit card systems, money service businesses, broker-dealer members of the Financial Industry Regulatory Authority (FINRA), broker-dealer members of the New York Stock Exchange, insurance companies, and dealers in precious metals, stones, or jewels.[11] But the AMLs were futile. For example, financial institutions are required to file a report concerning a transaction or series of related transactions in excess of $10,000 in currency. However, terrorist organizations such as the Tehreek-e-Taliban Pakistan (TTP) (the organization Shahzad was working with) transferred funds via hawalas, which is one of the most difficult IFTs to monitor and regulate.

Continued Failure to Regulate IFTs: The Costs to Local and Federal Governments as Well as Retailers

According to the BSA and Anti-Money Laundering Examination Manual for the Federal Financial Institutions Examination Council, the Patriot Act is "arguably the single most significant AML law that Congress has enacted since the BSA itself." Among other things, the Patriot Act criminalized the financing of terrorism and augmented the existing BSA framework by doing the following:

- Strengthening customer identification procedures
- Prohibiting financial institutions from engaging in business with foreign shell banks
- Requiring financial institutions to have due diligence procedures and, in some cases, enhanced due diligence procedures for foreign correspondent and private banking accounts
- Improving information sharing between financial institutions and the U.S. government[12]

The only problem was that BSAs couldn't tell authorities what was going on financially in countries like Pakistan, India, Afghanistan, and Somalia.

Even with India's recent appointment to the FATF, regulatory measures within the national banking system were in shambles. To get a firsthand look at just how bad it was, I took a trip to the State Bank of Hyderabad in India, to carry out an average retail banking transaction. What was most surprising was how the transaction was done: without computers. The day's transactions were written down in ledgers and filed away. When I asked to get an account balance "on behalf of someone else," my banker gave it to me without asking for my identification. But the most shocking part about my retail banking experience was that when I returned home, I realized that my banker had given me someone else's statement, complete with his name, account information, and *balance*.

"That's just the tip of the iceberg considering some of the stories we've heard," says Prashant Muddu, chief executive of Jocata, a financial and technology advisory company that specializes in helping banks become compliant with AML and Combating the Financing of Terrorism (CFT). "There are banks we've worked with that don't know how many customers they even have, much less know what type and the amount of funds are being transferred between accounts." Muddu, along with his colleague Gokul Kollayikal, explains while meeting with me over a cup of coffee in Hyderabad that many banks believe that extra paperwork required to track accounts and get them up to bank regulatory standards deters customers from wanting to bank with them. Therefore, they either refuse to embrace standards or turn a blind eye to them. "When you have a bank employee who is getting paid based on the amount of accounts he can bring in, why would he try and alienate potential business?" asks Kollayikal.

Failure to Regulate Hawalas

According to the World Bank, immediately following the failed bombing in Manhattan, investigators began unraveling the money trail to identify coconspirators in the attack planned and financed by the TTP. On September 15, 2010, prosecutors announced they had arrested and charged Mohamad Younis with helping finance the attack by serving as a hawaladar. Prosecutors said Younis had engaged in unlicensed hawala transactions with Shahzad and charged him with operating an unlicensed money transfer business between the U.S. and Pakistan.

As the investigation into the failed Times Square bombing shows, the use of hawalas remains a viable method for moving terrorist finances. Although expanded application of BSA reporting and recordkeeping requirements regulates hawalas and hawaladars, regulations need to start from outside the U.S. in addition to hawalas within the U.S.

"In the war on terrorism, a major challenge will be to infiltrate and monitor hawala networks in the Middle East," says Robert E. Looney, an analyst with the Center for Contemporary Conflict. "A crackdown by Arab and South Asian governments at the behest of Western governments is simply not feasible. The vast majority of the money is from legal, legitimate sources, and the hawala organizations are numerous and extremely powerful."[13]

But international cooperation from governments in countries that depend on the hawala system is difficult. People who live in rural areas of Afghanistan, Pakistan, Somalia, the Congo, and many Asian and Latin American countries use hawalas to transfer funds across borders because formal banking systems are nonexistent. Because hawalas are independently run and the networks are so vast, it is nearly impossible for governments to monitor transactions, how much money is being transferred, and to whom it is being transferred. Pakistan established a Special Investigation Group (SIG) in its Federal Investigation Agency (FIA) to counter terrorism. In addition to monitoring the cash flows of suspected terrorist groups, the group can enforce hawala regulations.[14] But currently the SIG is doing very little.

It wasn't until 2008 that the Pakistani government and the FIA cracked down on two business owners who allegedly transferred $10 billion out of Pakistan by way of hawalas. Javed Khanani and Munaf Kalia were partners in a foreign currency exchange business and were known to run their own separate and unregistered hawala counters. In addition, nine officials of the National Database and Registration Authority (NADRA) were arrested for allegedly making fake identity cards.[15]

Just months before the arrest, the SIG released a special report on the flight of dollars from the country. It stated that a forex (foreign exchange) crisis would occur in the country in the not-so-distant future.[16] The government reported that the smuggling of foreign currency has diminished the country's forex reserves from more than $16 billion in October 2007 to less than $7 billion at present.[17] In addition, Khanani and Kalia were known to have transferred millions of dollars in funds through hawalas for politicians, bureaucrats, army officers, and businessmen to send money for their children's education. They also paid installments on costly properties abroad.[18] Their actions prompted the Pakistani government to crack down on hawalas. In the wake of a global financial crisis, the mass exodus of foreign exchange from the banking system, along with rising inflation, was creating mounting financial instability in the country and costing it billions of dollars.[19]

Likewise, the government of Afghanistan was under investigation in late June 2010 regarding the nearly $3 billion in cash being transferred out of the country by airplane over three years from airport hawalas. With the economy in its infancy, Afghanistan depends on hawalas as its financial sector backbone. But the Afghan government has no way of tracking who sends money through hawalas and who is on the receiving end of transfers. According to Afghan customs records, between 2007 and 2010, close to $3.18 billion was recorded as leaving the airport. However, a courier was documented as carrying close to $2.3 billion between 2008 and 2009, and it went undocumented.[20]

Government officials also believe the money was siphoned off from money meant for Western aid projects and U.S., European, and NATO contracts providing security, supplies, and reconstruction work for coalition forces in Afghanistan.[21]

"It's virtually impossible to regulate the hawala system in countries that depend on it," says Looney. "A crackdown that attempts to ban the networks would simply drive them underground. And many of these citizens in these countries would view actions of this sort as caving to Western demands at the expense of Muslim tradition, and it could also create a backlash against the governments."[22]

IFTs Get Sophisticated: Stored Value Cards

According to the Commodity Futures Trading Commission (CFTC) web site, a financial institution and any "nonfinancial trade or business" must also report a transaction (or series of related transactions) in excess of $10,000 in currency.

In addition, the BSA requires the filing of a Form 105, Report of International Transportation of Currency and Monetary Instruments (CMIR), by anyone who physically transports, mails, ships, or causes to be physically transported, mailed, or shipped currency or other in an aggregate amount exceeding $10,000 on any one occasion, whether that transportation is into or out of the U.S. This includes the following:

- Coin or currency of the U.S. or any other country
- Travelers checks in any form
- Negotiable instruments (including checks, promissory notes, and money orders) in bearer form, endorsed without restriction, made out to a fictitious payee, or otherwise in such form that title thereto passes upon delivery
- Incomplete instruments (including checks, promissory notes, and money orders) that are signed but on which the name of the payee has been omitted
- Securities or stock in bearer form or otherwise in such form that title thereto passes upon delivery[23]

Even when you embark from an international flight, the first thing customs asks you is if you have anything more than $10,000 to declare. But criminals got sneaky.

The Patriot Act never took into consideration that money could be moved around on plastic cards that could be carried in a wallet, pocket, or handbag with amounts of up to $500,000 on them.

Bulk Cash Smuggling Comes in a Smaller Package

In the past, terrorist groups relied on methods such as bulk cash smuggling if they wanted to move large sums of money from one location to another. "Bulk cash smuggling" sounds exactly like what you would imagine it to be: thick wads of cash stashed in duffle bags, boxes, or suitcases making their way across borders undeclared and undetected by customs. As financial institutions started implementing AML programs and increased record-keeping and reporting requirements, terrorist groups realized moving money in that way was risky. Bulk cash smuggling would always be a part of their methods; it just needed more stealth. What better way to transport large sums of money than on a stored value card (SVC) that blends right into a billfold?

"No one is going to go through your wallet and ask you how much is on your credit cards," says Detective Amaury Guevara in the conference room at LAPD headquarters. He showed me all the different types of SVCs, ranging from American Express cash cards to debit cards that look similar to what I carry in my wallet. "Someone could be transporting millions of dollars a month overseas, and customs would never know, because the amounts are all on SVCs."[24]

The Treasury Department defines SVCs as "smart cards with electronic value... The technology eliminates coin, currency, scrip, vouchers, money orders, and other labor-intensive payment mechanisms."[25]

Similar to gift cards, SVCs can be obtained in a variety of locations, often without verifying identities, making them ideal as a conduit to move funds globally. The implications of this technological development in terms of terror financing and our government's inability to combat it are daunting. The threat is exacerbated by the fact that although the Treasury Department is reviewing these new products, SVCs are not currently considered "monetary instruments" for reporting and record-keeping purposes.[26]

To prove how antiquated government agencies and nongovernmental organizations (NGOs) are about trying to investigate potential terrorist financing, I read *Combating Money Laundering and the Financing of Terrorism*, the comprehensive workbook issued by the World Bank. Although this training manual was revised in 2009, it still doesn't take into consideration the new instruments terrorists are using to transfer funds. For example, the manual explains why money laundering has negative effects on developing nations, and what the FATF does. But when it comes to explaining what types of measures I should take if I encounter someone trying to smuggle more than $10,000 across the border, it lists the following tactics:

- Work with customs enforcement agents to identify the instruments (diamonds, cash, checks, and so on)
- File cash transaction reports (CTRs)
- Question clients if accounts seem to have suspiciously large sums of money being transferred
- Analyze bank records
- Work with Financial Intelligence Units (FIUs)

FATF regulations never mention funds transferred by other means, such as SVCs and online accounts, or through stolen merchandise such as DVDs, handbags, high-end clothing, and electronics.

According to Detective Guevara, what comes as a surprise to most law enforcement officials (but shouldn't) is the rapid evolution of these monetary instruments. He points out that today government officials and decision makers are talking about SVCs. Meanwhile, terrorist groups are looking at the online game Second Life, where members purchase fake items with real dollars online, as a way to move money. The terrorists' Internet and gaming savvy clearly is dwarfing the scope of law enforcement.

"Rather than simply [resting] on their laurels, terrorist groups have shown an incredible ability to adapt changing technologies to their needs and stay one step ahead of our regulatory and law enforcement officers," says Stephen I. Landman, Director, National Security Law and Policy at the Investigative Project on Terrorism. "The creation of stored value cards and the expansion of the Internet are just two of the problems that those tasked with countering terrorist financing will face over the next decade."

Although these figures are still difficult to track, the World Bank estimates that billions of dollars are illegally transferred on SVCs, with a loss of hundreds of millions of dollars to retailers in the U.S. and billions of dollars worldwide.

Retailers Feel the Pain of SVC Fraud

Stores within the U.S. felt the impact of SVC usage as money laundering instruments. In 2005, the National Retail Security Survey found that the average loss to retailers from gift card fraud (another form of SVC) was approximately $72,000. The cost increased in 2010 by nearly 2,000%. The retailers that responded to the survey attributed 62% of the losses to employee conduct, 13% to counterfeit or "skimmed" cards, and 13% to stolen cards.[27] Most of the fraud happens internally with clerks who remove the card's bar code and switch it with an item that is being purchased. When a customer purchases the item, he is actually putting value on the gift card. Employee fraud involving gift cards and stored value cards has grown sharply and is costing the retail industry an estimated $36 billion, or 1.51% of retail sales.[28]

"The recession really took a toll on regulating internal fraud, because there was so much employee turnover," says Joe LaRocca of the NRF. "By losing their most valuable and trustworthy employees because of staff cuts, retailers ended up taking a significant hit to their bottom lines. The lesson to be learned here is retailers need to get more sophisticated when it comes to tracking their sales and reporting if they want to stop this problem."[29]

Credit Card Fraud Is Even Worse

SVCs weren't the only digital monetary instruments that piqued the interest of potential fund-moving terrorists. In Los Angeles, Detective Guevara noticed how many of the criminals who had been investigated years ago and had since been jailed were using outside sources to devise and mastermind credit card fraud schemes.

"What's happening is that a lot of these once-violent criminals have aged and since learned a new, nonviolent way of stealing money," he says. "Money laundering has been around for centuries. This method is being handed to a new generation that does everything digitally."

In 2006, total credit card fraud losses in the U.S. alone were estimated at $3.718 billion.[30] Credit card companies paid the most dollar cost, along with point-of-sale (POS) merchants. Internet and mail order and telephone merchants were in second and third place.[31] The worldwide statistic is much higher.

Guevara notes that if there was a stereotype of a money laundering person, it doesn't apply to those involved in credit card fraud. From the financially desperate to kids younger than 20, people engaging in credit card fraud are unassuming and as average as someone sitting in a Starbucks with a Wi-Fi connection and a pair of headphones.

In November 2008, hackers broke into RBS Worldpay, a U.S. payment processing subsidiary of the Royal Bank of Scotland. They gained access to the data of 1.5 million cardholders and distributed the information to a network of "cashiers" working with them. As the "cashiers" created counterfeit payment cards, hackers went into the RBS Worldpay computer systems and modified the accounts so that the available funds on the cards and the limits on the cash were all raised. Over just 12 hours, the cashiers went on a spree, withdrawing $9 million from 2,100 ATMs in 280 cities worldwide.[32]

In June 2010, 178 individuals were arrested in a global credit card fraud ring based in Spain. The ring was broken into 14 different subgroups that were based in France, Italy, Germany, Ireland, Romania, Australia, Sweden, Greece, Finland, Hungary, and the U.S. Each group had a leader, who was the only one with direct contact to the larger ringleader. Individuals used stolen bank card numbers to create counterfeit cards and make ATM withdrawals and purchase items at retailers. The raid garnered 5,000 counterfeit cards and 120,000 stolen card numbers.[33] To give an example of how intricate this scheme was, the Spanish authorities found 11 laboratories where members of the group were producing the cards.[34] Overall, the group was said to have raked in close to $24.5 million for credit card fraud, along with extortion, robbery with force, and sexual exploitation. Says Guevara, "It's not just one crime like credit card fraud these criminals are involved in. It's just one of several."

Retailers such as GameStop and T.J. Maxx bore the brunt of international credit and identity fraud rings in a way that significantly affected their sales. According to LaRocca, in a separate incident, a ring of Vietnamese nationals fraudulently bought DVDs and games with stolen credit card information. Then they took the merchandise and resold it on online auction sites by setting up fake names. In addition, these nationals took the product and sent it back to Vietnam, costing the stores millions of dollars. Likewise, T.J. Maxx experienced a system hack in which a theft ring obtained customers' information and sold it to another ring in Eastern Europe. The Eastern European ring resold the information to Internet chat rooms and created fake credit card profiles, using them to acquire gift cards and then sold those cards online.

"These are very sophisticated rings that comprise field operatives and ringleaders working together," says LaRocca. "Typically the leaders will farm out the dirty work to the operatives, who are mostly illegal immigrants or foreign nationals. Their system purposefully has several technological layers, each done to throw off authorities. It's quick, virtually undetectable, and costs retailers a lot of money."

Even with the cooperation of the World Bank and International Monetary Fund (IMF), and mandatory compliance with FATF regulations, many countries have yet to effectively regulate money laundering and terrorist financing. The reasons for the lack of regulation are not complicated. Countries simply can't seem to define exactly what constitutes terrorist financing offenses. They can't figure out whether their laws already have clauses that allow potential terrorists to be prosecuted under the predicated FATF terrorist offenses list. Finally, if they don't have clauses, they can't seem to figure out how to be in sync with FATF regulations. Government bureaucracy is preventing money laundering from being suspended on an international level.

Domestically, retailers' loss of money is just the beginning of their worries. The ripple effect goes as far as the consumer psyche, says LaRocca. When consumers realize a retailer has been the target of credit card fraud, they tend to be more hesitant to go back to that retailer. At times it takes up to 90 days for consumers to get their money back if they have been a target of credit card fraud. Publicly, the retailer is lambasted in the media, and that sentiment doesn't go away easily.

"As retailers, all we can do is be vigilant about protecting our databases and continuously develop more sophisticated security measures.

We've done a lot of work, brought in partners for Immigration and Customs Enforcement (ICE) and the Federal Bureau of Investigation (FBI), and they knew who to reach out to, but the longer we let this problem go on, it's customers who end up paying the higher price for it," says LaRocca.[35]

RICO Defined

In 1970, the U.S. Congress passed the Racketeer Influenced and Corrupt Organizations Act (RICO). The statute provided extended penalties for criminal acts performed as part of an ongoing criminal enterprise. Its intent is to eliminate the influence of organized crime on interstate commerce.[36]

RICO was originally intended to target members of the mafia. The statute holds that "any person or organization who commits a combination of two or more crimes within a ten-year period can be charged with racketeering if the prosecution feels that those crimes were committed with a similar purpose or result."[37] Because the definition of "racketeering" is so general, 35 different crimes fall under its coverage, and sentencing can be steep. An individual found guilty of racketeering can be fined as much as $25,000 and sentenced to 25 years in prison. If an individual is found guilty of multiple crimes, jail time and fines could quadruple, depending on what he is being charged with.

Penalties for money laundering can also be severe. A person convicted of money laundering can face up to 20 years in prison and fines of up to $500,000.[38] Any property involved in a transaction or that can be traced to the proceeds of criminal activity—including property such as loan collateral, personal property, and, in some cases, entire bank accounts—may be subject to forfeiture. There are also criminal penalties for willful violations of the BSA and its implementing regulations under 31 USC 5322 and for structuring transactions to evade BSA reporting requirements under 31 USC 5324 (d). If a person, including a bank employee, willfully violates the BSA or its implementing regulations, they are subject to a criminal fine of up to $250,000 or five years in prison, or both.[39] Anyone who commits such a violation while violating another U.S. law or engaging in a pattern of criminal activity is subject to a fine of up to $500,000 or ten years in prison, or both.[40]

The RICO statute also allows the entire criminal organization to be prosecuted, as opposed to an individual. With its broad base and ability to go after an entire crime ring, it would seem like RICO would be a no-brainer when it comes to prosecuting ORC rings, especially those funding terrorism via money laundering schemes.

Guess again.

Why ORC Rings Still Exist: Money Laundering and the RICO Statute

"Money laundering is one area where the all-purpose cliché about 'September 11 changed everything' is certainly true," says Professor Ibrahim Warde. However, the change wasn't necessarily for the better. Professor Warde explains that money laundering is fundamentally different from terrorist financing. After 9/11, the government was pressed to do something immediate and drastic to reassure the public and project resolve. Focusing on the finances of terrorist organizations was the answer to a politically motivated need for a swift and muscular response, where the existing money laundering apparatus, as well as racketeering statutes and the Patriot Act, were the proverbial "hammer in a child's hand."[41]

"Terrorist financing now is a small part of a much broader, largely amorphous, and certainly ill-understood network," says Professor Warde. "The amounts needed to fund terrorist operations are small, and such amounts can easily bypass the formal banking system. Furthermore, terrorist financing is in many ways the opposite of money laundering: it is not about cleaning dirty money, but about soiling clean money. And clean money, by its very nature, is consistent with a customer's profile, and cannot be spotted by financial institutions."

The inadequacy of money laundering mechanisms are so general that they bypass the true backbone of terrorist funding. The organized crime rings use "clean" money and non-banking funding mechanisms to transfer money to terrorist groups overseas. Although the money might not be "dirty," the act of obtaining it is still illegal. Although the Patriot Act cracked down on unregistered money transmitters in the U.S. and bank accounts abroad, potential organizations funding terrorism without using bank accounts essentially fell through the cracks.

The RICO statute lists specific violations of federal law, including money laundering, violations of the BSA, and mail and wire fraud, among others.[42] But it doesn't include the use of supplementary mechanisms in its definition, such as unregulated Internet accounts, stored value cards, gift cards, and the other ways money can be transferred between terrorist groups without the need for banking systems. In addition, sentencing under the RICO statute can be less stringent compared to a sentence for providing material support for terrorism. Faisal Shahzad received a life sentence.

An umbrella enforcement of the RICO statute doesn't adequately sentence ORC members involved in terrorist acts. Instead, it protects them because of more lenient sentences.

More Problems with RICO: It's in the Definition

With any far-reaching law, the terms that are used to define and ultimately convict a group of people (in this case, a group of people funding and providing material support to al Qaeda) can get hazy. In

2001, a group of 3,000 individuals composed of survivors, family members, representatives of victims, and insurance carriers alleged that more than 200 defendants (including charities, banks, front organizations, terrorist organizations, and financiers who provided financial, logistical, and other support) directly or indirectly provided material support to al Qaeda. The plaintiffs sought to convict the defendants under the RICO conspiracy provision (18 U.S.C.A. 1962).[43] But language, and the way in which the RICO statute is structured, prevented the conviction from going through.

The court concluded that although the "complaints allege the moving defendants may have assisted al Qaeda ... they do not allege 'anything approaching active management or operation.'" In reaching this conclusion, the court relied on prior decisions of the Southern District to the effect that operation or management was not satisfied "merely by engaging in wrongful conduct that assists the enterprise" and that simply "providing services to [a] racketeering enterprise is not directing the enterprise." Accordingly, the court concluded that the plaintiffs had failed to satisfy the test of Reves and thus had failed to plead a viable RICO claim under section 1962(c) In re: TERRORIST ATTACKS ON SEPTEMBER 11, 2001. 392 F. Supp. 2d 539, 546 (S.D.N.Y. 2005).[44]

Despite 200 people allegedly funding al Qaeda, they were not convicted because they didn't fit into RICO's definition of an "enterprise." What's more, the 200 people funded the attack by not using a banking system. This model of financing is being duplicated not only in the U.S. but also internationally, and terrorist organizations engaging in it are not being scrutinized.

The trial of the Hammoud brothers highlights another loophole in the RICO statute, which has to do with how individuals funding a terrorist organization are tried and convicted. Mohamad Hammoud, the Lebanese immigrant based in North Carolina, became involved with Hezbollah at age 15.[45] After several years in the U.S., Hammoud recruited friends and family members to create his own cell of

Hezbollah sympathizers. This is when they got involved with cigarette smuggling as a way to generate income for the terrorist organization.

Hammoud also engaged in egregious fraud activities. He applied for a business loan of $1.6 million to build a BP gas station where the stolen cigarettes were to be sold. When the cell members were finally caught, authorities concluded that the cell purchased $7.5 million to $8 million worth of cigarettes for $1.5 million to $2.5 million in profits.[46]

What's more, authorities found that Hammoud and his accomplices were also committing immigration fraud by marrying American women just to stay in the country. In some instances, members of the cell had wives and children back in Lebanon.

The men were convicted under the RICO statute but were tried as thieves, not terrorists. Mohamad Hamoud received 155 years in prison for providing material support to Hezbollah. But his brother, Chawki Hammoud, who had just as much involvement in the scheme, was sentenced to 51 months for his role. The other brother, Said Harb, was sentenced to 46 months.[47]

The estimated cost to the state of Michigan was $20 million a year in tobacco tax.[48]

Like the Hammoud brothers, Ulises Talevera's Sony PlayStation 2 ring out of Miami might encounter the same loopholes when it comes to convicting them as a business entity providing material support to a terrorist organization as opposed to thieves. Until the RICO statute and the Patriot Act evolve to include crime rings that engage in theft to fund terrorism, funding on a massive scale will go unnoticed.

Laws That Once Protected Potential Terrorists Have Changed

The Antiterrorism and Effective Death Penalty Act of 1996 (AEDPA) says that ORC ring operatives may not provide "material support" in the form of service, training, explosives, lodging, communications equipment, or expert advice and assistance to a terrorist organization. Section 302 authorizes the Secretary of State to designate a group as a "foreign terrorist organization," and section 303 makes it a crime to provide "material support or resources" to nonviolent activities of a designated organization.[49] Congress passed an amendment to AEDPA known as the Intelligence Reform and Terrorism Prevention Act (IRTPA). It further clarified the Act, stating that individuals must "knowingly provide material support or resources" to violate the Act.

There are two issues when it comes to criminalizing potential terrorists under the RICO statute and the Patriot Act: knowledge of actually funding the act, and providing "material support." It's unclear how the terms "material support" and "coordination" are defined, so ultimately it's unclear what's legal or illegal according to the U.S. Constitution.

Defining "Material Support" and "Coordination"

In June 2010, the U.S. Supreme Court ruled that the government had the power to criminalize "material support" of a foreign terrorist organization in the decision *Holder v. Humanitarian Law Project*. This included those who provide service, training, expert advice, or assistance to groups designated and defined by the U.S. government as terrorist organizations.[50] The court ruling wasn't unanimous; the justices were divided. They applied "strict scrutiny" (the highest level of judiciary review the Supreme Court can issue) due in part to the definition of the words "support" and "coordination." For example, participating in coordinated speech with terrorist organizations might harm national security in the form of giving advice to designated terrorist organizations. Justice Stephen Breyer said the law could be interpreted too broadly for the sake of protecting Americans, asking "Precisely how does application of the statute to protected activities help achieve that important security-related end?" in the ruling.

The case came about when the Humanitarian Law Project, a nonprofit organization "dedicated to protecting human rights and promoting the peaceful resolution of conflict by using established international human rights laws and humanitarian law," decided to advocate on behalf of two ongoing cases. One case involved a collection of organizations supportive of the humanitarian and political activities of the Liberation Tigers of Tamil Eelam (LTTE) in Sri Lanka. The other involved a group headed by University of California professor Ralph Fertig, who wanted to advise the Kurdistan Workers' Party (PKK) on how to take its grievances against Turkey to the United Nations.[51] According to the Humanitarian Law Project, both activist groups were advocating for human rights and peacemaking. However, the Tamil separatists and the PKK had been designated as terrorist groups by former Secretary of State Madeleine Albright in 1996.

Chief Justice John Roberts Jr. stated in his ruling that "seemingly benign services" to a terrorist organization "bolsters the terrorist activities of that organization" by making it easier for the group to recruit members and raise funds.[52]

It's important to note that the Supreme Court ruling comes with a provision: Activities, even if deemed peaceful, can be banned if they are "coordinated with or controlled by foreign terrorist groups." The Supreme Court does not provide guidance on what "coordinating" specifically means. Also, the ban does not extend to domestic terrorist groups.[53]

Although many human rights activists deem the ban a violation of their First Amendment rights, Supreme Court Justice Elena Kagan argued before becoming a Chief Justice that any support of terrorist organizations, whether in the name of peace or otherwise, still supports terrorism.

"Hezbollah builds bombs," she said of the Lebanese militancy group. "Hezbollah also builds homes. What Congress decided was when you help Hezbollah build homes, you are also helping Hezbollah build bombs. That's the entire theory behind this statute, and it's a reasonable theory."[54]

The ruling puts an entirely new value on communication between ORC groups who collaborate with terrorist organizations. It also extends a ban on those who want to fund terrorism by providing funds through charitable organizations, secret accounts, hawalas, and wire transfers of money. "Providing material support" doesn't just come in the form of monetary assistance, according to the court ruling. Advice, as shown, can be just as powerful as the transfer of funds. But even with this ruling, the U.S. government must take steps to clarify what the parameters of intent or coordination truly are. In addition, this policy helps protect and bolster homeland security within the U.S., but without international support, protecting what is happening within our borders will be a futile mission.

Even though we know how deep ORC runs and the vast impact it has on our personal and global security, and although we have devised ways to respond to this threat, will the problem ever end?

Epilogue

On May 1, 2011, President Barack Obama announced that a team of Navy SEALs had stormed a compound in Abbottabad, Pakistan and assassinated the FBI's most wanted fugitive, Osama bin Laden. While the world celebrated, Jeannie Evans from Franklin Square, Long Island sat on her couch and, upon hearing the news, didn't react. "I thought to myself, 'So what?'" she said. "There are a million more we need to catch."

I met Jeannie on the afternoon that President Obama was scheduled to lay a wreath at Ground Zero in New York City. Her brother, Robert E. Evans, had been a firefighter at Engine 33, Ladder 9 in Lower Manhattan. The 36-year-old died while trying to leave the North Tower on 9/11, according to reports. Like any family member, Jeannie went through a range of emotions on that fateful day in 2001. But as she watched streams of people crowd Times Square and Ground Zero chanting "USA! USA! USA!" and holding up signs celebrating bin Laden's death, she could only describe her feelings as numb. "It's hard to celebrate when there is so much more work that needs to be done."

Jeannie's sentiment has been echoed by many fighting the war against terrorism and terrorist financing. "We cannot relax just because bin Laden is no longer in the picture," said Rep. Mac Thornberry (R-TX) in an interview with *Politico*. Referring to Anwar al-Awlaki's thwarted attacks in which he sent suicide bombers on planes and toner cartridges through the mail to blow people up, Thornberry points out that terrorism didn't begin and end with bin Laden.

Likewise, Pentagon top attorney Jeh Johnson affirmed what so many sources said when I interviewed them for this book: "The conflict against al Qaeda is evolving because that organization is evolving. It is more decentralized than it was ten years ago."[1]

Led by Baitullah Mehsud's Tehreek-e-Taliban, al Qaeda-inspired "independent cells" are spreading "Talibanization" across the Northwest Frontier Province (NWFP) and several of its districts next to the FATA regions. Almost 90 suicide attacks took place in various parts of the area between January and June of 2008. The abduction of the Pakistani ambassador to Afghanistan, the beheadings of suspected spies, and criminal acts in the Waziristan and Mohmand areas, as well as repeated attacks on video and music shops in and outside of the tribal areas, offer ample evidence that, however small in number, the Taliban zealots are out to spread their message and enforce their "code of life" with bombs and guns.[2]

But the Talibanization of regions of Afghanistan and Pakistan is just the tip of the iceberg. More factions of terrorist cells similar to al Qaeda are gaining momentum worldwide (the al Shabaab in Somalia, for example). Terrorist financing sources from wealthy, high-profile countries such as Saudi Arabia, Qatar, and Yemen are starting to lose interest in floating money to the larger organization and have started looking to more local politically minded cells. In an interview with the *Wall Street Journal*, Jean Charles Brisard, an international expert on terrorism finance, said organizations such as al Qaeda no longer frequently use the traditional financial system. Instead, they rely on couriers to take money to operatives. "[The traditional financial system] is basically useless," he said.[3]

Even with countries such as India joining the FATF and imposing more stringent banking regulations, there is no real way to regulate the black market despite tighter controls from the federal and local government. Yes, the U.S. Department of Justice may have been aware that proceeds of black market cigarettes and Viagra were being sent to the Hezbollah,[4] but was it tracking where the sale of OTC Prilosec and Pepcid AC was going? What about the sale of high-end handbags, clothing, and jewelry? My research took me to Mexican border towns, flea markets in less-than-desirable parts of town, Islamic communities in upstate New York, black market rupee exchanges in India, the back of LAPD undercover vehicles, and on tours of secret warehouses where stolen merchandise was being housed. But nothing resonated with me more than when I bought stolen OTC antacid from the Queen of Sheba grocery store. After doing extensive surveillance, the Walgreens organized retail crime division discovered that the store's owner had an estimated $14.5 million in the bank. And that wasn't from the sale of 40-ounce cans of beer. Boxes of stolen Prilosec OTC were found in the basement. A stream of potential sellers had been going to the back of the store and dropping off the stolen merchandise. But apart from the obvious charge of selling illicit OTC drugs, the store owner was never charged with money laundering because the Queens district attorney's office chose not to pursue it. "$14.5 million in the bank, and this guy wasn't involved in money laundering?" exclaimed a source close to the case. "I can't imagine how many cases the D.A.'s office allows to slip through the cracks because they don't feel like chasing down the money trail."

And therein lies the problem. High-profile busts of notorious terrorists may be good for the American psyche. But unless investigators at both the local and federal level as well as retailers band together to cut off terrorist financing at the grassroots level by regulating the black market, the cycle will continue.

Believe it or not, I was thinking about all this as I hurried down to the Christian Louboutin store on a sunny April day. It was the first really warm day after a bitterly cold winter. I wanted to celebrate not only the dogwoods blooming, but also finishing my second draft of this book. After a year of being holed up in a research library, I had decided to spend a bit of my savings on a pair of shoes I had coveted for nearly four years. The store was unusually crowded, with about 20 people milling about, trying on shoes and waiting to pay for their merchandise. At 6:42 PM, while most of the customers were near the cash register, a couple dressed in designer duds, sitting near the door (who, by the way, fit in perfectly with the other clientele) got up and walked out with three pairs of shoes. In shock, the manager went running after the couple, who ended up being, of all things, part of a booster ring. The manager returned to the store defeated. The total cost to the store was $3,000. Five members of the NYPD came to the store, joking about the merchandise ("Hey, where are my shoes?" yelled a female officer). They took as many notes as they could. They discussed monitoring web sites such as eBay and Craigslist to potentially track the sale of the shoes. But they all agreed there was pretty much no way to trace who took them.

As I was getting ready to pay for my shoes, I asked the manager if this type of situation happened a lot. He looked at me with an exhausted expression and said, "This is nothing. The other day someone came in here with a stolen credit card number on a real credit card and charged $10,000 worth of merchandise. I didn't press charges, though." Perplexed, I asked why not. "She was only 20 years old, and $10,000 is grand larceny. I would have ruined her life, and I didn't want that on my conscience."

And just like that, the cycle of retail crime repeats itself.

Glossary

Al Aqsa Martyrs Brigade

A coalition of Palestinian nationalist militias in the West Bank. The group's name refers to the Al Aqsa Mosque in Jerusalem. The organization has been designated as a terrorist group by the governments of Israel, the U.S., Canada, Japan, and the European Union. Many Palestinian people believe that the Al Aqsa Martyrs Brigade is a group that defends Palestinian rights by lawful resistance.

Al Farooq Mosque

A mosque in Brooklyn that came under scrutiny when it was discovered that several Brooklyn businessmen and a cleric from Yemen had funneled more than $20 million to al Qaeda, according to prosecutors.

al Khifa

A Muslim organization that had numerous branch offices, the largest of which was in the Al Farooq mosque in Brooklyn. In the mid-1980s, it was set up as one of the first outposts of Abdullah Yusuf Azzam and Osama bin Laden's Maktab al-Khidamat. (This organization was known to have raised money to recruit foreign mujahideen to fight the Soviets in Afghanistan. Then it became the main fundraising organization for al Qaeda.) Other cities with branches of al Khifa include Chicago, Pittsburgh, Tucson, Atlanta, and Boston. Al Khifa recruited American Muslims to fight in Afghanistan. Some of them participated in terrorist actions in the U.S. in the early 1990s and in al Qaeda operations elsewhere, including the 1998 attacks on U.S. embassies in East Africa.

Alpha Trading

A shell warehouse in Illinois where many Level 2 fences sold their merchandise.

al Qaeda

From the Arabic *al-qa`ida*, meaning "the base." A loosely knit militant Islamic organization led and funded by the late Osama bin Laden. It was established in the late 1980s and was made up of Arab volunteers who had fought the Soviet troops previously based in Afghanistan. Al Qaeda is known or believed to be behind a number of operations against Western (especially American) interests, including bomb attacks on two U.S. embassies in Africa in 1998 and the 9/11 attacks in 2001.

al Shabaab

Arabic for "the youth" or "the lads." Al Shabaab is an Islamist insurgent group fighting to overthrow the government of Somalia. The group is an offshoot of the Islamic Courts Union, which splintered into several smaller groups after its removal from power by Ethiopian forces in 2006. The group describes itself as waging jihad against "enemies of Islam." It is engaged in combat against the Somali Transitional Federal Government (TFG) and African Union Mission to Somalia (AMISOM). It has reportedly declared war on the UN and on Western nongovernmental organizations that distribute food aid in Somalia, killing 42 relief workers in 2008 and 2009 and is currently blocking Somalians' access to Western aid groups while it controls areas that have been declared famine zones since 2011. Several Western governments and security services have designated al Shabaab as a terrorist organization. It has been described as having ties to al Qaeda, which its leaders denied as of early 2010.

ARAPA

Albuquerque Retail Assets Protection Association. Karen Fischer is the brains behind ARAPA, the partnership which builds "local trust" for law enforcement and Albuquerque police to feel comfortable in exchanging information on incidents. Trust building on a local level allows personnel from both sides to feel comfortable in opening the door to proactive, public-private collaboration. It is also what LAAORCA is based on.

aspirational shopper
Someone who occasionally splurges on a purchase of an expensive handbag, a pair of shoes, or a piece of clothing to feel and seem the same as those who can regularly buy such goods.

BAD-CATS (Burglary Auto Detail, Commercial Auto Thefts)
The Los Angeles police department cargo theft squad.

Bank Secrecy Act (BSA) of 1970
Also known as the Currency and Foreign Transactions Reporting Act. Requires U.S. financial institutions to assist U.S. government agencies to detect and prevent money laundering. Specifically, the act requires financial institutions to keep records of cash purchases of negotiable instruments, to file reports of cash transactions exceeding $10,000 (daily aggregate amount), and to report suspicious activity that might indicate money laundering, tax evasion, or other criminal activities. It was passed by the U.S. Congress in 1970. The BSA is sometimes called an anti-money laundering (AML) law.

BAORCA (Bay Area Organized Retail Crime Association)
San Francisco's organized retail crime database system, modeled after Los Angeles' LAAORCA.

Bertelsmann Transformation Index (BTI)
An international ranking of 125 developing and transition countries. It considers the political and economic status of each country and the political management performance by the relevant actors by publishing two rankings, the Status Index and the Management Index.

Bloods

A street gang founded in Los Angeles, California, widely known for its rivalry with the Crips.

booster

Someone who steals merchandise from stores. Also known as a *runner*.

A Level 1 booster fits the image of a typical shoplifter—an emotionally needy starlet, the little old lady across the hall, the neighborhood heroin addict. The person usually has a drug, gambling, or alcohol addiction and steals to fund fixes. The Level 1 booster may steal on her own or in a group.

A Level 2 booster is more organized, tends to travel to different states, and takes an entrepreneurial approach to boosting by creating a small business out of it. Level 2 boosters work in groups of two or three people made up of a man and two women or all women. They coordinate a hit on a store that takes three or four minutes, stealing anywhere from a couple items all the way up to a hundred items (if they are stealing OTC drugs). Because Level 2 boosters operate in a group, their mission is to pull as many products as possible in a short amount of time and then later sell them.

A Level 3 booster is tactical and strategic, having boosted for many years. He now runs a larger organization that recruits Level 1 and Level 2 boosters. Most Level 3 fences make profits of $2.5 to $18 million, according to the NRF and RILA. Level 3 fences and boosters include all races and involve international organized criminals, gangs, Nigerian criminal enterprises, Irish travelers, and traditional mobsters such as La Cosa Nostra. Level 3 boosters organize at a high level, have a tight and organized network, and tend to send much of their profits to support overseas terrorist groups in Latin America, Africa, the Middle East, Ireland, or Italy.

booster bag

A common tool that Level 2 and Level 3 boosters use. It is made from an actual store bag taken from a prior boosting hit or obtained through a legitimate purchase. It is lined with several layers of sensor-eclipsing material such as aluminum foil or cellophane. This masks the security tags on the clothing, CDs, DVDs, or other items and keeps the store's security detection systems at the front from being set off.

Bureau of Economic Analysis
A branch of the U.S. Department of Commerce that reports the GDP (gross domestic product) every quarter.

Cargonet
A database created by the FBI and ICE in conjunction with RILA and local police departments.

cargo theft
For statistical purposes, the FBI defines cargo theft as "the criminal taking of any cargo including, but not limited to, goods, chattels, money, or baggage that constitutes, in whole or in part, a commercial shipment of freight moving in commerce, from any pipeline system, railroad car, motortruck, or other vehicle, or from any tank or storage facility, station house, platform, or depot, or from any vessel or wharf, or from any aircraft, air terminal, airport, aircraft terminal, or air navigation facility, or from any intermodal container, intermodal chassis, trailer, container freight station, warehouse, freight distribution facility, or freight consolidation facility." After 9/11, cargo theft was estimated to be between $30 and $50 billion annually. ORC accounts for almost half of these losses.

Ciudad del Este
Spanish for "city of the east." The second-largest city in Paraguay and capital of the Alto Paraná department, located at the Rio Paraná. It is part of a triangle known as the Triple Frontera (Triple Border), or *Tríplice Fronteira* in Portuguese.

clan-based militia

A militia rooted in an ethnic group in countries such as Somalia, created to overthrow the government. With more than 15 years of civil war and the absence of a central government, the rights of the Somali population have been left in the hands of sharia courts and clan-based local authorities with militia powers. Clan rivalries and the inefficiency of institutions that might otherwise establish a consistent rule of law have exposed Somalia's civilian population to human rights abuses without effective legal recourse.

Coalition of Law Enforcement and Retail (CLEAR)

A partnering organization between law enforcement and loss prevention professionals.

Combating Organized Retail Crime Act of 2009

Introduced to Congress in February 2009 in an effort to curb the illegal activity taking place in flea markets, pawnshops, and online marketplaces such as Craigslist and eBay.

credit card fraud

In 2006, total credit card fraud losses in the U.S. alone were estimated at $3.718 billion. Credit card companies paid the most, along with point-of-sale (POS) merchants. Internet and mail order and telephone merchants were in second and third places. The worldwide numbers are much higher.

Crips

Primarily, but not exclusively, an African-American gang founded in Los Angeles, California in 1969. Now a loosely connected network of individual sets, often engaged in open warfare with other gangs, such as the Bloods. The Crips are one of the largest and most violent associations of street gangs in the U.S., with an estimated 30,000 to 35,000 members. The gang is known to be involved in murders, robberies, and drug dealing, among many other criminal pursuits. The gang is known for its members' use of the color blue in their clothing.

Department of Homeland Security (DHS)

A cabinet department of the U.S. federal government created in response to the 9/11 attacks. Its primary responsibility is to protect the territory of the U.S. from terrorist attacks and to respond to natural disasters. Whereas the Department of Defense is charged with military actions abroad, the DHS works in the civilian sphere to protect the U.S. within, at, and outside its borders.

deployed counterfeit ORC ringleader

Someone who supervises booster crews and is involved in cashing in fraudulent receipts from retail stores.

drug trafficking organization (DTO)

The major DTOs (drug cartels) are Mexican and Colombian and are said to generate a total of $18 to $39 billion in wholesale drug proceeds per year. Mexican cartels are currently considered the greatest organized crime threat to the U.S.

e-fencing

Describes boosters who sell stolen items on Internet sites such as eBay, DHgate, and Alibaba.

FARC (Revolutionary Armed Forces of Colombia)

Also known as the People's Army (in Spanish, *Fuerzas Armadas Revolucionarias de Colombia – Ejército del Pueblo*) or FARC-EP. A Marxist-Leninist revolutionary guerrilla organization based in Colombia that is involved in the ongoing Colombian armed conflict. FARC-EP is a peasant army that has proclaimed itself to be a revolutionary agrarian, anti-imperialist Marxist-Leninist organization of Bolivarian inspiration. It claims to represent the rural poor in a struggle against Colombia's wealthier classes. It opposes U.S. influence in Colombia (Plan Colombia), neo-imperialism, monopolization of natural resources by multinational corporations, and paramilitary or government violence. It funds itself principally through ransom kidnappings and taxation of the illegal drug trade. FARC-EP remains the largest and oldest insurgent group in the Americas.

FATA (Federally Administered Tribal Areas)
A semiautonomous tribal region in the northwest of Pakistan between the province of Khyber Pakhtunkhwa, Balochistan, and the neighboring country of Afghanistan. FATA comprises seven agencies (tribal districts) and six FRs (frontier regions). The territory is almost exclusively inhabited by Pukhtoon (Pathan) tribes who are predominantly Sunni Muslims by faith.

fatwa
A legal pronouncement in Islam issued by a religious law specialist on a specific issue.

FBI's Joint Terrorism Task Force (JTTF)
A partnership between various U.S. law enforcement agencies that is charged with taking action against terrorism. This includes investigating crimes such as wire fraud and identity theft. The agencies that comprise a JTTF generally include the FBI, other federal agencies (notably, Department of Homeland Security components such as the U.S. Coast Guard Investigative Service, U.S. Immigration and Customs Enforcement, U.S. Customs and Border Protection, Transportation Security Administration, U.S. Secret Service, and the Department of State's Diplomatic Security Service), state and local law enforcement, and specialized agencies such as railroad police. JTTFs engage in surveillance, electronic monitoring, source development, and interviews in their pursuits. FBI task forces obtain written memoranda of understanding (MOUs) between participating law enforcement agencies. The FBI provides funds to pay for participating agencies' expenses, such as officer overtime, vehicles, fuel, cell phones, and related office costs.

Federal Motor Carrier Safety Administration (FMCSA)
Established January 1, 2000 to regulate the U.S. trucking industry.
FMCSA is headquartered in Washington, D.C. and employs more
than 1,000 people in all 50 states and the District of Columbia. Its
primary mission is improving the safety of commercial motor vehicles
(CMVs) and truck drivers through enactment and enforcement of
safety regulations.

fence
Someone who purchases the items boosters steal and sells them on
the black and gray markets. Fences and fencing operations are the
point people who sell stolen merchandise to consumers at flea markets, swap meets, pawnshops, and online auction sites (a practice also
known as *e-fencing*). Fences often operate legitimate businesses in
conjunction with illegitimate enterprises. Fences can be either commercial or residential.

A Level 1 fence is a low-level fence often called a *street fence*. This
kind of fence steals merchandise in small quantities and either sells
or exchanges it quickly for cash. Most Level 1 fences are drug addicts
and sell the merchandise on the street at swap meets or flea markets.

A Level 2 fence, also known as a *mid-level* fence, works with accomplices, often using cell phones, wireless devices, and e-mail to communicate and lift product across state borders.

A Level 3 fence is a *high-level* fence who works in an organized group
of up to eight people. They cover large geographic areas such as the
Eastern and Western Seaboards or big sections of the Midwest. They
move tens of thousands of dollars worth of merchandise a day.

Financial Action Task Force (FATF)
An intergovernmental body whose purpose is to develop and promote
national and international policies to combat money laundering and
terrorist financing. The FATF is a policy-making body that works to

generate the necessary political will to bring about legislative and regulatory reforms in these areas.

Galeria Page mall

In the Tri-Border Area of Paraguay, a mall owned by a Hezbollah sympathizer who employed other Hezbollah sympathizers to manage the mall and staff stores. He would send money back to Iran as part of Hezbollah aid.

gift card fraud

A type of fraud that occurs in all types of retailers. There are several ways to commit gift card fraud, but most thieves obtain a stolen gift card, activate it, and sell it online. Alternatively, they obtain stolen credit card numbers, create gift cards, and sell them on online auction sites or gift card exchange sites.

gray market

Unlike the black market, where goods are channeled through illegal means, the gray market allows regulated product from a legal source to be sold to an unauthorized marketplace or channel. Walk through a tourist area of any major city, and you will notice electronics stores that have TVs, DVD players, and computers all drastically underpriced. According to an NYPD source, most of those stores are selling gray market products. Products intended for a specific market are "diverted" and sold to a different unauthorized marketplace through an intermediary.

hawala

Also known as *hundi*. An informal value transfer system based on the performance and honor of a huge network of money brokers who are located primarily in the Middle East, North Africa, the Horn of Africa, and South Asia. Can also be made up of a network of hawala brokers, or *hawaladars*.

Hezbollah

Arabic for "party of God." A Shi'a Muslim militant group and political party based in Lebanon. It leads the March 8 Alliance, which withdrew from the government in January 2011 over its refusal to reject the Special Tribunal for Lebanon. It receives financial and political support from Iran and Syria. Its paramilitary wing is regarded as a resistance movement throughout much of the Arab and Muslim worlds. Multiple countries, including predominantly Sunni Arab nations such as Saudi Arabia, Egypt, and Jordan, have condemned Hezbollah's actions.

hired booster

Usually a former driver from countries such as Cuba, Colombia, Ecuador, and Mexico. These boosters are hired by shell warehouses and are paid $500 to lift merchandise, dispose of its packaging, and ship it to another address, where the warehouses then resell it. The warehouses report the merchandise as stolen and collect the insurance money, creating another fraudulent revenue stream.

Ihsan

An Arabic derivative of the verb *ahsana*, which means "to do things better." Ihsan is considered the highest of the three levels of the Muslim faith (the other two are Islam and Iman) and the closest to God.

illegal Internet pharmacy

A web site that sells controlled prescription drugs such as Xanax, Oxycontin, Vicodin, Ritalin, and Valium without a license to sell them. Illegal Internet pharmacies do not require the purchaser to provide a valid prescription and often sell OTC medicines as well.

Immigration and Customs Enforcement (ICE)

A federal law enforcement agency under the U.S. Department of Homeland Security (DHS) that identifies, investigates, and dismantles vulnerabilities regarding the nation's border, economic,

transportation, and infrastructure security. The largest components within DHS are Homeland Security Investigations (HSI) and
Enforcement and Removal Operations (ERO). Headquartered in
Washington, D.C., ICE investigates and enforces more than 400
federal statutes within the U.S. and maintains attachés at major U.S.
embassies overseas. ICE is led by a director who is appointed at the
sub-Cabinet level by the President and is confirmed by the Senate.
The director reports directly to the Secretary of Homeland Security.
The mission of ICE is to protect the U.S. and uphold public safety by
enforcing immigration and customs laws.

insurance fraud through cargo theft
A way for terrorists to obtain funding. Fences who own shell warehouses swindle millions of dollars of insurance money to fund terrorist fronts.

International Center for the Prevention of Crime (ICPC)
Founded in 1994 as an international forum for national governments,
local authorities, public agencies, specialized institutions, and nongov-
ernment organizations to exchange experience, emerging knowledge,
policies, and programs to prevent crime and promote community
safety. It helps cities and countries reduce delinquency, violent crime,
and insecurity.

International Islamic Relief Organization (IIRO)
Also known as the International Islamic Relief Organization of Saudi
Arabia (IIROSA). A charity based in Saudi Arabia. The United
Nations has listed its branch offices in Indonesia and the Philippines
as belonging to or associated with al Qaeda.

International Monetary Fund (IMF)
An international organization created to promote global monetary and
exchange stability, to facilitate the expansion and balanced growth of
international trade, and to help establish a multilateral system of payments for current transactions.

Islamberg
A Muslim community in Hancock, New York.

Jamaat al Fuqra
Arabic for "community of the impoverished." A paramilitary organization of mostly African-American Muslims based in Pakistan and the
U.S. Some of the approximately 3,000 members have planned various
acts of violence, often directed at rival factions. Two al Fuqra members were convicted of conspiring to murder Rashad Khalifa in 1990,
and others are alleged to have assassinated Ahmadiyya leader Mozaf-
far Ahmad in 1983. The group itself is not listed as a terror group by
the U.S. or the EU, but it was listed as a terrorist organization in the
1999 "Patterns of Global Terrorism" report by the U.S. State Department. It operates two front groups: Muslims of the Americas and
Quranic Open University. The group also has been known to operate
in Canada and the Caribbean.

Jam'iyyat Ul-Islam Is-Saheeh (JIS)
Translates into "the assembly for authentic Islam."

LAAORCA (Los Angeles Organized Retail Crime Association)
In January 2009, Captain Bill Williams and Detective Kent Oda established LAAORCA, a database that tracks the frequency of ORC crime,
where it is happening, and possible perpetrators. It communicates the
information in real time to its agency and private-sector partners. The
idea was to provide a proactive partnership between police and community. In addition, LAAORCA exposes the root causes of crime and
disorder and creates efficiencies between prosecutors, courts, corrections, and media.

Lashkar-e-Taiba (LeT)
Urdu for "Army of the Good," "Army of the Righteous," or "Army
of the Pure." Also known as Lashkar-i-Tayyaba, Lashkar-e-Tayyaba,
Lashkar-e-Tayyiba, Lashkar-i-Taiba, and Lashkar Taiba. One of

the largest and most active militant Islamist terrorist organizations in South Asia, operating mainly from Pakistan. Responsible for the attacks on Mumbai in 2008.

LEAPS

Recognizing that change needed to be implemented, and quickly, the LAPD created the Law Enforcement and Private Security conference to promote discussions and information sharing between government agencies and private security entities within retailers.

Lebanese Shi'a

Shi'a Islam constitutes some 35% to 49% of Lebanon's population. Most of its adherents live in the northern area of the Beqaa Valley and southern Lebanon. The majority of Shi'a Muslims in Lebanon are Twelvers, with a community of hundreds of Ismailis. Druze, often accounted for as Ismailis, constitute a further 5% of the population.

loss prevention staff

Executives and associates who are responsible for detecting, reporting, and resolving matters in the areas of safety, inventory shortage (shrinkage), cash handling, and theft, and for providing customer service as per company standards.

M-18

Also known as the 18th Street gang, named after a street in Los Angeles, California. Considered the largest transnational criminal gang in Los Angeles, with an estimated thousands of members in Los Angeles County alone. Approximately 200 individual, autonomous gangs operate under the same label within separate barrios in the San Fernando Valley, the San Gabriel Valley, the South Bay, South Los Angeles, Downtown Los Angeles, Pico Union, Inglewood, Cudahy, and Orange County, according to the latest figures from the National Drug Intelligence Center (NDIC).

Maniac Latin Disciples

The largest Latin street gang in Chicago.

Mara Salvatrucha

Also known as MS, Mara, and MS-13. A transnational criminal gang that originated in Los Angeles and has spread to other parts of the U.S., Canada, Mexico, and Central America. The majority of the gang is ethnically composed of Central Americans and is active in urban and suburban areas.

matricula consular

Also known as the *Matrícula Consular de Alta Seguridad* (MCAS) (consular identification card [CID]). An identification card issued by the Mexican government through its consulate offices to Mexican nationals residing outside of Mexico. The card's issuance has no bearing on immigration status in the foreign country the person is residing in. The purpose of the card is to demonstrate that the bearer is a Mexican national living outside of Mexico. It includes a Government of Mexico-issued ID number and bears a photograph and address of the Mexican national to whom it is issued.

Mexican Zetas

The Los Zetas Cartel is a criminal organization in Mexico dedicated mostly to international illegal drug trade, assassinations, and other organized crime activities. This drug cartel was founded by a small group of Mexican Army special forces deserters and now includes corrupt former federal, state, and local police officers, as well as ex-Kaibiles from Guatemala. This group of highly trained gunmen was first hired as a private mercenary army for Mexico's Gulf Cartel. After the arrest of the Gulf Cartel's leader, Osiel Cárdenas Guillen, as well as other events, the two entities became a combined trafficking force, with the Zetas taking a more active leadership role in drug trafficking. In February 2010, Los Zetas became independent and became enemies of their former employer/partner, the Gulf Cartel. Los Zetas are led by Heriberto "El Lazca" Lazcano. The Drug Enforcement Administration (DEA) considers Los Zetas as probably the most violent paramilitary enforcement group in Mexico.

MS-13

A street gang. The number 13 refers to a street in Los Angeles. See *Mara Salvatrucha*.

Mujahadeen-e-Khalq (MEK)

A militant Islamic-Marxist or Islamic-Socialist organization in Iran that advocates the overthrow of the Islamic Republic of Iran. Founded in 1965 by a group of Iranian college students as an Islamic-Marxist political movement, MEK was originally devoted to armed struggle against the Shah of Iran, capitalism, and "Western imperialism." In the aftermath of the 1979 Iranian Revolution, at first the MEK and the Tudeh Party chose to side with clerics led by the Ayatollah Khomeini against the liberals, nationalists, and other moderate forces within the revolution. The MEK endorsed the taking of American embassy personnel hostage in 1979 and subsequently condemned Khomeini's decision to release the hostages in January of 1981. A power struggle ensued, and by mid-1981, MEK was fighting street battles against the Islamic Revolutionary Guards. Since then, more than 10,000 people have been killed in fighting between the MEK and the Iranian government. During the Iran-Iraq War, the group was given refuge by Saddam Hussein and mounted attacks on Iran from within Iraqi territory. They continued to mount attacks inside Iran until 1999, when they assassinated the chief of staff of the Iranian military, Brigadier General Ali Sayad Shirazi. The group claims to have renounced violence in 2001. Today it is the main organization in the National Council of Resistance of Iran (NCRI), an "umbrella coalition" calling itself the "parliament-in-exile dedicated to a democratic, secular, and coalition government in Iran." The group has had thousands of members for many years in bases in Iraq, but according to the British Broadcasting

Corporation, they were disarmed in the wake of the U.S.-led invasion and are said to have adhered to a cease-fire.

National Retail Federation (NRF)
The world's largest retail trade association. Its members include department store, specialty, discount, catalog, Internet, and independent retailers, as well as chain restaurants and grocery stores. Members also include businesses that provide goods and services to retailers. The NRF represents an industry made up of over 1.6 million U.S. retail establishments with more than 24 million employees and 2005 sales of $4.4 trillion. The NRF is also an umbrella group that represents more than 100 associations of state, national, and international retailers.

National Security Law and Policy at the Investigative Project on Terrorism
The Investigative Project on Terrorism is a nonprofit research group founded by Steven Emerson in 1995. It is recognized as the world's most comprehensive data center on radical Islamic terrorist groups. The IPT has investigated the operations, funding, activities, and front groups of Islamic terrorist and extremist groups in the U.S. and around the world.

Operation Blackbird
The FBI uncovered an ORC ring that specialized in reselling infant formula to warehouses. The proceeds were wired back to countries in the Middle East where Hezbollah and Hamas were active.

Operation Greenquest
Targeted financiers of al Qaeda and other international terrorist groups. The FBI identified and interviewed 18 people led by families of Middle Eastern origin who bought and sold (in addition to infant formula) razor blades, nicotine patches, and Viagra stolen from supermarkets in North Texas.

ORC Annual Report

A report created by the NRF that tracks organized retail crime developments and statistics throughout the year. Retailers that are members of the NRF fill out the Organized Retail Crime Survey. Its purpose is to understand the impact of organized retail crime on retailers across the country by measuring trends and operational methods of criminal enterprises.

Organisation for Economic Co-operation and Development (OECD)

A forum in which governments can work together to share experiences and seek solutions to common problems. The OECD works with governments to understand what drives economic, social, and environmental change. It also measures productivity and global flows or trade and investment while analyzing and comparing data to predict future trends.

organized retail crime (ORC)

Organized retail crime tends to be discussed in terms of criminal networks engaged in large-scale theft. Descriptions of ORC also generally entail criminals fraudulently obtaining goods in quantities beyond what would normally be intended for personal consumption; reselling these ill-gotten goods; receiving, concealing, transporting, or disposing of these goods; or coordinating individuals to commit these retail crimes. Federal law enforcement agencies, such as the FBI, tend to limit discussions of ORC to situations in which boosters steal merchandise from retail establishments and resell it. Currently, ORC is not a federal crime. For data collection purposes, Congress has defined ORC as the following:

- Violating a state ban on shoplifting or retail merchandise theft—if the quantities of items stolen are of an amount that would not normally be purchased for personal use or consumption—and stealing for the purposes of reselling the items or re-entering them into commerce

- Receiving, possessing, concealing, bartering, selling, transporting, or disposing of any property that is known to have been taken in the violation just outlined

- Coordinating, organizing, or recruiting persons to undertake either of the two violations just outlined

Patriot Act
Established to help curtail terrorism by creating a federal law to prosecute criminals who finance terror.

PPK
Partiya Karkeren Kurdistan (Kurdistan Workers' Party). Also known as KGK, and formerly known as KADEK or Kongra-Gel. A Kurdish militant separatist organization that fights an armed struggle against the Turkish state for the creation of an independent Kurdistan. The group was founded on November 27, 1978 and was led by Abdullah Öcalan. The PKK's ideology is founded on revolutionary socialism and Kurdish nationalism. The PKK's goal has been to create an independent Kurdish state. Kurdistan is a geographic region that comprises southeastern Turkey, northeastern Iraq, northeastern Syria, and northwestern Iran, where the Kurdish population is the majority. This goal has now been moderated to claiming cultural and political rights for the ethnic Kurdish population in Turkey. In 2010, however, after the PKK stepped up its military activities, Murat Karayilan threatened that the PKK would declare independence if their demands were not met by the Turkish state. The PKK is listed as a terrorist organization internationally by a number of states and organizations, including the U.S.

Red House
An alleged 50-acre Muslim commune in Charlotte County, Virginia.

remittance

A transfer of money by a foreign worker to his home country. Money sent home by migrants constitutes the second-largest financial inflow to many developing countries, exceeding international aid.

Retail Industry Leaders Association (RILA)

A U.S. trade association headquartered in Arlington, Virginia, that promotes consumer choice and economic freedom through public policy and industry operational excellence. Executives participate in RILA for its educational forums, public policy advocacy, and advancement of the industry.

retail returns fraud

Returning merchandise by presenting receipts that have been falsified, stolen, or reused.

RICO

Racketeer Influenced and Corrupt Organizations Act. A U.S. federal law that provides for extended criminal penalties and a civil cause of action for acts performed as part of an ongoing criminal organization. The RICO Act focuses specifically on racketeering. It allows the leaders of a syndicate to be tried for crimes they ordered or helped others to carry out. This closed a perceived loophole that, for example, allowed someone who told a man to murder someone to be exempt from trial because he didn't commit the crime himself.

runner

An alternative name for *booster*.

shell store

Many fences who run nonlegitimate warehouses also own or are affiliated with stores geared toward tourists who want to buy inexpensive batteries, electronics, clothing, and household appliances.

shell warehouse
A location where mid- and high-level fences sell their stolen merchandise. These warehouses, which seem like legitimate businesses from the outside, are actually fronts for the sale of stolen goods.

Shipper's Export Declarations (SED)
Generally required by the U.S. Census Bureau for shipping single commodities valued at more than $2,500, or for commodities requiring a license or license exception.

specially designated global terrorist (SDGT)
In effect since December 6, 2006 under Executive Order 13224. Empowers the U.S. Secretary of State to designate certain individuals or entities as having committed or who pose a significant risk of committing acts of terrorism that threaten national security.

stored value card (SVC)
Monetary value on a card not from an externally recorded account. Differs from prepaid cards, where money is on deposit with the issuer, similar to a debit card. One major difference between stored value cards and prepaid debit cards is that prepaid debit cards are usually issued in the name of individual account holders, whereas stored value cards are usually anonymous. The funds and/or data are physically stored on a stored value card. With prepaid cards, the data is maintained on computers affiliated with the card issuer. The value associated with the stored value card can be accessed using a magnetic strip embedded in the card, on which the card number is encoded; using radio frequency identification (RFID); or by entering a code number, printed on the card, into a telephone or other numeric keypad.

Street Vendor Project
A membership-based project with more than 750 active vendor members who are working together to create a vendors' movement for

permanent change. They reach out to street vendors and storage garages and teach them about their legal rights and responsibilities. They hold meetings to plan collective actions for making their voices heard. They publish reports and file lawsuits to raise public awareness about vendors and the enormous contribution they make to a city. Finally, they help vendors grow their businesses by linking them with small-business training and loans. The Street Vendor Project is part of the Urban Justice Center, a nonprofit organization that provides legal representation and advocacy for various marginalized groups of New Yorkers.

Taliban

Arabic for "students." An Islamist militia group that ruled large parts of Afghanistan starting in September 1996. Although in control of Afghanistan's capital (Kabul) and most of the country for five years, the Taliban's Islamic Emirate of Afghanistan gained diplomatic recognition from only three states: Pakistan, Saudi Arabia, and the United Arab Emirates. After the 9/11 attacks, the Taliban regime was overthrown by Operation Enduring Freedom. The Taliban mostly fled to neighboring Pakistan, where they regrouped as an insurgency movement to fight the Islamic Republic of Afghanistan (established in late 2001) and the NATO-led International Security Assistance Force (ISAF).

TOMCATS

Due to the significant increase in organized commercial cargo theft in Miami-Dade County, Florida, and its negative impact on commerce, the Cargo Crimes Section (CCS) took on a leadership role. It joined with the FBI, U.S. Customs and Border Protection, the Florida Department of Law Enforcement (FDLE), the Florida Highway Patrol (FHP), and the Florida Department of Transportation (FDOT) to form a South Florida cargo theft task force called the Tactical Operations Multi-Agency Cargo Anti-Theft Squad (TOMCATS).

Tri-Border Area
The South American border intersection of Argentina, Brazil, and Paraguay.

TSA
Transportation Security Administration, an agency of the U.S. Department of Homeland Security. Responsible for the safety and security of the traveling public in the U.S.

Tupas
The Tupamaros street gang, which originated in Caracas, Venezuela. Today, its primary center of operations is on the west side of Caracas. This is a decidedly political gang. It identifies with a kind of Robin Hood mythology that surrounds how peasants and the urban poor in Uruguay and elsewhere romanticize the exploits of the original Tupamaros based in Uruguay.

UNESCO
United Nations Educational, Scientific, and Cultural Organization, a specialized agency of the United Nations established on November 16, 1945. Its purpose is to contribute to peace and security by promoting international collaboration through education, science, and culture. It hopes to further universal respect for justice, the rule of law, and human rights, along with fundamental freedoms proclaimed in the UN Charter.

Uniform Crime Reporting System
Used by the FBI to track and monitor trends in crime.

United Nations Office on Drugs and Crime (UNODC)
UNODC is a global leader in the fight against illicit drugs and international crime and is mandated to assist Member States in their struggle against illicit drugs, crime and terrorism. Established in 1997 through a merger between the United Nations Drug Control Programme and

the Centre for International Crime Prevention, UNODC operates in all regions of the world through an extensive network of field offices.

U.S. Customs and Border Protection (CBP)

A federal law enforcement agency of the U.S. Department of Home-land Security. Regulates and facilitates international trade, collecting import duties, and enforcing U.S. regulations, including trade, drug, and immigration laws.

USIA

The United States Information Agency, which existed from 1953 to 1999, was devoted to "public diplomacy." In 1999, USIA's broadcasting functions were moved to the newly created Broadcasting Board of Governors, and its exchange and nonbroadcasting information functions were given to the newly created Undersecretary of State for Public Affairs and Public Diplomacy at the U.S. Department of State.

zakat

Muslims are required to give away 2.5% of their earnings as a form of *zakat*, or alms.

Endnotes

Introduction

1. This IM exchange has been edited to include the most relevant aspects of the conversation.

2. *Cincinnati Enquirer*, "Retailers Reining in Sophisticated Theft Rings," Laura Baverman, May 7, 2011.

Chapter 1

1. *New York Times*, "Taliban Leader Flaunts Power Inside Pakistan," Jane Perlez, June 2, 2008.

2. The Tehreek-e-Taliban held a two-day "Ghazi Islam Conference" in April 2008, attended by Taliban leaders and delegations from the Tank and Swat districts of NWFP, North and South Waziristan, Kurram, Orakzai, and Bajaur tribal agencies.

3. *Forbes* magazine, "Is al Qaeda Bankrupt?," Nathan Vardi, February 2010.

4. Author interview with Bill Martel, June 24, 2010.

5. An informal value transfer system of Islamic origin facilitated by brokers.

6. All groups who were at one point al Qaeda sympathizers and were responsible for terrorist attacks in India, the U.S., and South America.

7. *Terror Incorporated: Tracing the Dollars Behind the Terror Networks*, Loretta Napoleoni (Seven Stories Press, 2005).

8. Author interviews with Jerry Biggs, head of Loss Prevention at Walgreens, November 15, 2009; Read Hayes, the National Association for

Shoplifting Prevention, November 17, 2009; Larry C. Johnson, former analyst at the U.S. Department of State, January 7, 2010.

9. Author interviews with Read Hayes, Ph.D. University of Florida and the Loss Prevention Research Council, November 17, 2009 and Gary Weisbecker, FBI agent working on organized retail crime cases, October 20, 2009.

10. Author interview with Joe LaRocca, April 6, 2011.

11. Author interview with Casey Chroust, April 18, 2009.

12. Chris spoke to me on the condition of anonymity for fear of incriminating himself or his colleagues.

13. Bertelsmann Stiftung, BTI 2010, Somalia Country Report. Gutersloh: Bertelsmann Stiftung, 2009.

14. United Nations Development Programme, "The Economic Crisis in the Arab States."

15. CIA World Fact Book on Somalia, November 2010.

16. I witnessed Faisal Shahzad make this statement when he answered to charges in a ten-count indictment on June 21, 2010.

17. CNN.com, "N.J. men planned to 'wage violent jihad,' feds say," June 6, 2010.

18. In a conversation with James L. Patton, attorney representing Carlos Eduardo Almonte, after their indictment June 7, 2010 in New Jersey, he mentioned funding came from the sale of stolen items.

19. Videotaped interview with Taliban leader Mullah Muhibullah, August 21, 2008, translated into English on the web site www.islamicawakening.com.

20. "Militancy in Pakistan's Federally Administered Tribal Areas (FATA) and Afghanistan," Magnus Norell, Swedish Defence Research Agency (FOI), February 2010.

21. "Islamberg" is a community in upstate New York composed of mostly African-Americans who converted to Islam and choose to live by strict religious codes apart from regular society. The sister town called "Red House" in Virginia is home to a sect called "Muslims of the Americas" who are followers of Sheikh Mubarik Gilani. The news on Islamberg was initially reported by FOX 5 News, February 2006.

22. "No Trespassing: U.S. facing homegrown terror," Wajid Ali Syed, Foreign Policy Association, Pakistan.foreignpolicyblogs.com, January 18, 2011.

23. FBI Affidavit from special agent David J. Glawe outlining his investigation into a $7 million fraud operation involving counterfeit and stolen apparel by three people living in Red House, Virginia, Muslim community.

24. A Review of Current and Evolving Trends in Terrorism Financing: Written testimony submitted to the House Committee on Financial Services, Subcommittee on Oversight and Investigations, Stephen I. Landman, September 28, 2010.

25. "Countering Ideological Support to Terrorism in the Circum-Carribbean," John T. Fishel and Mary Grizzard, 2005.

26. "Kevin James and the JIS Conspiracy," Frontline's "The Enemy Within," Rob Harris, with contributed reporting by Neil MacFarquhar of the *New York Times*.

27. FBI Deputy Assistant Director Donald Van Duyn, statement before the Senate Committee on Homeland Security and Governmental Affairs and Related Agencies, September 19, 2006, http://www.fbi.gov/congress/congress06/vanduyn091906.htm (accessed March 26, 2010).

28. Greg Grandin, "The Narcissism of Violent Differences," in *Anti-Americanism*, Andrew Ross and Kristin Ross, editors, (New York University Press, 2004), p. 19.

29. Ibid.

30. Pew Global Attitudes Project, "America Admired, Yet Its New Vulnerability Seen as Good Thing, Say Opinion Leaders," December 19, 2001.

31. "Countering Ideological Support to Terrorism in the Circum-Carribbean," John T. Fishel and Mary Grizzard, 2005.

32. "El Rukns Had Early Terror Ties," *Chicago Sun Times*, Carlos Sadovi, June 11, 2002.

33. MS-13 stands for Mara Salvatrucha, an organized criminal gang composed largely of Central Americans who operate in U.S. urban areas.

34. A matricula consular is an identification card issued by the government of Mexico through its consulate offices to Mexican nationals residing outside of Mexico, regardless of their immigration status.

35. "A Line in the Sand: Confronting the Threat at the Southwest Border," prepared by the majority staff of the House Committee on Homeland Security Subcommittee on Investigations, Michael T. McCaul, Chairman, http://www.fbi.gov/news/testimony/consular-id-cards-in-a-post-9-11-world.

36. *Strategic Insights,* "The Maras and National Security in Central America," Thomas C. Bruneau, Volume IV, Issue 5 (May 2005).

37. Ibid.

38. Ibid via the PNC in El Salvador.

39. Ibid.

40. Ibid.

41. Erick Stakelback, "Unholy Border Alliance," frontpagemagazine.com, Jan. 3, 2005.

42. Author interview with Samuel Logan, November 2009.

43. Ibid.

44. Author interview with Samuel Logan, March 21, 2010.

45. GAO, Terrorist Financing: U.S. Agencies Should Systematically Assess Terrorists' Use of Alternative Financing Mechanisms, November 2003.

46. GAO, Report to the Chairman, Committee on the Judiciary, House of Representatives, International Financial Crime Treasury's Role and Responsibilities Relating to the Selected Provisions of the USA Patriot Act, July 29, 2005.

47. Author interview with John Tobon, July 1, 2010.

48. CNN.com, "South America's 'Tri-Border' Back on Terrorism Radar," Mike Boettcher, November 7, 2002.

49. MSNBC.com, "Hezbollah Builds a Western Base," Pablo Gato and Robert Windrem, May 9, 2007.

50. Ibid.

51. CIA paper from 2004.

52. A legal pronouncement in Islam issued by a religious law specialist on a specific issue.

53. "Hezbollah: Social Services as a Source of Power," JSOU Report, James B. Love, 2010.

54. Hezbollah: Financing Terror Through Criminal Enterprise, Testimony of Dr. Matthew Levitt, Senior Fellow and Director of Terrorism Studies, the Washington Institute for Near East Policy, May 25, 2005.

55. *Philadelphia Inquirer,* "Ex-Camden County Resident Indicted in Alleged Terror Cell Held in Paraguay," Mike Newall, June 17, 2010.

56. Ibid.

57. Ibid.

58. Levitt conducted an interview with a former U.S. law enforcement official, Washington D.C., April 27, 2004 for his testimony on May 25, 2005.

Chapter 2

1. According to a Fendi spokesperson, only one public event took place in 2009 and again in 2010. There was no event in 2008.

2. *Bloomberg BusinessWeek,* "LVMH's Fendi Is 'Very Positive' on Luxury Outlook, Burke Says," February 26, 2010.

3. Interview with Milton Pedraza, April 28, 2011.

4. Department of Justice press release, "Jury Convicts Two New York Importers in One of the Largest Counterfeit Goods Prosecutions in U.S. History," June 11, 2010.

5. Ibid.

6. Author interview with an ICE investigator, April 15, 2011.

7. Fendi corporate press release, "Fendi and Burlington Coat Factory Warehouse Settle Fendi's Trademark Counterfeiting Lawsuit Against Burlington for $10,050,000.00," October 20, 2010.

8. Ibid.

9. Speech Michael Burke gave on Fendi 2010.

10. United States District Court for the Northern District of Illinois, Eastern Division, Coach, Inc. and Coach Services, Inc., v. City of Chicago, d/b/a New Maxwell Street Market, Cong Wu, Xiao Yang, and DOES 1 through 100, May 19, 2010.

11. Author interview with an anonymous source (NYPD detective), August 20, 2010.

12. National Income and Product Accounts, Table 2.3.1, Percent Change from Preceding Period in Real Personal Consumption Expenditures by Major Type of Product.

13. From "The Future of Luxury" in Marketing Daily. Richard, Baker April 30, 2009. Follow up interview with Richard Baker, May 17, 2011.

14. "The Globalization of Crime: A Transnational Organized Crime Threat Assessment," United Nations Office on Drug and Crime, June 2010.

15. Ibid.

16. Ibid.

17. Ibid.

18. Ibid.

19. FBI 2009 report done by the Internet Crime Complaint Center (IC3), a partnership of the FBI and the National White Collar Crime Center.

20. United Nations Security Council, Security Council Committee Pursuant to Resolutions 751 (1992) and 1907 (2009) concerning Somalia and Eritrea, July 18, 2011.

21. "The Globalization of Crime: A Transnational Organized Crime Threat Assessment," United Nations Office on Drug and Crime, June 2010.

22. A terrorist organization in Somalia with ties to al Qaeda that most recently took responsibility for the attacks in Uganda during the 2010 World Cup.

23. Interview with Jack Gee, June 25, 2010.

24. eBay Q2 2009 earnings report.

25. Inteview with Paul Jones at the NRF conference in Atlanta on June 14th, 2010.

26. Interview with Kris Buckner, August 5, 2010 at his office in Torrence, CA.

27. Reuters, "Drugs, Terrorism and Shadow Banking," Bernard Debusmann, March 26, 2010.

28. Ibid.

29. Ibid.

30. This conversation took place during a small breakout session at the NRF conference in Atlanta, Georgia, June 15, 2010. The subject of the breakout session focused on employee theft.

31. Ibid.

32. *Los Angeles Times*, "Court cases shed light on money transferring systems," Tina Susman, May 24, 2010.

33. The Cornerstone Report (a division of ICE), Volume III: No. 2, December 2006, "Prepaid Cards an Emerging Threat."

34. Interview with Joe LaRocca, April 6, 2010.

35. *New York Times*, "Street Vending as a Way to Ease Joblessness," Jennifer 8. Lee, April 29, 2009.

36. Author interview with Ali Issa, staff organizer with the Street Vendor Project, July 12, 2010.

37. Performance and Accountability Report Fiscal Year 2008, U.S. Customs and Border Protection.

38. Ibid.

39. "KC police bust what they call an organized retail crime ring operating in a nice neighborhood," NBC Action News, July 1, 2010.

40. Author interview with Dr. Read Hayes, National Association for Shoplifting Prevention, November 15, 2009.

41. Phone interview with Jack Gee, June 29, 2010.

42. Ibid.

Chapter 3

1. I spoke with Detective Hahn at the LEAPS conference in Los Angeles August 5, 2010, where he described the scene at the Arden Fair mall in Sacramento.

2. Ibid.

3. University of Florida National Retail Survey 2009. "Shrinkage" refers to losses from both ORC rings and theft not related to ORC.

4. Cargo Theft Training National Insurance Crime Bureau, Texas Department of Insurance, Fraud Conference Supervisory Special Agent Jerry Allen, November 12, 2010.

5. Bureau of Justice Statistics Criminal Victimization in the United States, 2008 Statistical Tables and U.S. Census Bureau National Crime Victimization Survey 2010.

6. I spoke to Timothy Elliot when he was working at Barneys on August 17th, 2010. After he left, I touched base with the current spokesperson, who confirmed Barneys does not comment on loss prevention matters.

7. *Traffic World*, "Cargo Security Unlocked," A.G. Keane, 269(13), 2005, p. 10 (via the CRISP report "Organized Retail Crime: Assessing the Risk and Developing Effective Strategies").

8. CRISP report: "Organized Retail Crime: Assessing the Risk and Developing Effective Strategies."

9. Author interview with a human resources representative at Bloomingdale's, April 21, 2011.

10. *New York Times*, "Shoplifters? Studies Say Keep an Eye on Workers," Steve Greenhouse, December 29, 2009.

11. Associated Press, "A Guilty Plea in Wal-Mart Case," February 1, 2006.

12. NRF 2008 National Retail Security Survey

13. National Retail Security Survey 2010 by Dr. Richard Hollinger professor of Criminology at the University of Florida.

14. Conversation with Paul Cogswell at the NRF Loss Prevention EXPO June 15th, 2010 in Atlanta, Georgia.

15. Phone interview with Jack Gee, June 29, 2010.

16. Interview with Saks Fifth Avenue employee, September 2010.

17. Interview with Kevin Tyrell, Section Chief, ICE-HSI Illicit Finance and Proceeds of Crime Unit, May 22, 2010.

18. "Is Black-Market Baby Formula Financing Terror?" The *Christian Science Monitor*, Clayton, Mark. June 29, 2005.

19. LPRC Organized Retail Crime Report.

20. FinCEN Form 105, otherwise known as the Report of International Transportation of Currency or Monetary Instruments (CMIR), requires people who physically transport (carry, mail, or ship) funds or who cause the money to be physically transported, mailed, shipped, or received, in currency or travelers checks exceeding $10,000, into or out of the U.S., to file a CMIR. The Bank Secrecy Act of 1970 does not cover cash, debit cards, or gift cards.

21. *The World's Most Threatening Terrorist Source Networks and Criminal Gangs*, eds. Michael T. Kindt, Jerrold M. Post, and Barry Schneider, Palgrave Macmillian, 2009.

22. Phone interview with Jerry Biggs, July 22, 2010.

23. Interview with Gary Weisbecker on March 11th, 2010

24. RILA Loss Prevention Research Council, Organized Retail Crime Annual Report 2009, Reed Hayes, Ph.D., CPP Loss Prevention Research Council and University of Florida.

25. Ibid.

26. Coalition Against Organized Retail Crime, U.S. House of Representatives Committee on the Judiciary Subcommittee on Crime, Terrorism, and Homeland Security, hearing on "Combating Organized Retail Crime: The Role of Federal Law Enforcement," November 5, 2009.

27. Statement of The National Association of Chain Drug Stores, Alexandria, VA, to the U.S. House of Representatives House Committee on the Judiciary Subcommittee on Crime, Terrorism, and Homeland Security.

28. For statistical purposes, the FBI defines cargo theft as "the criminal taking of any cargo including, but not limited to, goods, chattels, money, or baggage that constitutes, in whole or in part, a commercial shipment of freight moving in commerce, from any pipeline system, railroad car, motortruck, or other vehicle, or from any tank or storage facility, station house, platform, or depot, or from any vessel or wharf, or from any aircraft, air terminal, airport, aircraft terminal or air navigation facility, or from any intermodal container, intermodal chassis, trailer, container freight station, warehouse, freight distribution facility, or freight consolidation facility."

29. Interview with Jared Palmer, April 10, 2010.

30. ASIS Foundation, Connecting Research in Security to Practice, CRISP report: "Organized Retail Crime: Assessing the Risk and Developing Effective Strategies," Walter E. Palmer, CPP CFI, CFE, and Chris Richardson, CPP, 2009.

31. CRS Report Prepared for Members and Committees of Congress on Organized Retail Crime, Kristin M. Finklea, Analyst in Domestic Security, January 6, 2011.

32. Interview with Detective Marc Zavala, August 9, 2010.

33. Press release: "Stearns' Cargo Theft Provision to Be Enacted as Part of Patriot Act Reauthorization," July 21, 2005.

34. Interview with Jared Palmer, April 13, 2010.

35. Speech given by Joe LaRocca at the NRF Loss Prevention conference in Atlanta, Georgia, June 2010.

36. Interview with James Cooper at LAPD headquarters, August 10, 2010.

37. In *The 9/11 Commission Report* the government lists communication and private sector preparedness as one of the ways to prevent terrorist attacks: "We believe that compliance with the standard should define the standard of care owned by a company to its employees and the public for legal purposes. Private-sector preparedness is not a luxury; it is a cost of doing business in the post 9/11 world. It is ignored at a tremendous potential cost in lives, money and national security."

38. Interview with James Featherstone at the city of Los Angeles emergency management headquarters, August 9, 2010.

39. Speech given by James Featherstone at the LEAPS conference in Los Angeles, August 5, 2010.

40. Interview with Steve Sambar, Captain, Major Crimes Division, at LAPD headquarters, August 9, 2010.

41. Author interview, August 6, 2010.

42. Author interview with Detective Kent Oda, June 22, 2010.

43. Interview with Joe LaRocca from National Retail Federation, April 6, 2010.

Chapter 4

1. Author interview with Gary Weisbecker, June 2010.

2. Phone interview with Jerry Biggs, November 20, 2009.

3. U.S. Census Bureau e-stats report 2007.

4. Sheriff Ed Dean of Marion County, Florida, at the 2009 National Cargo Theft Summit.

5. *Fleet Owner* magazine, "Target: Cargo Theft," Sean Kilcarr, October 21, 2009.

6. FreightWatch International, "South Florida Cargo Theft Gangs."

7. FreightWatch International, "U.S. Cargo Theft: A 2009 Review."

8. Ibid.

9. Ibid.

10. *Wall Street Journal*, "Lilly Drugs Stolen in Warehouse Heist," March 17, 2010.

11. Author interview with Chuck Forsaith, June 15, 2010.

12. *Wall Street Journal*, "Lilly Drugs Stolen in Warehouse Heist," March 17, 2010.

13. *International In-house Counsel Journal*, Vol. 2 No. 8, Summer 2009, 1169-1174, "The Effects on Cargo Theft in a Down Global Economy," Jared S. Palmer, General Counsel, AFN, LLC, USA.

14. Interview with Author, July 2004.

15. *International In-house Counsel Journal*, Vol. 2 No. 8, Summer 2009, 1169-1174, "The Effects on Cargo Theft in a Down Global Economy," Jared S. Palmer, General Counsel, AFN, LLC, USA.

16. Interview with Joe LaRocca, April 6, 2010.

17. Coalition on Organized Retail Crime report 2009.

18. ORC Annual Report, Dr. Read Hayes, January 12, 2009, and author interview with Hayes, November 17, 2009.

19. *Chicago Tribune*, "Streamwood Man Used His Business to Sell Stolen Items Online," October 1, 2009.

20. Online security newsletter, CSOONLINE.com.

21. *The Daily News*, "Prosecutors: He's Victoria's Secret Bra Thief," Nicole Bode, September 2, 2008.

22. *New York Times*, "Vendors at Aqueduct Flea Market Seek New Home as Closing Nears," Elizabeth Harris, December 16, 2010. Street Vendor Project, streetvendor.org.

23. NBC New York, December 10, 2010.

24. Fifth annual Organized Retail Crime survey. Methodology: completed by loss prevention executives from 115 companies, including department, discount, drug, grocery, restaurant, and specialty retailers.

25. Author interview with Frank Muscato, April 3, 2009.

26. Interview with Jerry Biggs, March 24, 2010.

27. NRF Organized Retail Crime survey.

28. Author interview with Joe LaRocca, June 23, 2010.

29. *Wall Street Journal*, September 29, 2009.

30. Maguire Woods LLP.

31. California Civil code section 1797.8-1797.86 definition of "gray market goods" means the consumer goods bearing a trademark and normally accompanied by an express written warranty valid in the U.S. through channels other than the manufacturer's authorized U.S. distributor and that are not accompanied by the manufacturer's express written warranty valid in the U.S.

32. From the *Journal of Technology Law & Policy*, section 1526 of the Tariff Act of 1930, controlling gray market goods.

33. Retail Industry Leaders Association 2010 Organized Retail Crime Survey.

Chapter 5

1. Interview with Harold Prudencio at Albuquerque Police Department headquarters, August 18, 2010.

2. *FBI Law Enforcement Bulletin*, "ROP-ing fences," J. Trainum, N. Brown, and R. Smith, Jr., 60(6), 1991, p. 7.

3. ASIS CRISP report: "Organized Retail Crime: Assessing the Risk and Developing Effective Strategies," Walter E. Palmer, CPP, CFI, CFE, and Chris Richardson, CPP, 2009.

4. Taken from an interview Paul Jones did with NBC.

5. Phone interview with Frank Muscato, March 10, 2010.

6. ASIS CRISP report: "Organized Retail Crime: Assessing the Risk and Developing Effective Strategies," Walter E. Palmer, CPP, CFI, CFE, and Chris Richardson, CPP, 2009.

7. Phone interview with Jerry Biggs, March 9, 2010.

8. NRF report on Organized Retail Crime Survey 2009.

9. Ibid.

10. *Palm Beach Post*, "4 Held in String of CVS Thefts," Eliot Kleinberg, November 19, 2009.

11. Author interview with Dr. Read Hayes on May 6, 2011, and Read Hayes and King Rogers, "Catch Them if You Can: This Study of Organized Retail Crime Looks at How These Criminal Groups Operate and What Measures Might Help Stores Fight Back," *Security Management*, vol. 47, no. 10(2003), hereafter "Catch Them if You Can."

12. Interview with Detective Marc Zavala, August 11, 2010 in a Los Angeles Police Department warehouse for stolen items. The location was undisclosed.

13. FreightWatch 2010 Bi-Annual Cargo Theft Report.

14. Federal Bureau of Investigation Uniform Crime Report, Crime in the United States, 2009.

15. E-Fencing Enforcement Act of 2008, the Organized Retail Crime Act of 2008, and the Combating Organized Retail Crime Act of 2008, Hearing before the Subcommittee on Crime, Terrorism, and Homeland Security of the Committee on the Judiciary House of Representatives.

16. National Retail Crime survey 2010.

17. Interview with Detective Guevara at Los Angeles Police Department Headquarters, August 10, 2010.

Chapter 6

1. Terrorist and Organized Crime Groups in the Tri-Border Area (TBA) of South America: A Report Prepared by the Federal Research Division, Library of Congress, under an Interagency Agreement with the U.S. government, July 2003.

2. Ibid.

3. Ibid.

4. Ibid.

5. Interview with Larry Johnson, co-owner and chief executive of BERG Associates, February 11, 2010.

6. BBC Monitoring Service, UK, September 15, 2001.

7. Ibid.

8. *Middle East Intelligence Bulletin* (a monthly publication of the United States Committee for a Free Lebanon), "Hezbollah's Global Finance Network: The Triple Frontier," Blanca Madani, 4 No. 1, January 2002.

9. "Paraguay: Lack of Control System on the Border with Brazil Allows for Currency Flight," BBC Monitoring Americas: Political (London), January 23, 2003. Citing ABC Color web site, January 22, 2003.

10. Terrorist and Organized Crime Groups in the Tri-Border Area (TBA) of South America: A Report Prepared by the Federal Research Division, Library of Congress, under an Interagency Agreement with the U.S. government, July 2003.

11. Ibid.

12. CNN.com, "Sources: Terrorists Find Haven in South America," November 7, 2001.

13. http://paraguay.usembassy.gov/hizballah_fundraising_network_in_the_triple_frontier2.html, Hezbollah Fundraising Network in the Triple Frontier, U.S. Treasury Department Office of Public Affairs, which specifically identifies active members of the terrorist organization.

14. Interview with FBI source, August 23, 2010.

15. United States District Court Southern District of Florida United States of America vs. Samer Mehdi, Khaled T. Safadi, Cedar Distributors, Inc., Ulises Talavera, Transamerica Express of Miami, Emilio Jacinto Gonzalez-Neira, and Jumbo Cargo, Inc., Case No. 09-20852, October 1, 2009.

16. *Homeland Security and Terrorism*, Russell D. Howard, James J.F. Forest, and Joanne C. Moore (McGraw-Hill, 2005).

17. Interview with professor Ibrahim Werde, April 9, 2010.

18. International Journal of Comparative and Applied Criminal Justice Spring 2008, Vol. 32, No. 1, "The Nexus of Organized Crime and Terrorism: The Case Studies in Cigarette Smuggling" Louise I. Shelly, and Sharon A. Melzer,

19. Interview with Detective Amaury Guevara at LAPD headquarters, August 12, 2010.

20. Foxnews.com, "Congresswoman Raises Red Flag on Hezbollah-Cartel Nexus on U.S. Border," June 25, 2010.

21. *The 9/11 Commission Report*

22. Ibid.

23. Ibid.

24. Ibid.

25. "The Nexus of Organized Crime and Terrorism: Two Case Studies in Cigarette Smuggling," Louise Shelley and Sharon Meltzer.

26. Ibid.

27. Ibid.

28. *Homeland Security and Terrorism*, Russell D. Howard, James J.F. Forest, and Joanne C. Moore (McGraw-Hill, 2005).

29. Quote taken from a document entitled "Al Qaeda en Argentina" on Horatio Calderon's web site www.horaciocalderon.com.

30. United States District Court of Florida Indictment, Safadi, Cedar Distributors, Ulises Talavera, Transamerica Express of Miami, Emilio Jacinto Gonzalez-Neira, Jumbo Cargo.

31. SDGT entity pursuant to Executive Order 13224. "Seven Charged for Illegal Export of Electronics to U.S. Designated Terrorist Entity in Paraguay," Department of Justice, February 19, 2010.

32. *The 9/11 Commission Report*.

33. Ibid.

34. AJB, "Terrorismo: Egípcio é capturado pela PF" (Terrorism: Egyptian Is Captured by PF), Correiro Braziliense (Brasília), April 16, 2002, http://www2.correioweb.com.br/cw/EDICAO_20020416/pri_ult_160402_259.htm.

35. Interview with Professor William Martel, June 29, 2010.

36. R.A. Merritt report, Statement of Detective Randy Merritt, Pasadena Police Department Community Defense Unit (C.D.U.) Multi-Agency Task Force Special Investigations Bureau.

37. Ibid.

38. Interview with Randy Merritt at the LAPD LEAPS conference, August 6, 2010.

39. Quote from Robert C. Scott, Congressionl Representative from Virginia, taken from "Combating Organized Retail Crime-The Role of Federal Law Enforcement" hearing before the Subcommittee on Crime, Terrorism, and Homeland Security, November 5, 2009.

Chapter 7

1. Interview with attorney James Patton, May 5, 2010.

2. Interview with a source close to the case outside of the Newark, NJ courthouse, June 17, 2010.

3. Interview with Taliban commander Mullah Munibullah, August 2009, translated on the web site www.islamicawakening.com.

4. Interview with professor William Martel, May 4, 2010.

5. *Hide & Seek: Intelligence, Law Enforcement, and the Stalled War on Terrorist Finance*, John Cassara (Potomac Books, Inc., 2007).

6. Interview with William C. Martel, September 2011.

7. *Hide & Seek: Intelligence, Law Enforcement, and the Stalled War on Terrorist Finance*, John Cassara (Potomac Books, Inc., 2007).

8. CBC Radio Canada, "Money-Transfer Systems, Hawala Style," June 11, 2004.

9. Interpol.

10. 9/11 Commission's Monograph on Terrorist Financing.

11. Ibid.

12. "The Financial War Against Terrorism," Reyko Huang, CDI (Center for Defense Information) research analyst, March 5, 2002.

13. *Evil Money: The Inside Story of Money Laundering & Corruption in Government, Banks & Business*. Dr. Rachel Ehrenfeld, (HarperCollins, 1992, 1994).

14. Associated Press, "Farooque Ahmed Described as a Quiet Suburban Dad," October 28, 2010.

15. Interview with source in the Global Risk department at JP Morgan Chase, March 15, 2010.

16. International Convention for the Suppression of the Financing of Terrorism, G.A. Res. 109.

17. Financial Task Force on Money Laundering: Combating the Abuse of Alternative Remittance Systems: International Best Practices, June 20, 2003.

18. Author interview with an anonymous source, April 1, 2011, Hyderabad, India.

19. Statement of Secretary Paul O'Neill on signing the Executive Order Authorizing the Treasury Department to Block Funds of Terrorists and Their Associates, September 24, 2001, via *Terrorist Financing*, edited by Mary B. Erlande (Gazelle Distribution, 2006).

20. International Narcotics Control Strategy Report, March 2005.

21. "USA Patriot Act and Its Impact on Sound Anti-Money Laundering Programs," presentation by the Comptroller of the Currency Administrator of National Banks.

22. Testimony of John F. Moynihan and Larry C. Johnson before the House Committee on Finance Subcommittee on Oversight and Investigations hearing on "Progress Since 9/11: The Effectiveness of U.S. Anti-Terrorist Financing Efforts."

23. Phone interview with Kevin Tyrrell, April 5, 2010.

24. A non-federally regulated account has mandatory compliance with filing regulations contained within the Money Laundering Control Act of 1986, according to a spokesperson for FinCEN.

25. *Forbes* magazine, "Richest List," July 10, 1989.

26. "Prepared Remarks of Attorney General John Ashcroft DEA/Drug Enforcement Rollout," March 19, 2002.

27. Author interview with Samuel Logan, MS-13 expert and author of *This Is for the Mara Salvatrucha* (Hyperion, 2009), November 15, 2009.

28. *The Al Qaeda Connection: International Terrorism, Organized Crime and the Coming Apocalypse*, Williams, Paul L., Prometheus Books, 2005.

29. Larry C. Johnson, former analyst for the U.S. Central Intelligence Agency. In 1989 he moved to the U.S. Department of State and served four years as the deputy director for transportation security, antiterrorism, assistance training, and special ops in the State Department's Office of Counterterrorism.

30. Financial Crimes Enforcement Network advisory from the U.S. Department of the Treasury, June 1999.

31. "A Line in the Sand: Confronting the Threat at the Southwest Border," Prepared by the Majority Staff of the House Committee on Investigations, Michael T. McCaul, Chairman, 2006.

32. New Mexico Auto Theft Statistics, Rocky Mountain Insurance Information Association.

33. *McAllen (TX) Monitor*, "Police bust auto theft ring with ties to Zetas," Ryan Holeywell, August 2, 2007.

34. "A Line in the Sand: Confronting the Threat at the Southwest Border," Prepared by the Majority Staff of the House Committee on Investigations, Michael T. McCaul, Chairman, 2006.

35. "Colombia Rebels, al Qaeda in 'Unholy' Drug Alliance," Hugh Bronstein, January 4, 2010.

36. U.S. Department of the Treasury Financial Crimes Enforcement Network (FinCEN) Advisory, Columbian Black Market Peso Exchange.

37. *Maghreb Politics Review*, "U.S. Arrests Malians in Terror Drugs 'Link,'" Tommy Miles.

Chapter 8

1. Author interviews with Samuel Logan, MS-13 and narcoterrorism expert and author of *This Is for the Mara Salvatrucha*, October 7, 2009; Thomas Ruskin, owner of the CMP group, November 15, 2009; Larry C. Johnson, January 7, 2010.

2. www.islamicawakening.com.

3. Speech given prior to 9/11 titled "Jihad: Aims and Objectives," audio excerpt from Flashpoint Global Partners, www.globalterroralert.com.

4. NPR, "'Revolution Muslim' A Gateway For Would-Be Jihadis" Dina, Temple-Raston, October 13, 2010.

5. Ibid.,

6. Interview with Aaron Klein, WABC Radio, May 4, 2010.

7. *New York Daily News*, "Brooklyn Men Busted in Dubai May Be New Faces of Terror: Experts," Alison Gendar and Samuel Goldsmith, May 2, 2010.

8. U.S. Attorney Southern District of New York, "Manhattan U.S. Attorney Charges Faisal Shahzad with Attempted Car Bombing in Times Square."

9. *Wall Street Journal.*

10. Interview with the author outside of the Newark Federal Courthouse, June 10, 2010.

11. Author interview with Kris Buckner, August 6, 2010.

12. *New York Times*, "Brooklyn Mosque Becomes Terror Icon, But Case Is Unclear," Andy Newman with Daryl Khan, March 9, 2003.

13. Interview with NYPD commissioner Raymond W. Kelly at the WWD CEO Summit, November 1, 2010.

14. *The Military Observer*, "Funding Pakistan's Jihad Against the West," Ali K. Chishti, October 27, 2010.

15. Ibid.

16. Typologies and Open Source Reporting on Terrorist Abuse of Charitable Operations in Post-Earthquake Pakistan and India.

17. Financial Action Task Force on Money Laundering, *Combating the Abuse of Non-Profit Organizations: International Best Practices*, 7 (October 11, 2002).

18. On April 26, 2006, the U.S. Treasury designated the Jamaat-ud-Dawa as a terrorist organization. In December of 2008, the UN Security Council added the Jamaat-ud-Dawa to the list of entities and organizations known to support al Qaeda and the Taliban and listed the group as an alias of the Lashkar-e-Taiba terror group.

19. Spending figures published by the Punjab provincial government.

20. BBC, "Pakistan 'Gave Funds' to Group on UN Terror Blacklist." June 16, 2010.

21. Al-Shorfa.com, "The Taliban's Income All Termed Illegal," Amjad Bashir Siddiqi, April 17, 2010.

22. *PBS News Hour*, "Militant Groups Aid Pakistan Flood Victims," September 15, 2010.

23. *Al-Qaida's Jihad in Europe: The Afghan-Bosnian Network*, Evan Kohlman, Berg 2004.

24. *The True Face of Jihadis*, Amir Mir (Mashal Books, Lahore, 2004).

25. *Wall Street Journal*, "Money Eludes Pakistan's Crackdown on Accused Terror Group," Mathew Rosenberg and Glenn R. Simpson, December 13, 2008.

26. Ibid.

27. Globalsecurity.org.

28. United States District Court of Minnesota, United States of America v. Amina Farah Ali, a/k/a Amina Aden, a/k/a Amina Adan, a/k/a Amina Wadaado and Hawo Mohamed Hassan a/k/a Halima Hassan, a/k/a Halimo Hassan, September 14, 2009.

29. Associated Press, "Two Minnesota Women Among 14 Charged in Terror Probe," August 7, 2010.

30. IPT News, "Minneapolis Somalis Played Key Role in al Shabaab Investigation," Investigative Project, August 6, 2010.

31. Executive Order 13224.

32. "Terrorist Abuse of Non-Profits and Charities: A Proactive Approach to Preventing Terrorist Financing," Jennifer Lynn Bell.

33. Ibid.

34. Interview with Jerry Biggs, March, 2010.

35. Interview with John Tobon, July 1, 2010.

36. GAO report: "Terrorist Financing: U.S. Agencies Should Systematically Assess Terrorists' Use of Alternative Financing Mechanisms," November 2003.

37. Interview with John Tobon, July 1, 2010.

38. GAO report: "Terrorist Financing: U.S. Agencies Should Systematically Assess Terrorists' Use of Alternative Financing Mechanisms," November 2003.

39. USAID letter to Mr. Shukri Baker, President of Holy Land Foundation of Relief.

40. USAID Audit of the Adequacy of USAID's Antiterrorism Vetting Procedures, Audit Report No. 9-000-08-001-P, November 6, 2007.

41. Ibid.

42. Ibid.

Chapter 9

1. *Seven Days Illustrated* magazine, 1969.

2. RAND Note, "The Mitrone Kidnapping in Uruguay," David Ronfeldt, August 1987, prepared for the U.S. Department of State Defense Advanced Research Projects Agency.

3. U.S. District Court Eastern District of New York, The European Community v. RJR Nabisco, Inc., R.J. Reynolds Tobacco Company, R.J. Reynolds Tobacco International, Inc., RJR Acquisition Corp., f/k/a Nabisco Group Holdings Corp., RJR Nabisco Holdings Corp., R.J. Reynolds Tobacco Holdings, Inc.

4. *At Home in the World*, Daniel Pearl (Wall Street Journal Books, 2002).

5. *Daily Times Pakistan*, "Smuggling Under Afghan Transit Trade Agreement: Pakistan Bearing Annual Revenue Loss of $2.3 Billion," January 23, 2010.

6. *At Home in the World*, p. 75.

7. *At Home in the World*.

8. *Miami Herald*, "Miami-Dade Businessman to Plead Guilty to Terror-Related Smuggling," Jay Weaver, October 1, 2010.

9. *Washington Post*, "Hezbollah Official Indicted on Weapons Charge," Spencer S. Hsu, November 25, 2009.

10. Indictment filed in U.S. District Court for the Eastern District of Pennsylvania vs. Criminal No.: 09 United States of America v. Hassan Hodroj, Dib Handi Harb, Hasan Antar Karaki, Moussa Ali Hamdan, Hamze El-Najjar a/k/a "Hamze Al-Majjar," Moustafa Habib Kassem, Latif Kamel Hazime, a/k/a "Andanan," Alaa Allia Ahmed Mohamed a/k/a "Ataa Ahmed Mohamed Abouelnagaa," Maodo Kane Michael Katz, November 4, 2009.

11. Ibid.

12. United States District Court Southern District of Florida, USA v., Samer Mehdi, Khaled T. Safadi, Cedar Distributors, Inc., Ulises Talavera, Transamerica Express of Miami, Emilio Jacinto Gonzalez-Neira and Jumbo Cargo, Inc., October 1st, 2009.

13. "Tobacco and Terror: How Cigarette Smuggling Is Funding Our Enemies Abroad," prepared by the Republican Staff of the U.S. House Committee on Homeland Security, U.S. Rep. Peter T. King (IR-NY), Ranking Member.

14. Ibid.

15. United States District Court Eastern District of New York, The European Community v. RJR Nabisco, Inc., R.J. Reynolds Tobacco Company, R.J. Reynolds Tobacco International, Inc., RJR Acquisition Corp., f/k/a Nabisco Group Holdings Corp., RJR Nabisco Holdings Corp., R.J. Reynolds Tobacco Holdings, Inc.

16. Ibid.

17. *International Journal of Comparative and Applied Criminal Justice*, "The Nexus of Organized Crime and Terrorism: Two Case Studies in Cigarette Smuggling," Louise I. Shelley and Sharon A. Melzer, Spring 2008, Vol. 32 No. 1.

18. United States District Court Eastern District of New York, The European Community v. RJR Nabisco, Inc., R.J. Reynolds Tobacco Company, R.J. Reynolds Tobacco International, Inc., RJR Acquisition Corp., f/k/a Nabisco Group Holdings Corp., RJR Nabisco Holdings Corp., R.J. Reynolds Tobacco Holdings, Inc.

19. Ibid.

20. Ibid.

21. Ibid.

22. The PKK was established in the 1970s as a Marxist-Leninist insurgent group composed of Turkish Kurds. On October 8, 1999, Secretary of State Madeleine Albright designated the PKK as a Foreign Terrorist Organization (FTO). On May 10, 2001, Secretary of State Colin L. Powell reaffirmed the designation of the PKK as an FTO.

23. United States District Court Eastern District of New York, The European Community v. RJR Nabisco, Inc., R.J. Reynolds Tobacco Company, R.J. Reynolds Tobacco International, Inc., RJR Acquisition Corp., f/k/a Nabisco Group Holdings Corp., RJR Nabisco Holdings Corp., R.J. Reynolds Tobacco Holdings, Inc.

24. Economics of Tobacco Control, World Bank Group, Chapter 5, "Measures to Reduce the Supply of Tobacco."

25. South African Revenue Service media release, "Destruction of Illegal Cigarettes."

26. *Wall Street Journal*, "States Go to War on Cigarette Smuggling," Gary Fields, July 20, 2009.

27. Economics of Tobacco Control, World Bank Group, Chapter 5, "Measures to Reduce the Supply of Tobacco."

28. World Health Organization Framework Convention on Tobacco Control Intergovernmental Negotiating Body (Article 15 of the WHO FCTC).

29. United Nations Office on Drugs and Crime Newsletter on the fight against money laundering and terrorism financing in West Africa.

30. "Terrorism and Tobacco: How Cigarette Smuggling Finances Jihad and Insurgency Worldwide," Kate Wilson Center for Public Integrity, June 29, 2009.

31. Ibid.

32. Report of the Group of Experts to the UN Security Council, July 21, 2004.

33. Ibid.

34. "Prepared Testimony of Ralf Mutschke, Assistant Director, Criminal Intelligence Directorate, International Criminal Police Organization, Interpol, before the House Committee on the Judiciary Subcommittee on Crime, "The Threat Posed by the Convergence of Organized Crime, Drug Trafficking and Terrorism," Federal News Service, Ralf Mutschke, December 13, 2000.

35. *Daily Mail*, "U.S. Businessman Funded Real IRA Soldier Killers by Smuggling Cigarettes into Ireland," Paul Thomson, March 13, 2009.

36. *Irish Times*, "The High Cost of Cheap Fakes," October 4, 2010.

37. CBS News, *60 Minutes*, "The Price of Bananas" transcript, August 9, 2009.

38. Reuters, "Chiquita Faces New Lawsuit, $1 Billion Damages Sought," April 14, 2010.

39. Bloomberg, "Murders May Lead to Damages Tailspin for Chiquita," Erik Larson and Joshua Goodman, April 2, 2008.

40. Reuters, "Chiquita Sued Over Killing of U.S. Missionaries," reported by Tom Brown, edited by Mohammad Zargham, March 12, 2008.

41. *Palm Beach Post News*, "Judge Rules Families Can Proceed with Suit Against Banana Giant Chiquita," Jane Musgrave, February 4, 2010.

42. Bloomberg "Murders May Lead to Damages Tailspin for Chiquita," Larson, Erik, Goodman, Joshua April 2nd, 2008

43. *Narco News*, "Congressman William Delahunt to Investigate U.S. Corporations' Support for Colombian Paramilitaries," Dan Feder, January 22, 2008.

44. CBS News, *60 Minutes*, "The Price of Bananas" transcript, August 9, 2009.

45. Ibid.

46. The William Rivas Front was run by AUC paramilitaries in the banana zone of Magdalena.

47. Superior Court of the State of California for the County of Los Angeles, Juana Perez v. Dole Food Company.

Chapter 10

1. Interview with Steven Reed at the LEAPS conference in Los Angeles, CA, August 5, 2011.

2. Interview with Captain Daniel Hahn at the LEAPS conference in Los Angeles, CA, August 5, 2011.

3. NRF 2010 survey of organized retail crime.

4. Phone interview with Alan Herbach, CEO of American Theft Prevention, September 9, 2009.

5. Author interview with Alan Herbach, October 22, 2009.

6. "Sarah" is the younger sister of a contact who has been involved in organized retail crime for five years. She went from stealing YSL handbags to working at JCPenney and stealing there.

7. DigitalPersona White Paper "Combating Retail/Restaurant Fraud with Fingerprint Biometrics: A Cost-Effective Approach to Loss Prevention for Payroll Theft and Point- of-Sale (POS) Shrink," July 2009.

8. NRF 2009 National Retail Security Survey.

9. Ibid.

10. University of Florida 2005 National Retail Security Survey.

11. NRF Survey 2010.

12. Costco Q3 2009 quarterly earnings report.

13. *SFGate*, "Shoplifting Ring Pocketed Millions Worth of Products," Peter Fimrite, June 6, 2008.

14. Coalition Against Organized Retail Crime, Hearing on Organized Retail Theft Prevention, October 25, 2007.

15. "Sales Tax Decline in Late 2008 Was the Worst in 50 Years: Early Data for 2009 Show Further, Sharp Drop in Tax Revenues for Most States," Donald J. Boyd and Lucy Dadayan, April 2009.

16. Statistics from Crime Stoppers of Houston, www.crime-stoppers.org.

17. Retail Industry Leaders Association (RILA) Crime Trends Survey 2009.

18. Retail Industry Leaders Association (RILA) Crime Trends Survey 2010.

19. Retail Crime Congressional research.

20. Ibid.

21. WakeUpWalMart.com, "Crime and Wal-Mart—'Is Wal-Mart Safe?' An Analysis of Official Police Incidents at Wal-Mart Stores," May 1, 2006.

22. Interview with Joe LaRocca, April 7, 2010.

23. Congressional Research Service, paper on organized retail crime by Kristin Finklea, June 16, 2010.

24. Author interview with a Brooklyn mother who is primarily dependent on formula for her infant, October 2010.

25. LawFuel, The Laws News Network, "Estimated More Than 20 Tractor-Trailer Loads of Merchandise Seized."

26. Frank Muscato testimony, Subcommittee on Crime, Terrorism, and Homeland Security.

27. Ibid.

28. NRF Report 2009.

29. ASIS Foundation, "Organized Retail Crime: Assessing the Risk and Developing Effective Strategies," Walter E. Palmer and Chris Richardson.

30. ASIS Foundation Research Council, Strategies, 2009, p. 4.

31. "Shoplifting, Inc.," March 4, 2010, Bernice P.L. Yeung, 109-162, section 1105, codified at 28 U.S.C. section 509 note. In the Violence Against Women and Department of Justice Reauthorization Act of 2005, Congress defined organized retail theft and directed the Attorney General and FBI to establish a task force to combat organized retail theft as well as a clearinghouse within the private sector.

32. Interview with Jerry Biggs, April 5, 2010.

Chapter 11

1. World Bank, "A Review of Current and Evolving Trends in Terrorism Financing," testimony submitted to the House Committee on Financial Services, Subcommittee on Oversight and Investigations, U.S. Gen. Accounting Office, Terrorist Financing: U.S. Agencies Should Systematically Assess Terrorists' Use of Alternative Financing Mechanisms, at 3 (2003), available at http://www.gao.gov/new.items/d04163.pdf ("[The FBI] do[es] not systematically collect and analyze data on alternative financing mechanisms.").

2. *Terrornomics*, edited by Sean S. Costigan and David Gold (Ashgate Publishing Co., 2007).

3. Ibid.

4. Ibid.

5. Ibid.

6. Ibid.

7. GAO Report to the Chairman, Committee on the Judiciary, House of Representatives, International Financial Crime: Treasury's Roles and Responsibilities Relating to Selected Provisions of the USA Patriot Act.

8. Napoleoni estimates that before 9/11 the new terror economy was at $500 million and growing at a rate of 5–6%. Compounded, the number came out to be $850 billion.

9. World Bank, Combating Money Laundering and the Financing of Terrorism: A Comprehensive Training Guide.

10. U.S. Commodity Futures Trading Commission Anti-Money Laundering Industry Oversight.

11. Ibid.

12. Anti-Money Laundering Examination Manual for the Federal Financial Institutions Examination Council.

13. Strategic Insight, "Following the Terrorist Informal Money Trail: The Hawala Financial Mechanism," Robert E. Looney, November 1, 2002.

14. Combating Money Laundering and the Financing of Terrorism: A Comprehensive Training Guide, World Bank.

15. *Daily Times Pakistan*, "Money Laundering Scam Worth $10 Bn," Faraz Khan, November 9, 2008.

16. *Pakistan Daily*, "Khanani Remanded in FIA Custody," November 10, 2008.

17. Ibid.

18. Ibid.

19. Ibid.

20. *Wall Street Journal*, "Corruption Suspected in Airlift of Billions in Cash from Kabul," Matthew Rosenberg, June 25, 2010.

21. Ibid.

22. Strategic Insight, "Following the Terrorist Informal Money Trail: The Hawala Financial Mechanism," Robert E. Looney, November 1, 2002.

23. The Commodity Futures Trading Commission web site lists the AML programs and what U.S. financial institutions should adhere to.

24. Interview with Detective Amaury Guevara at LAPD headquarters, August 8, 2010.

25. Combating Money Laundering and the Financing of Terrorism: A Comprehensive Training Guide, World Bank.

26. Ibid.

27. *Retail Crime, Security, and Loss Prevention: An Encyclopedic Reference*, Charles A. Sennewald and John H. Christman (Butterworth-Heinemann, 2008).

28. *New York Times*, "Gift-Card Cons on the Rise as Employees Find Them Easy to Swipe," Steven Greenhouse, December 29, 2009.

29. Interview with Joe LaRocca, June 28, 2010.

30. *Economic Review-Federal Reserve Bank of Kansas City*, "The Changing Nature of U.S. Card Payment Fraud: Industry and Public Policy Options," Richard J. Sullivan.

31. Ibid.

32. Ibid.

33. *SC Magazine*, "Police Bust Massive Global Credit Card Fraud Ring," Angela Moscaritolo, June 16, 2010.

34. Ibid.

35. Interview with Joe LaRocca, June 28, 2010.

36. *Organized Crime: From Trafficking to Terrorism*, Volume 2, Frank Shanty (ABC-CLIO, 2007).

37. Ibid.

38. 18 USC 1956.

39. 18 USC 981 and 982.

40. 31 USC 5322(a).

41. *The Price of Fear: al Qaeda and the Truth Behind the Financial War on Terror*, Ibrahim Warde (I.B. Tauris & Co. Ltd., 2007).

42. Ibid.

43. Application of Racketeer Influenced and Corrupt Organizations Act (RICO), 18 U.S.C.A. section 1961 et seq., to Terrorists and Acts of Terrorism, Jay M. Zitter, J.D.

44. Ibid.

45. *International Journal of Comparative and Applied Criminal Justice*, "The Nexus of Organized Crime and Terrorism: Two Case Studies in Cigarette Smuggling," Louise I. Shelly and Sharon A. Melzer, Spring 2008, Vol. 32, No. 1.

46. Bell, 2003; Broyles and Rubio, 2004; United States of America v. Mohamad Youssef Hammoud, 2004.

47. Ibid.

48. Ibid.

49. The Antiterrorism and Effective Death Penalty Act of 1996 substantially amends the federal habeas corpus law as it applies to both state and federal prisoners whether on death row or imprisoned for a term of years, according to Charles Doyle, senior specialist, American Law Division, June 3, 1996.

50. CNN, "High Court: Law Banning 'Support' of Terror Groups Constitutional," Bill Mears, June 21, 2010.

51. "Terror and Free Speech," *Los Angeles Times* editorial, June 22, 2010.

52. Ibid.

53. CNN, "High Court: Law Banning 'Support' of Terror Groups Constitutional," Bill Mears, June 21, 2010.

54. Holder v. Humanitarian Project, Supreme Court Opinion, October Term 2009.

Epilogue

1. Politico.com, "GOP Seeks to Redefine War on Terror," Josh Gerstein, May 10, 2011.

2. Swedish Defence Research Agency (FOI), "Militancy in the Pakistani Federally Administered Tribal Areas (FATA) and Afghanistan," Magnus Norell, February 2010.

3. *Wall Street Journal*, "Bin Laden Left Legacy of Stronger Controls on Terrorist Finance," Samuel Rubenfeld, May 3, 2011.

4. CNN.com, "Terrorism Groups Helped by Black Market Goods," Randi Kaye, July 19, 2006.

Index

A

Abd al Hamid Al Mujil, 9
Abdinur, Abdifatah, 172
Abdullah al Muhajir, 21
Abdullah Faisal, 161
Abdullah Yusuf Azzam, 135
Abelrahman, Idriss, 156
Abu Abdul Aziz, 171
Abu Talhah Al-Amirikee, 162
Abu Zubaydah, 129
Advantage Freight Network, 65, 86, 111, 126
AEDPA (Antiterrorism and Effective Death Penalty Act) of 1996, 239-241
Afghan Transit Trade (ATT), 165, 181
Africa, cigarette smuggling in, 190-191
Agilence, Inc., 209
Aguirre, Fernando, 193
Ahmed, Farooque, 145
Akhdar, Elias Mohamad, 184
Al Barakaat, 144
Al Farooq Mosque, 168
al Khifa, 135
al Qaeda
   AQIM (al Qaeda in the Islamic Maghreb), 156, 189
   connection with MS-13 (Mara Salvatrucha), 21-25
   effect of global recession on, 9-11
   funding by Muslim charities, 174-175
   fundraising activities of, 134-135
   independent cells, 121
al Qaeda in the Islamic Maghreb (AQIM), 156, 189
al Shabaab, 11, 18, 41, 161, 174
Al Taqwa, 144
al-Awlaki, Anwar, 166-167
Albright, Madeleine, 193, 240
Albuquerque Police Department, 72-74
Albuquerque Retail Assets Protection Association (ARAPA), 72
Alessa, Mohamed Mahmood, 18, 163
Alfred Bossert money laundering organization, 186
Ali, Amina Farah, 172-173
Almonte, Carlos Eduardo, 18, 163
Alpha Trading, 82
Amazon, 43
American Theft Prevention Products, 3, 206
AMI (anti-money laundering) programs, 222
anti-American sentiment among immigrant communities, 15-17, 21
anti-money laundering (AML) programs, 222

Antiterrorism and Effective Death
Penalty Act of 1996 (AEDPA),
239-241
Anti-Terrorism Clause (ATC), 174
Aponte, Anthony, 107
Aponte, Harry, 107
Appo Import Export, 123-127
AQIM (al Qaeda in the Islamic
Maghreb), 156, 189
Aqueduct Flea Market, 91
ARAPA (Albuquerque Retail Assets
Protection Association), 72
Arden Fair Mall (Sacramento, CA),
201-205
Arellano Felix, 155
Arostequi, David Nil-Jose, 107
aspirational shoppers, 38
At Home in the World (Pearl), 181
ATC (Anti-Terrorism Clause), 174
Atef, Mohammed, 129
ATT (Afghan Trade and Transit), 165
Atta, Mohammad, 128-129
auto theft, 113-115
Avanguardia Nazional, 140
Ayabatwa, Tibert Rujugiro, 190
Ayala, Janice, 214
Ayatollah Khomeini, 28

B

B. Rosen and Sons, 86-87
baby strollers, use by boosters, 107
BAD-CATS, 64, 112
Baker, Richard, 38
Bank of New York, 171
The Bank of New York, money
laundering through, 185-188
Bank Secrecy Act (BSA) of 1970,
144-145, 185
Banki, Mahmoud Reza, 47
banking regulations, 145-150
banking systems
anti-money laundering (AML)
programs, 222

circumvention of. *See* money
laundering
hawalas. *See* hawalas regulation
failures
hawalas, 219-227
*in Pakistan, India, Afghanistan,
and Somalia, 223-224*
Barakat, Assad Muhammad,
123-127, 135
Barakat, Hamzi, 124
Barakat, Hatim Ahmad, 124-125, 135
Barakat, Muhammad Fayez, 125
Barakat Import Export Ltd, 124
Barneys, 54-56, 116
Benevolence International
Foundation, 175
BERG Associates, 120
Bergman, Jay, 156
Bianchi, Corrado, 187
Biegelman, Martin T., 132
Biggs, Jerry, 13, 61, 78-79, 88, 90, 92,
98-99, 217
Bihi, Abdirizak, 173
Black Market Peso Exchange,
152-155
blame game, 54
Bloomingdale's, 57
Boies Schiller & Flexner LLP, 197
Bomez, Julio, 86-87
booster bags, 107
boosters. *See also* cargo theft
booster bags, 107
case studies
June, 80
Maria, 77-80, 97-98
Marin Moreno, 73
Nick Jojola, 98-99
definition of, 97
deterring, 115-118
legal penalties for convictions,
101-103
Level 1 boosters, 98-99
Level 2 boosters, 104-108

Level 3 boosters, 108-115
  tools and theft techniques, 107
Borodkin, Alice, 45
Brazil, Muslim population in, 120
Breyer, Stephen, 240
BSA (Bank Secrecy Act) of 1970,
  144-145, 185
Buckner, Kris, 44, 166-167
bulk cash smuggling, 228
Burke, Michael, 32, 34
Burlington Coat Factory, 34
Bush, George W., 173

C

Calderon, Horacio, 132
Caltagirone, Tom, 63
Canara Bank, 147
cargo theft, 83-84, 112-113, 172
  cargo theft rings, 84
  case study: cargo theft of B. Rosen
    and Sons, 86-87
  costs of, 64-67, 93
  as national security threat, 93
  of over-the-counter drugs, 84-86
  USA Patriot Improvement and
    Reauthorization Act, 93
cartels, 152-155
Casa Apollo, 124
Casa Hamze, 124
cash cards, 45-48
Cassara, John A., 141
CCTV (closed-circuit television
  system) at Arden Fair Mall
  (Sacramento, CA), 202-203
Cedar Distributors, 133
Center for Contemporary
  Conflict, 225
CFT (Combating the Financing of
  Terrorism), 224
CFTC (Commodity Futures Trading
  Commission), 227

CFTRA (Currency and Foreign
  Transaction Reporting Act), 148
Chambers Ireland, 192
Chan, Siu Yung, 33, 64
Chanel, 59
charitable donation loopholes,
  173-175
charities (Muslim)
  charitable donation loopholes,
    173-175
  funding of terrorist organizations,
    169-172
  online solicitation of donations, 175
  U.S. fundraising for, 172-173
  USAID Antiterrorism Vetting
    Procedures, 175-177
Chase Manhattan Bank, money
  laundering through, 185-188
Chesnut, Rob, 42
Chesser, Zack, 161
Chiquita, involvement with
  Columbian paramilitary groups,
  192-195
"Chris from the Congo" (counterfeit
  handbag dealer), 13-15, 34-37, 49,
  137, 166
Chroust, Casey, 13
cigarette smuggling, 183-192
  in Africa, 189-191
  costs of, 183-185, 188-189
  history of, 188-189
  in Ireland, 191-192
  in Latin America, 191
  by RJR Corp., 183-188
circumvention of banking systems.
  See money laundering
Citibank N.A., money laundering
  through, 185-188
Clarke, Ronald V., 55, 213
CLEAR (Coalition of Law
  Enforcement and Retail),
  42, 58, 168

closed-circuit television system (CCTV) at Arden Fair Mall (Sacramento, CA), 202-203

CNDP (Congress National Pour la Defence du Peuple), 190

Coach, 34-36, 59

Coalition of Law Enforcement and Retail (CLEAR), 42

Coalition on Organized Retail Crime, 58, 89, 168

Coco USA, 33, 62

Cogswell, Paul, 46, 58

Cohen, Joey (Yousef al-Khattab), 161-163

Collette, 38

Collingsworth, Terry, 196

Colombia
cigarette smuggling in, 191
extortion by paramilitary groups, 192-197

Combating Money Laundering and the Financing of Terrorism, 229

Combating Organized Retail Crime Act of 2009, 95

Combating the Financing of Terrorism (CFT), 224

Commandant Jerome (FAPC), 190

Commodity Futures Trading Commission (CFTC), 227

Community Oriented Notification Network Enforcement Communication Technology (CONNECT), 74

Congo Tobacco Company, 190

Congress National Pour la Defence du Peuple (CNDP), 190

Congressional Research Service on Organized Retail Crime, 207

CONNECT (Community Oriented Notification Network Enforcement Communication Technology), 74

consumer demand for counterfeit/ pirated merchandise, 38-39

Copaxone, theft of, 85

Cornerstone, 71

Costco, 210

costs of ORC (organized retail crime), 4, 53-54, 63, 207-208
cigarette smuggling, 188-189
credit card fraud, 231-234
decrease in state tax revenues, 210-212
health costs, 212-215
labor costs, 208-210
per-employee theft case versus average shoplifter, 208
stored value card fraud, 230

Coughlin, Tom, 57

counterfeit merchandise
case study: Fendi, 31-32
Coach case study, 34-36
consumer demand for, 38-39
eBay response, 42-44
and funding of terrorist organizations, 48-51
handbags, 13-16
online sales of, 40-42
passports, 127-132
policing of, 39-40
sales by street vendors, 48-51

Couric, Katie, 219

Cox, Kenneth, 73-74

Craigslist, 89

CRAVED goods, 213

credit card fraud, 231-234

criminal penalties, 101-103, 248. *See also* legislation
for boosters, 101-103
for fences, 101-103

cross-border gangs
M-18, 22
MS-13 (Mara Salvatrucha), 21-25
Zetas, 23

Cruz, Julian Rivera, 107

CTR (currency transaction report), 145

Cuomo, Gerardo, 187

Currency and Foreign Transaction Reporting Act (CFTRA), 148
currency transaction report (CTR), 145
cutouts, 187
CVS, 107
Cymbalta, theft of, 85

D

Dar-ul-Islah Mosque, 168-169
Deckers, 44
Del Monte, involvement with Colombian paramilitary groups, 195
Delahunt, William, 195
Denz, Martin, 187
Denz, Werner, 187
Department of Homeland Security (DHS), 71
DHS (Department of Homeland Security), 11, 71
DigitalPersona, 207
discretionary versus nondiscretionary spending, 38
documents, forging of, 127-132
Dole Foods, involvement with Colombian paramilitary groups, 195-197
domestic terrorism, 17-19
    anti-American sentiment among immigrant communities, 15-17
    Islamberg compound (Hancock, New York), 19
    Red Compound (Virginia), 19
drug cartels, 152-155
drugs, theft of, 84-86
Duyn, Donald Van, 21

E

eBay, 89
    monitoring of illegal merchandise, 42-44
    response to e-fencing, 44

e-fencing, 40-42, 89-91
    E-fencing Enforcement Act of 2009, 95, 116-118
    recognizing, 51-52
E-fencing Enforcement Act of 2009, 95, 116-118
18th Street gang, 22
El Lasca, 154
electronic sensors, 206
Eli Lilly & Co., 85
Elias, Samuel, 104-105
Elliot, Timothy, 56
El-Najjar, Hamze, 182
employee theft
    costs of, 208
    insider information, 54-56
    scope of, 56-59
Epoch USA Trading Company, 39
Escobar, Pablo, 151
Essabar, Zakariya, 129
European Community v. RJR Corp, 185-188
Evans, Jeannie, 243
Evans, Robert E., 243
Executive Order 13224, 133, 173
extremism (Muslim). See Muslim extremism

F

fakeidsite.com, 132
family crime networks, 119-121
    case study: Assad Muhammad Barakat, 123-127
    Morel family, 119
    in Tri-Border area of South America, 120-123
    trust factor, 136-
FAPC (Forces Armees du Peuple Congolais), 190
FARC (Fuerzas Armadas Revolucionarias de Colombia), 11, 60, 151-152, 191, 194

FATA (Federally Administered Tribal Areas), 18

FATF (Financial Action Task Force), 26, 147, 221

Fayad, Sobhi Mahmoud, 125

FBI
Joint Terrorism Task Force, 60
and LAAORCA (Los Angeles Area Organized Retail Crimes Association), 71
Uniform Crime Reporting System, 67

Featherstone, James, 69-70

Federal Bureau of Investigations. *See* FBI

Federal Financial Institutions Examination Council, 223

Federal Motor Carrier Safety Administration (FMCSA), 65

Federally Administered Tribal Areas (FATA), 18

Feey Town, 98

fences
deterring, 115-118
legal penalties for convictions, 101-103
Level 3 fences, 108-112
professional fences, 100
role of, 100-101

Fendi, 31-32

Fertig, Ralph, 240

Filene's Basement, 34

Financial Action Task Force (FATF), 26, 147, 221

Financial Action Task Force on Money Laundering, 170

Financial Industry Regulatory Authority (FINRA), 222

financing. *See* banking systems

FINRA (Financial Industry Regulatory Authority), 219-221

Fischer, Karen, 72-74

flea markets, 91

FMCSA (Federal Motor Carrier Safety Administration), 65

Forces Armees du Peuple Congolais (FAPC), 190

forged documents, 127-132

Forsaith, Chuck, 85

"44 Ways to Support Jihad" (Anwar al-Awlaki), 167

Friedheim, Cyrus Jr., 193

Fuerzas Armadas Revolucionarias de Colombia (FARC), 11, 151-152, 191, 194

funding of terrorist organizations
fundraising activities of terrorist organizations, 134-135
Muslim charities
charitable donation loopholes, 173-175
foreign charities. See terrorist organizations
online solicitation of donations, 175
U.S. fundraising for, 172-173
USAID Antiterrorism Vetting Procedures, 175-177

fundraising activities of terrorist organizations, 134-135

Funes, Mauricio, 154

G

Galeria Page mall, 124, 133, 135, 182

GameStop, 59, 233

gangs
M-18, 22
MS-13 (Mara Salvatrucha), 21-25
Zetas, 23

Garcia, Luis, 187

Gee, Jack, 42, 44, 50, 51, 58, 168

ghost companies, 132-133

ghost exports, 189

gift cards, 45-48

Global Relief Foundation, 175

Gonzalez, Carlos Espinoza, 109-110

Gonzalez-Neira, Emilio, 30, 50, 63, 126, 133, 182

gray market, 90, 94

Group of Experts (U.N.), 190
growth of ORC (organized retail crime), 4-5
Guevara, Amaury, 116, 128, 228-232
Gulf cartel, 155

H

Hahn, Daniel, 53, 204
Hamas, 11
Hamdan, Moussa Ali, 29-30, 182
Hammoud, Chawki, 238
Hammoud, Mohamad, 131, 184, 238
Hamzime, Latif Kamel, 182
handbags
  counterfeit. See counterfeit merchandise
  stolen, 1-3
Haq, Abdul, 181
Harb, Dib Hani, 29, 182
Harb, Said, 238
Hassan, Hawo Mohamed, 172-173
hawaladar, 47, 143
hawalas, 10, 142-144, 219-221, 224-227
Hayes, Jack L., 208
Hayes, Read, 49
health costs of ORC (organized retail crime), 212-215
Herbach, Alan, 3, 206
Hernandez Operation, 72
Hezbollah, 11
  activity in Latin America, 24
  activity in South America, 27-30, 120-123
  case study: Assad Muhammad Barakat, 123-127
  counterfeiting by, 29-30
  decentralization of, 10
  funding by sales of pirated/counterfeit merchandise, 50

  funding from ORC (organized retail crime), 166-167
  fundraising activities of, 135
Hide & Seek: Intelligence, Law Enforcement, and the Stalled War on Terrorist Finance (Cassara), 141
Hill, Roderick, 193
Hodroj, Hassan, 29, 182
Holder v. Humanitarian Law Project, 239-241
Hollinger, Richard, 58, 208
Holy Land Foundation, 60, 170, 174, 176
"homegrown terrorism", 160-165
hoodies, use to circumvent security cameras, 201-204
Hooper, James, 68, 107,
hot products, 55
Howard, Russell D., 220
human smuggling, 129-132
Humanitarian Law Project, 239-241
Hussein, Saddam, 11, 188
Hussein, Uday, 11, 188

I

ICE (Immigration and Customs Enforcement), 11, 59, 214
Idara Khidmat-e-Khalq (IKK), 171-172
Identity Theft Handbook: Detection, Prevention, and Security (Biegelman), 132
IFTs (informal funds transfers). See hawalas
IIRO (International Islamic Relief Organization), 9
IKK (Idara Khidmat-e-Khalq), 171-172
illegal entry into U.S.
  counterfeit passports, 127-132
  human smuggling, 129-132

IMF (International Monetary Fund), 141, 233

immigrant communities, anti-American sentiment among, 15-17, 21

Immigration and Customs Enforcement (ICE), 11, 59, 214

India, banking regulation failures in, 223-224

informal funds transfers (IFTs). *See* hawalas

inmates, recruitment by Muslim extremists, 19-21

Intelligence Reform and Terrorism Prevention Act (IRTPA), 239

International Convention for the Suppression of the Financing of Terrorism, 146, 219

International Islamic Relief Organization (IIRO), 9

International Monetary Fund (IMF), 141, 233

Investigative Project on Terrorism, 230

IRA (Irish Republican Army), 11, 140, 191-192

Ireland, cigarette smuggling in, 191-192

Irish Republican Army (IRA), 140, 191-192

IRTPA (Intelligence Reform and Terrorism Prevention Act), 239

Islamberg compound (Hancock, New York), 19

Islamic charities. *See* Muslim charities

Islamic extremism. *See* Muslim extremism

islamicjihad.com, 161

Issa, Ali, 48

Issa, Oumar, 156

J

Jaish-I-Mohammed, 181

Jamaat al Fuqra, 19

Jamaat-ud-Dawa, 170-172

James, Kevin Lamar, 20

Jam'iyyat Ul-Islam Is-Saheeh (JIS), 20

Jerome (leader, FAPC), 190

Jimenez, Caros Mario, 195

JIS (Jam'iyyat Ul-Islam Is-Saheeh), 20

Jocata, 224

Johnson, Larry, 120, 152, 192

Joint Terrorism Task Force, 60

Jojola, Nick, 73, 98-99

Jomana Import Export, 126, 133

Jones, Paul, 43-44, 101

Juarez Cartel, 113

Jumbo Cargo, 126, 133

June (booster), 80

K

Kagan, Elena, 241

Kalia, Munaf, 225

Kassem, Moustafa Habib, 182

Kelly, Raymond W., 169

Keskes, Ahmet M., 89

Khalid Sheikh Mohammed, 128

Khan, Aftab, 47, 139, 142

Khan, Khalid, 181

Khan, Pir, 47, 139, 142

Khanani, Javed, 225

Kollayikal, Gokul, 224

Kresevich, Millie, 216

Kris, David, 183

Kroft, Steve, 195

Kurdistan Workers' Party (PKK), 186, 240

L

LAAORCA (Los Angeles Area Organized Retail Crimes Association), 70-72

labor costs of ORC (organized retail crime), 208-210

Lam, Chong, 33, 64

Landman, Stephen I., 19-21, 230

LAPD (Los Angeles Police Department), 68-72

LaRocca, Joe, 12, 48, 88, 92, 100, 106, 212, 231, 233-234

Lashkar-e-Taiba (LeT), 11, 41, 170

Latin America
cigarette smuggling in, 191
ORC (organized retail crime) and, 151-152

Latin American immigrant communities, anti-American sentiment among, 21

Laurent, Patrick, 187

Law Enforcement and Private Security (LEAPS) conference, 69-70

LEAPS (Law Enforcement and Private Security) conference, 69-70

legislation. *See also* criminal penalties
Antiterrorism and Effective Death Penalty Act of 1996 (AEDPA), 239-241
Bank Secrecy Act (BSA) of 1970, 144-145, 185
Combating Organized Retail Crime Act of 2009, 95
E-fencing Enforcement Act of 2009, 95, 116-118
Intelligence Reform and Terrorism Prevention Act (IRTPA), 239
Money Laundering Control Act, 150
Organized Retail Theft Investigation and Prosecution Act of 2010, 212
RICO (Racketeer Influenced and Corrupt Organizations Act). *See* RICO (Racketeer Influenced and Corrupt Organizations Act)
Tariff Act of 1930, 94
USA Patriot Improvement and Reauthorization Act, 66-67, 93, 148-150, 220-222

LeT (Lashkar-e-Taiba), 11, 41, 170

Level 1 boosters, 98-99

Level 2 boosters, 104-108

Level 3 boosters, 108-115

Levis, theft of, 64

Levitt, Matthew, 28, 30

Liberation Tigers of Tamil Eelam (LTTE), 240

license plate recognition software, 202-203

Llorens, Gilbert, 187

Logan, Samuel, 23, 152

Looney, Robert E., 225-227

Los Angeles Area Organized Retail Crimes Association (LAAORCA), 70-72

Los Angeles Police Department (LAPD), 68-72

Loss Prevention Research Council, 49

Loyd, Ed, 194

LTTE (Liberation Tigers of Tamil Eelam), 240

Luxottica Retail, 216

Luxury Institute, 32

LVMH, 32

Lynch, Stephen F., 142

M

M-18, 22

Madoff, Bernie, 95

Maktab al-Khidamat, 135

Malik, Abdul, 62

Malik, Rehman, 171

Mancuso, Salvatore, 195

Mangones, Jose Gregorio, 196

Manson, Charles, 163

Mansur family, 187

Mara Salvatrucha. *See* MS-13 (Mara Salvatrucha)

Maras. *See* cross-border gangs

Maria (booster), 60, 77-80, 97-98

Markaz-e-Dawa Irshad, 171

Markaz-ud-Dawa-wal-Irshad, 172

Marra, Kenneth, 194

Martel, Bill, 10

Martel, William, 135, 140

Masood, Talat, 171

Mastermind Tobacco Company, 190

material support, 239-241

matricula consulars, 22

Medellin drug cartel, 151

Mehdi, Samer, 111, 126, 133

Mehsud, Baitullah, 9-10

MEK (Mujahadeen-e-Khalq), 80

Merritt, Randy, 137

Mervyns, 64

Mexican Zetas, 152-155

Modern Jihad: Tracing the Dollars Behind the Terror Networks (Napoleoni), 220

Mohamed, Abderahman, 169

Mundial (World) Engineering and Construction, 123, 135

money brokers, 187

money laundering, 25-27, 139-141, 185-188

  banking regulations and, 145-150

  Black Market Peso Exchange, 152-155

  with cigarette smuggling, 183-192

  credit card fraud, 231-234

  hawalas, 142-144, 219-221, 224-227

  RICO (Racketeer Influenced and Corrupt Organizations Act), 234-235-238

  on Second Life, 230

  South American, Mexican, and African connection, 155-157

  stored value cards, 227-231

Money Laundering Control Act, 150

Monnier, Patrick, 187

Monograph on Terrorist Financing, 144

Monsoor, Ahmed, 165-166

Moore, Michael, 70

Morel family, 119

Moreno, Marin, 73

Morton, Jesse. *See* Younous Abdullah Mohammed

mosques, funding of terrorist organizations, 168-169

motor vehicle theft, 113-115

Moynihan, John, 122

MS-13 (Mara Salvatrucha), 21-25, 60, -152

Muddu, Prashant, 224

Mueller, Robert, 45

Mujahadeen-e-Khalq (MEK), 80

Mullah Minbullah, 18

Murillo, Diego Fernando, 195

Murphy, Sean, 192

Muscato, Frank, 92, 103, 214-215

Muslim charities

  charitable donation loopholes, 173-175

  funding of terrorist organizations, 169-172

  online solicitation of donations, 175

  U.S. fundraising for, 172-173

  USAID Antiterrorism Vetting Procedures, 175-177

Muslim extremism. *See also* terrorist organizations

  domestic terrorism, 17-19

  recruitment of prison inmates, 19-21

  in U.S., 160-165

Mutschke, Ralf, 191

Myrick, Sue, 128

N

NADRA (National Database and Registration Authority), 225

Napolitano, Janet, 128, 220

National Cargo Theft Task Force, 67
National Database and Registration
  Authority (NADRA), 225
National Insurance Crime Bureau
  (NICB), 83, 154
The National Movement for
  the Restoration of Pakistani
  Sovereignty, 181
National Retail Federation (NRF),
  54, 88, 205
National Retail Security Survey
  (NRSS), 207
Nelson A. Rockefeller Institute, 210
The New Tribes Mission Group, 194
NICB (National Insurance Crime
  Bureau), 83, 154
Nixon, Richard, 67
Nkunda, Laurent, 190
NRF (Nationals Retail Federation),
  54, 88, 205
NRSS (National Retail Security
  Survey), 207

O

Obama, Barack, 243
OCRs (organized crime rings), 24
Oda, Kent, 64, 70, 213
online sales of pirated/counterfeit
  merchandise, 40-42. *See also*
  e-fencing
Operation Blackbird, 60
Operation Greenquest, 60
Operation Polar Cap, 145
opium trade, 140
ORC (organized retail crime), 216
  anti-American sentiment and, 15-17
  boosters, 77-80
    auto theft, 113-115
    booster bags, 107
    case study: June, 80
    case study: Maria, 97-98
    case study: Marin Moreno, 73
    case study: Nick Jojola, 98-99

  definition of, 97
  deterring, 115-118
  legal penalties for convictions,
    101-103
  Level 1 boosters, 98-99
  Level 2 boosters, 104-108
  Level 3 boosters, 108-115
  tools and theft techniques, 107
  cargo theft, 83-84, 112-113
    cargo theft rings, 84
    case study: cargo theft of B.
      Rosen and Sons, 86-87
    costs of, 64-67, 93
    as national security threat, 93
    of over-the-counter drugs,
      84-86
    USA Patriot Improvement and
      Reauthorization Act, 93
  costs of, 4, 53-54, 63, 207-208
    credit card fraud, 231-234
    decrease in state tax revenues,
      210-212
    health costs, 212-215
    labor costs, 208-210per-
      employee theft case versus
      average shoplifter, 208stored
      value card fraud, 230
  counterfeit merchandise. *See*
    counterfeit merchandise
  criminal penalties, 101-103, 234
  definition of, 216
  e-fencing, 40-42, 89-91
  employee theft
    costs of, 208
    insider information, 54-56
    scope of, 56-59
  family crime networks. *See* family
    crime networks
  fences
    definition of, 97
    deterring, 115-118
    legal penalties for convictions,
      101-103
    Level 3 fences, 108-112

professional fences, 100
role of, 100-101
funding of terrorist organizations,
59-61, 159-160
correlation between ORC and
terrorism, 168
"homegrown terrorism,"
160-165
Somalian connection, 165-167
gray market, 94
growth of, 4-5
in Latin America, 151-152
legislation combating
Combating Organized Retail
Crime Act of 2009, 95
E-fencing Enforcement Act of
2009, 95
USA Patriot Improvement and
Reauthorization Act, 93
as low-risk crime, 91-93
money laundering, 139-141, 185-188
banking regulations and,
145-150
Black Market Peso Exchange,
152-155
credit card fraud, 231-234
hawalas, 142-144, 224-227
RICO (Racketeer Influenced
and Corrupt Organizations
Act), 234-238
South American, Mexican, and
African connection, 155-157
stored value cards, 227-231
via cigarette smuggling,
183-192
overview of, 4
pirated merchandise. *See* pirated
merchandise
policing of, 67-68
case study: Albuquerque Police
Department, 72-74
case study: Los Angeles Police
Department, 68-72

preventative measures
case study: Arden Fair Mall
(Sacramento, CA), 201-205
defining ORC versus shopliting
and shrinkage, 215-216
failures, 204-207
regulation of resale market,
216-217
retail returns fraud, 106-108
shell stores, 87-91
shell warehouses
explained, 80-81
profile of, 81-83
smuggling
bulk cash smuggling, 228
cigarette smuggling, 183-192
of PlayStations into South
America, 180-182
of TVs into Pakistan, 183
stolen merchandise. *See* stolen
merchandise
threat of, 11-13
trust factor, 136-138
wholesalers, 61-63
Ordine Nuovo (New Order), 140
organized crime rings (ORCs), 24
organized retail crime. *See* ORC
(organized retail crime)
Organized Retail Theft Investigation
and Prosecution Act of 2010, 212
Osama bin Laden, 129, 134, 170,
189, 243
over-the-counter drugs, theft of,
84-86
Oxycontin, theft of, 85

P

Padilla, Jose, 21
Pakistan Electronics Manufacturers
Association, 181
Palmer, Jared, 65, 67, 85
Parker, Trey, 162
Partiya Karkeren Kurdistan. *See* PKK
(Partiya Karkeren Kurdistan)

Parvonis Research, 93

passive terrorist sympathizers, 140

passports, counterfeit, 127-132

Patriot Act, 66-67, 93, 148-150, 220-222

Patterson, Gregory, 20

PayPal, 43

Pearl, Daniel, 19, 181-182

Pedraza, Milton, 32

Peekaboo handbag (Fendi), 32

Perez, Pablo, 196

pharmaceuticals, theft of, 84-86

pirated merchandise
    case study: Fendi, 31-32
    Coach case study, 34-36
    consumer demand for, 38-39
    eBay response, 42-44
    and funding of terrorist organizations, 48-51
    online sales of, 40-42
    policing of, 39-40
    sales by street vendors, 48-51

PKK (Partiya Karkeren Kurdistan), 11, 186, 240

Plan Satan, 180

PlayStations, smuggling into South America, 182

policing of ORC (organized retail crime), 67
    case study: Albuquerque Police Department, 72-74
    case study: Los Angeles Police Department, 68-72
    pirated/counterfeit merchandise, 39-40

Premium Knowledge Group, 38

preventative measures
    against boosters/fences, 115-118
    case study: Arden Fair Mall (Sacramento, CA), 201-205
    defining ORC versus shoplifting and shrinkage, 215-216
    failures, 204-207
    regulation of resale market, 216-217

Prilosec, street value of, 104

prison inmates, recruitment by Muslim extremists, 19-21

professional fences, 100

Prudencio, Harold, 99, 113

Purdue Pharma Technologies, Inc., 85

Q-R

Queen of Sheba (store), 62

Raad, Mohammed, 28

Racketeer Influenced and Corrupt Organizations Act (RICO). *See* ICE (Immigration and Customs Enforcement)

Rahim al-Nashiri, 129

Rasulullah, 167

RBS Worldpay, 232

Red Brigade, 140

Red Compound (Virginia), 19

Reed, Steven, 201-205

regulation
    banking regulation failures
        hawalas, 224-227
        in Pakistan, India, Afghanistan, and Somalia, 223-224
    of resale market, 216-217

Report of International Transportation of Currency and Monetary Instruments (CMIR), 227

resale market, regulation of, 216-217

Rescorla, Rick, 69

Retail Industry Leaders Association (RILA), 13, 62, 211

Retail Information Systems (RIS) Store Systems Study, 205

retail returns fraud, 106-108

Retail Ventures Inc. (RVI), 34

retailers
    blame game, 54
    costs of ORC (organized retail crime), 53-54

employee theft
  insider information, 54-56
  scope of, 56-59
  flea markets, 91
  shell stores, 87-91shrinkage, 54
  stolen merchandise. *See* stolen
    merchandise
returns fraud, 106-108
Revolutionary Armed Forces of
  Colombia (FARC), 60
revolutionmuslim.com, 160-163
RICO (Racketeer Influenced and
  Corrupt Organizations Act), 216,
  234-238
RILA (Retail Industry Leaders
  Association), 13, 62, 211
RIS (Retail Information Systems)
  Store Systems Study, 205
risk of ORC (organized retail
  crime), 91-93
R.J. Reynolds Tobacco, cigarette
  smuggling, 183-188
RJR companies
  cigarette smuggling, 183-188
  money laundering, 185-188
Robbin, Bema, 19
Roberts, John Jr., 240
Rockefeller, Nelson, 179
Rodner, Derek, 209
Rodriguez, George, 65-66
Rosemont Wholesale, 214
rotteneggs.com, 107
Roundtree, Ronald Gerald, 19
round-tripping, 189
Royal Bank of Scotland, 232
runners. *See* boosters
RVI (Retail Ventures Inc.), 34
Ryder, Winona, 92

S

Sacramento Police Department
  (SACPD), partnership with Arden
  Fair Mall, 202-204

Safadi, Khaled T., 30, 50, 63, 126,
  133, 182
Saks Fifth Avenue, 57
sales tax revenues, effect of ORC
  (organized retail crime) on, 210-212
Samana, Hammad, 20
Sanaullah, Rana, 170
SARs (suspicious activity
  reports), 147
Schultz, Ray, 74
Scott, Bobby, 212
Scott, Robert C., 138
SDGT (Specially Designated Global
  Terrorist), 133
Sears, 57
Second Life, 230
Secret Service, 71
SED (Shipper's Export
  Declarations), 126
shadow banking, 45
Shahzad, Faisal, 17, 25, 47, 139-142,
  162-165, 219-220
Shaykh Ahmed Nur Jimale, 144
shell corporations, 26
shell stores, 87-91
shell warehouses
  explained, 80-81
  profile of, 81-83
Shipper's Export Declarations
  (SED), 126
shoplifting
  costs of, 208
  as low-risk crime, 92
  versus ORC (organized retail crime),
    215-216
shopping.com, 43
shrinkage, 54, 215-216
Simcox, David, 130
Simms, Keisha Janelle, 19
Sinaloa, 155
Sindhi people, 120
Singleton, Terri Lynn, 19
Sintrainagro, 196

The Smoke Shop, 183
smuggling
  bulk cash smuggling, 228
  cigarette smuggling, 183-192
    in Africa, 189-191
    costs of, 183-185, 188-189
    history of, 188-189
    in Ireland, 191-192
    in Latin America, 191
    by RJR Corp.183-188
  of PlayStations into South America,
    180-182
  of TVs into Pakistan, 180-182
sob-ids.com, 132
social media, use by Muslim
  charities, 175
Somalia
  instability in, 16
  ORC (organized retail crime) in,
    159, 165-167
Sony Gulf FZE
  smuggling of PlayStations into South
    America, 182
  smuggling of TVs into Pakistan,
    180-182
South America
  Hezbollah activity in, 27-30, 120-123
  theft rings, 110
  Tri-Border Area of South
    America, 119
South Park, 162-163
Specially Designated Global Terrorist
  (SDGT), 133
State Bank of Hyderabad, 224
state budgets, effect of ORC
  (organized retail crime) on, 63,
  210-212
Stearns, Cliff, 66
stolen merchandise. *See also*
  boosters; fences
  auto parts, 113-115

cargo theft, 83-84, 112-113
  cargo theft rings, 84
  case study: cargo theft of B.
    Rosen and Sons, 86-87
  costs of, 64-67, 93
  as national security threat, 93
  of over-the-counter drugs,
    84-86
  USA Patriot Improvement and
    Reauthorization Act, 93
eBay response, 42-44
e-fencing, 40-42, 89-91
employee theft
  insider information, 54-56
  scope of, 56-59
funding of terrorist organizations,
  59-61
gift cards, 45-48
handbags, 1-3
recognizing, 51-52
retail returns fraud, 106-108
sales at flea markets, 91
sales by shell stores, 87-91
shell warehouses
  explained, 80-81
  profile of, 81-83
Stone, Matt, 162
stored value cards, 45-48, 227-231
Stored Value Systems, 46, 58
The Street Vendor Project, 48
StubHub, 43
Sudafed, street value of, 104
suspicious activity reports
  (SARs), 147
SVCs. *See* stored value cards

T

T. J. Maxx, 233
Tactical Operations Multi-
  Agency Cargo Anti-Theft Squad
  (TOMCATS), 112

Tahir, Anjun, 114
Talavera, Ulises, 30, 50, 63, 111, 126, 133, 182, 238
Taliban, decentralization of, 10
Talibanization, 244
Talib's Sportswear, 19
Target, 205
Tariff Act of 1930, 94
tax revenues, effect of ORC (organized retail crime) on, 210-212
Tehreek-e-Taliban, 9, 18, 165, 222, 244
television sets, smuggling into Pakistan, 180-182
terror watch lists, 220
terrorist organizations
anti-American sentiment among immigrant communities, 21
association with drug cartels, 155
bulk cash smuggling, 228
circumvention of banking systems, 25-27, 219-221
effect of global recession on, 9-11
financial needs of, 127
funding by Muslim charities
charitable donation loopholes, 173-175
foreign charities, 169-172
online solicitation of donations, 175
U.S. fundraising for, 172-173
USAID Antiterrorism Vetting Procedures, 175-177
funding by sales of pirated/counterfeit merchandise, 48-51, 59-61
funding from mosques, 168-169
funding from ORC (organized retail crime), 11, 159-160
correlation between ORC and terrorism, 168
"homegrown terrorism", 160-165
Somalian connection, 165-167

fundraising activities of, 134-135, 244-245
ghost companies, 132-133
illegal entry into U.S.
counterfeit passports, 127-132
human smuggling, 129-132
material support for, 239-241
money laundering, 139-141
banking regulations and, 145-150
Black Market Peso Exchange, 152-155
credit card fraud, 231-234
hawalas, 142-144, 219-221
RICO (Racketeer Influenced and Corrupt Organizations Act), 234-238
South American, Mexican, and African connection, 155-157
stored value cards, 227-231
passive sympathizers, 140
shadow banking, 45
theft. See stolen merchandise
Third World Relief Agency (TWRA), 134
This Is for the Mara Salvatrucha: Inside the MS-13, America's Most Violent Gang (Logan), 23
Thornberry, Mac, 243
Times Square Bomber. See Shahzad, Faisal
Tobon, John, 26-27, 40, 160, 174, 175
Tod's, 59
TOMCATS (Tactical Operations Multi-Agency Cargo Anti-Theft Squad), 112
Toure, Harouna, 156
Tovar, Rodrigo, 195
tradeboss.com, 133
Transamerica Express, 111, 133
Transportation Security Administration (TSA), 65

Tri-Border Area of South America, Hezbollah activity in, 27-30, 119, 120-123

trucking industry, regulation of, 65. *See also* cargo theft

trust, 136-137

TSA (Transportation Security Administration), 65

TTP. *See* Tehreek-e-Taliban

Tupamaro, 179

Tutaya, George, 90

TVs, smuggling into Pakistan, 180-182

TWRA (Third World Relief Agency), 134

Tyrrell, Kevin, 150

U

UAC (United Self-Defense Forces) of Colombia, 192-195

Uganda, cigarette smuggling in, 190-191

Uniform Crime Reporting System, 67

United Nations

Group of Experts, 190

International Convention for the Suppression of the Financing of Terrorism, 146, 219

Office on Drugs and Crime (UNODC), 32

United Self-Defense Forces (AUC) of Colombia, 192-195

United States Agency for International Development (USAID), Antiterrorism Vetting Procedures, 175-177

UNODC (United Nations Office on Drugs and Crime), 32

Urban Justice Center, 48

USA Patriot Improvement and Reauthorization Act. *See* Patriot Act

USAID (United States Agency for International Development), Antiterrorism Vetting Procedures, 175-177

V

van Gogh, Theo, 162

Velosa, Edgar, 195

Verisk Analytics, 93

Victoria's Secret, 90

Vidal, Roman, 192

W

Walgreens, 13, 60-61, 78, 92, 94, 98, 205, 215

Walmart, 57, 211-212

Walt money laundering conspiracy, 186

Warde, Ibrahim, , 144, 235

warehouses

explained, 80-81

profile of, 81-83

Washington, Levar, 20

Wehrle, Joe, 83

Weisbecker, Gary, 61, 62

wholesalers, 61-63, 80, 82

Williams, Bill, 70-72

Wolosky, Lee, 197

wonderhowto.com, 107

X-Y

Younis, Mohamad, 224

Younous Abdullah Mohammed, 161-165

Yousef al-Khattab, 161-163

Z

Zakaria, Abe, 79
zakat funds, 28
Zappos.com, 43
Zavala, Marc, 64-66, 112
Zetas, 23, 152-155
Zyprexa, theft of, 85

FINANCIAL TIMES

In an increasingly competitive world, it is quality
of thinking that gives an edge—an idea that opens new
doors, a technique that solves a problem, or an insight
that simply helps make sense of it all.

We work with leading authors in the various arenas
of business and finance to bring cutting-edge thinking
and best-learning practices to a global market.

It is our goal to create world-class print publications
and electronic products that give readers
knowledge and understanding that can then be
applied, whether studying or at work.

To find out more about our business
products, you can visit us at www.ftpress.com.